George Southern B.E.M.
Sandridge Court
9 Blenheim Terrace
SCARBOROUGH
North Yorkshire YO12 7HF

+. 352266

Poisonous
Inferno

Poisonous Inferno

World War II Tragedy at Bari Harbour

To JOHN & HILARY.
With kindest wishes
George Southern
Sept 2012

George Southern

Airlife

Copyright © 2002 George Southern

First published in the UK in 2002
by Airlife Publishing Ltd

British Library Cataloguing-in-Publication Data
  A catalogue record for this book
  is available from the British Library

ISBN 1 84037 389 X

Typeset by Phoenix Typesetting, Burley-in-Wharfedale, West Yorkshire
Printed in England by MPG Books Ltd., Bodmin, Cornwall.

Contact us for a free catalogue that describes the complete range of Airlife books.

Airlife Publishing Ltd
101 Longden Road, Shrewsbury, SY3 9EB, England
E-mail: sales@airlifebooks.com
Website:www.airlifebooks.com

ACKNOWLEDGEMENTS

H OW is it possible that a disaster such as that which occurred in the Italian Adriatic port of Bari on 2 December 1943 is unknown to the vast majority of the British public, and indeed to most ex-servicemen too?

Strict censorship applied for thirty years, and even after that time information was scarce and extremely difficult to obtain. I gathered valuable details from the Public Record Office, who were most cooperative, but I drew a blank in obtaining any service records. I did not have time during that fateful night in Bari to take in fully what was happening around me; it was enough that I was alive at the end of it. Only in the last few years have I realised how heavily involved I was.

First I must thank the British press for publishing my appeals for information. Without their help I could not have contacted the survivors and participants whose personal stories form the basis of this book, especially the following:

Bristol Observer	*Brighton News*
Belfast Telegraph	*Epping Gazette*
Glasgow Herald	*Glasgow Daily Record*
Hull Daily Mail	*Norfolk Guardian and Gazette*
Manchester Evening News	*Leicester Mercury*
Liverpool Echo	*Portsmouth Evening News*
Evening Chronicle Newcastle	*Scarborough Evening News*
South Wales Argus	*Thurrock Gazette*
Western Evening Herald	*South Western Mail*
Plymouth Evening Herald	*Wolverhampton Mail*
Worthing Gazette	*Yorkshire Evening Post*

I am also grateful to *The Navy News, Ships Monthly, La Gezetta Del Mezzogiorno,* Bari, and to the *Independent on Sunday* for allowing me to quote from Patrick Cockburn's article concerning mustard gas experiments on US Navy personnel.

My thanks for information supplied by: Patricia Edwards, Army Historical Branch, Ministry of Defence; Annet Gould of the Navy

Records Society; George Drewett, President of the 1st Destroyer Flotilla Association for his searches on my behalf at the Public Records Office; the British Library; the New Zealand Defence Staff; the Queen Elizabeth II Army Memorial Museum, Waiouri, New Zealand; Barry L. Zerby, Military Reference Branch, the National Archives Washington DC; the Naval Historical Centre, Washington Navy Yard; and the National Archives at College Park Maryland.

Sheral Kendall allowed me to quote from her book *New Zealand Military Nursing*; Gay Trevithic from her diary; the National Museum of Scotland from an article in *Blackwood's Magazine* 'Big Bang at Bari', and Gwladys Rees Aikens of Halifax Nova Scotia, from her book *Nurses in Battledress.*

Many others helped me with information, among them: Jean-Jacques Breuet, Les Fontaines, France; Otto Kragt Harlingen, Holland; Wing Commander Douglas Blackwood; J.E. Cantley, Chumbly, Canada; Mrs M. Walkington, Senior Clerk, Lloyd's Register of shipping; Reg Hanson Exeter Branch, Merchant Navy Association; John Thorpe, *Yorkshire Evening Post*; Douglas Bertram; Len Walters; and Major Harry Wilkinson RA (Rtd).

I am indebted to Ted Fry for his maps and sketches of the moles, jetties, harbour installations and discharging berths, and without Bob Wills' marvellous memories and descriptions of the 98th British General Hospital this book would be all the poorer. I am grateful to him for allowing me to record this vitally important aspect.

Help in research in Italy came from: Professor Giorgio Assennato of Instuto di Medicini del Lavoro, Facolta di Medicina e Chirurgia, Universita Degli Studi di Bari; Dr Donato Sivo, who allowed me to quote from his doctoral dissertion 'Effeti dell' Esposizione al Sollfuro di Biclioturato on una Coorte di Pescatori'; Angelo Neve, Coordinator of Marine Studies, Barletta, for sending me videos of wrecks on the seabed and for photographs and information on present-day contamination. Thanks also to Ray Bennet, my man on the spot in Bari (then and now) for taking time and trouble to ferret out information. He also supplied me with photographs of the present-day harbour and the sad ones taken in the military cemetery near Bari. Ray in return received help from the Principal of the Instituto Pugliese, Professor Enzo Mazzocoli, and his deputy, Dr Leuzzi.

My old shipmate, Bob Davies, obtained copies of derestricted official British accounts and other valuable information. I cannot thank enough my son Paul for his encouragement and for his many translations and expert advice regarding research and writing over a period of years, all given with his consummate good humour.

Acknowledgements

Last but not least, my thanks go to my dear wife Kay, my finest companion of fifty-three years, who sorted my mail, encouraged me and was unfailingly enthusiastic. She never lost her innate good humour, even though her valuable time was running out and I disturbed the calm and orderly household with word-processor chatter and untidy manuscripts. As my self-imposed proofreader and corrector she was of the opinion that this story should be told, but sadly in April 1995, she died suddenly. To that fine woman I dedicate this book.

FOREWORD

THOUGH it is more than half a century since VE Day, there seems to be an endless market for books about the war. Many describe long campaigns, the exploits of generals and details of long-drawn-out battles. But George Southern has chosen a different technique – to concentrate on one single, extraordinary night, to put one particular event under the microscope. And it is this which makes this book so interesting.

The combination of circumstances – so many ships crammed together, hundreds of tons of high-octane petrol, liquid mustard gas floating on oil from sunken ships – all combined to produce a ghastly scenario which is most vividly described. But the horrors are balanced by the courage displayed by the participants. This was not a matter of killing more enemy, but of trying to save our own men.

The deeds thus described, the risks taken to save the lives of others, the heroic efforts of doctors and nurses in the hospital, all add up to a huge tapestry of horror and of heroism. A particular aspect is that the vast majority of the men involved were acting on their own initiative. The conditions were such that the usual communication and command structure was almost non-existent. Soldiers and sailors just had to 'get on with it' – and they did magnificently.

Readers will realise that many years of careful and patient research has been put into producing such a detailed account. George Southern's descriptions come 'from the horse's mouth', because he was there himself, and so were the people whose stories he has collected.

We are all indebted to him for producing a book which will be a revelation to the younger generation – and which will be all too readily understood by those who served in war. The latter will share the admirable philosophy of John Adams of the Royal Corps of Signals, wisely quoted by George Southern: 'Bearing in mind what happened to so many in Bari, I was content to be in one piece.'

Rear Admiral Sir Morgan Giles, OBE DSO GM

CONTENTS

INTRODUCTION

GAETANO Lacaita had set out before dawn on his boat, the *Campanella* from the small fishing town of Molfetta, 18 miles north of Bari in the Apulian region of southern Italy. He cast his nets and settled down to listen to the early morning news on his transistor radio. A dramatic sunrise heralded another brilliant, cloudless day in the summer of 1994.

Towards midday the sea began to swell and Gaetano decided to haul in his nets prior to making for home. As he pulled at the nets he became aware of a pungent smell which at first he could not recognise. As he continued to haul at them the smell became stronger. In the bottom of the boat he noticed a dull grey-greenish metallic object among the shimmering fish. With a sigh of recognition he dug out a pair of torn rubber gloves from a wooden locker behind the motor and, stretching forward, removed with some difficulty the jagged metal ensnared in the net and let it sink back into the sea.

Gaetano inspected his silvery catch writhing and wriggling about in the bottom of the boat, removed some small fish and threw them back into the sea where they were immediately seized upon by the ever watchful greedy seagulls. After deftly gutting the fish and throwing the innards overboard, he started up the motor and began the return journey to Molfetta. As the tiny *Campanella* rode the increasing swell, Gaetano was pleased to have an excuse for returning home: more football! Italy's World Cup game from the USA live on television. It was a pity his wife did not like football.

Gaetano landed his catch, called in at the bar for a quick glass or two of wine and drove the short distance from the waterfront to his home on Via Santa Caterina. That afternoon as he watched the build-up to the match – Baggio endlessly scoring goals in slow motion to music – he was aware of a burning sensation in his eyes and his eyelids felt as if they were coated in sand. His hands, which he had thoroughly scrubbed only a couple of hours before, were blotchy, itchy and red. He had lost interest in the game well before half-time, his eyes streaming and his eyelids swollen and blistered. His hands and especially his right arm and elbow were also badly blistered, his throat felt raw and he had difficulty breathing.

By this time his wife had telephoned her brother and asked him to take her husband to the occupation clinic in Bari. During the journey Gaetano's breathing became more laboured and his pulse began to race. By the time they reached the clinic he was in an extremely distressed condition.

The following day, after checking his patient's progress, Dr Domenico Silvestrelli returned to his office at the occupational clinic and, turning on his computer, opened up the file entitled 'Mustard gas contamination'. As he pressed down on the cursor, the statistics rapidly passed before his eyes.

1944–1945: 6 cases of mustard gas contamination to workers involved in salvage operations

1955–1994: 144 cases of mustard gas contamination of fishermen

Area of injury of 135 cases, Molfetta: Statistics:

Eyes	28.8%
Scrotum	6.6%
Face	32.5%
Upper joints	45.1%
Lower joints	5.9%
Abdominal region	0.7%
Hands	39.2%
Feet	1.4%

Dr Silvestrelli updated his information by adding Gaetano Lacaita's case to the other 144 mustard gas-contaminated victims.

The mustard gas bombs and shells were lying at the bottom of the sea at depths ranging from 50 to 700 feet, between 2 and 10 miles off the Apulian coast in a wide arc off Bari, Molfetta and Trani. The list of chemical cases had been thoroughly documented at the University of Bari's Institute for Occupational Medicine, and Dr Silvestrelli knew full well that the ghastly legacy of the German air raid on Bari on 2 December 1943, twenty-five years before his birth, would continue to defile the waters of the Adriatic Sea.

As usual, on Armistice Sunday 1990, my wife and I attended the traditional church service at Scarborough's well-known Queen Street Methodist Church. Most of the town's seafaring interests were represented: the local Sea Cadet Force, the Royal and Merchant Navies, the Royal National Lifeboat Institution and local fishermen and townspeople. During the service their standards and wreaths were blessed. Afterwards the various groups mustered outside the church and as always marched down the hill to the windy seafront. The next phase of the commemoration was the short service and two minutes' silence at the eleventh hour.

The lifeboat house, with its wooden, barnacled slipway leading down to the sea, had itself been the scene of many of Scarborough's maritime tragedies, and on this day formed the focal point of the service. The Sea Cadets lined both sides of the ramp in front of the clergy, and the rest of us gathered round for hymn singing and prayers. Wreaths were simultaneously being laid at sea, just outside the harbour. My family joined Kay and me for this part of the service, and we stood together on that cold, breezy but fine November morning. The maroon fired, signalling the two minutes' silence. Normally it summoned the volunteer lifeboat crew to duty. That particular day it disturbed a more than usual number of seagulls.

The scavenging birds flew noisily around, squawking and calling and at that moment, as I remembered lost shipmates, my mind flashed back forty-seven years. The raucous call of the seagulls became the cries of despair, desperate men in the water screaming and shouting for help as the flames enveloped them, and as I raised my eyes to the water's edge, I saw not the boat from which the wreaths were placed over the side but a rescue boat picking up injured and dying sailors in another harbour, in another time, a long way from home. For the rest of the day my family found me in a quiet, subdued and reflective frame of mind, unable to shake off the feelings I had experienced during the service of remembrance. By the end of the day I had come to a decision.

As is usual on these occasions, the clergy had reiterated in the service the debt owed by the nation to the dead of both wars: 'They will not be forgotten' and 'We will remember them'. Ironically the men my thoughts had flown to on that morning had been the victims of one of the worst disasters of the war, but had been deliberately forgotten by the Government and their sacrifice had certainly not been remembered in any way. The War Cabinet had ordered the episode to be swept under the carpet as if it was something to be ashamed of.

On Panel No. 106 of the Tower Hill Memorial, London, commemorating the 30,000 men of the Merchant Navy who have no known grave but the sea, is the name Peter Kenyon Green. He was serving aboard the SS *Testbank.* He died on 2 December 1943; he was a Scot from Glasgow, aged sixteen. He was one of the hundreds of men the War Cabinet and successive governments did not want to remember. The decision I came to on that Armistice Day was to tell the story of this secret episode, describing the actual experiences of the men concerned. I did not want it to be told by some ghost writer, or someone who was miles away at the time, but first-hand by the survivors who had been involved in this most horrifying and bizarre disaster.

My feeling was that if one of us did not write the account soon, the truth would be lost for ever, as I know full well all we survivors are in our sunset years. This then is the story of Bari, 2 December 1943.

1

THE SCENE IS SET

HIGH in the sky, at 20,000 feet (6,100 metres), the German pilot saw below him, from his cockpit in the 300 mph (480 kph) Me 20 reconnaissance plane, the tiny outlines of ships moving around inside and outside the harbour. The vessels' wakes, even at that altitude, told the airman that the ships were heading for the harbour: another convoy had arrived at Bari.

The port of Bari, on the Adriatic coast of Italy, was at that time, 2 December 1943, a most important strategic port supplying the 8th Army. During the weeks preceding, the Allied High Command had uppermost in their planning, the need to draw as many enemy troops and materials as possible from the English Channel areas in preparation for Operation Overlord the following year. The landings in Italy were a vital part of this plan and the swift capture of ports on the Italian mainland were of paramount importance to sustain the Allied forces once they had landed.

At the beginning of September 1943, the Allied armies had landed at the bay of Salerno. Heavy fighting took place, as the Germans stubbornly defended every high inch of the bridgehead the Allies had created. Meanwhile, further south the 8th Army had crossed the straits of Messina to land unopposed at Reggio di Calabria; once inland they had swung north in an attempt to link up with the 5th Army at Salerno. The mountainous country was ideal for defence. The Germans had mined the roads and gulleys, making progress slow and costly for the Allies.

In the heel of Italy, British troops had landed from the sea some miles from the large Italian naval base of Taranto and quickly taken it, allowing shipping to use the port and dockyard. The troops moved on northwards to reach the Adriatic ports of Brindisi and Bari. By 10 September the three ports, together with the Salerno bridgehead, were in Allied hands.

With supplies coming ashore at the small port of Salerno, the 5th Army had swept north to take the great prize of Naples. This city's magnificent harbour, with its miles of jetties, docks, discharging berths and facilities to take over 100 ships, became the most important port for supplying the Allied armies in the push for their next objective – the 'Eternal City', Rome. Fortunately all the coastal railway systems were found to be intact and in working order, very little had been destroyed by the retreating forces.

The 5th Army had pushed on further north until it met stubborn resistance in the Lira Valley, before Cassino, where the enemy were holding superb defensive positions in the hills and mountains. Field Marshal Albert Kesselring had taken over command of the German forces from Field Marshal Erwin Rommel, who had been recalled to northern France by Hitler. Kesselring's first order was for his troops to dig in. Bunkers and pill boxes were constructed in the hillsides covering the valleys below and any movement by Allied forces in daylight brought down on their heads an immediate bombardment.

Meanwhile, on the other side of Italy the 8th Army was now under the command of General Oliver Leese, who had taken over from Field Marshal Bernard Montgomery; the latter had been recalled to Britain for the planning of Operation Overlord. The 8th Army quickly captured the Foggia air base, some 70 miles (110 km) north-west inland of Bari. This large complex, with thirteen airstrips, was absolutely vital for the continuation of the rapid advance up the Adriatic coast of Italy. Still advancing, it had made a landing near the small port of Termoli and entered the town, which the Germans contested bitterly. The enemy had then fallen back to prepared defensive positions along the Sangro River, where the mountainous country combined with deteriorating weather had slowed down the British advance. It was late November before the 8th Army had completed the crossing of the river.

The 8th Army's rapid advance and long lines of communication meant that Bari, though well over 100 miles (160 km) from the front line, was of paramount importance as a main supply base. Because the supply and maintenance of the armies and air forces was imperative, the usual precautions of blacking out the port were waived. Bari was a blaze of light during the hours of darkness in order to facilitate the discharging of vessels, which carried on round the clock. The same applied in the port of Brindisi, some 70 miles (110 km) south of Bari.

Though not fully operational at that time, a small number of bomber and fighter aircraft were based at Foggia. However, the US Air Force was beginning to transfer its large bomber squadrons from bases in North Africa. They needed a constant supply of spares, tools and equipment, jeeps and trucks, bombs and rockets and the vast array of materials needed to support the ground troops in Italy and the intended bombing of targets in Germany. The overriding requirement, however, was for a constant supply of high-octane fuel.

The petrol for the hundreds of planes expected in the next few weeks was shipped not only in tankers but in other vessels, which carried it in drums and cans, and sometimes as deck cargo. To save space, all vehicles carried aboard the merchant ships – tanks, ambulances, lorries, jeeps, vans and tracked vehicles – had full petrol tanks.

In Bari harbour on the eastern mole, Molo San Cataldo, there were facilities for discharging fuel from the tankers into container areas just outside the dockyard by means of a pipeline. This ensured a quick turn-round of tankers, another important factor at the Adriatic port.

The pilot of the German plane did not ponder over the logistic problems facing the Allied forces. After all, the Axis forces had enough problems of their own, one of which was to slow down and stop the Allied advance northwards towards Rome and beyond. They were doing their utmost to stop supplies arriving at their intended destinations. The more they could delay the war in Italy the more time was gained for the new weapons promised by Hitler to become operational. Rumours of rockets and jet-propelled planes were being talked about openly among the German forces. The convoys entering the Mediterranean were harried by submarines and aircraft all along the North African coast. The tonnage lost during this period reached alarming proportions. Another hazard when the convoys reached Sicily and Italy was the danger of ships striking mines. Hundreds of them were sown by planes, submarines and E-boats in the path of approaching convoys and in the comparatively shallow waters around the shores of Italy's 'heel and toe', where the loss of many ships proved their efficiency.

This situation set the stage for what was to follow. The pilot, high in the sky, his photographs taken, sped off to his northern Italian base. An hour or so later he was in the debriefing room reporting to his superiors on the state of Bari harbour. Little did he know that he was the catalyst for a train of events which would lead to one of the most successful German air raids of the war.

With the rest of my shipmates I joined the newly built destroyer HMS *Zetland* when she left the Clydeside shipbuilding yard of Yarrow and Company and commissioned in May 1942. After sea and gunnery trials she sailed to become part of the group of convoy escorts for the Western Approaches based at the Northern Ireland port of Londonderry. I was given the post of loader on 'A' gun which was a twin 4 in (100 mm) gun turret sited on the forecastle. In early August 1942 she was temporarily withdrawn to form part of the destroyer screen during the most famous Malta convoy, code-named Operation Pedestal, after which she resumed Atlantic convoys once again. At dawn on 8 November 1942 she was close inshore guarding the landing of troops on the beaches east of Algiers during Operation Torch.

HMS *Zetland* (Hunt class) destroyer, built at the Glasgow shipyard of Yarrows. She had a displacement of approximately 1,000 tons. Her armament was three twin 4 inch gun turrets, one forward, two aft, a four-barrel pom-pom and two twin 20 mm Bofors. *(G. Southern)*

Author aged 23, in 1944, serving at that time as a store assistant after leaving *Zetland* to be admitted to hospital in Syracuse to have his infected hand drained of poison. *(G. Southern)*

HMS *Broke,* without power and listing badly, several miles north-east of Algiers, taken from HMS *Zetland* one hour before being sunk by depth charges discharged from *Zetland.* All survivors, including stretcher cases, had previously been transferred to *Zetland* for passage to Gibraltar. *(G. Southern)*

German soldiers being transported to Malta after being picked up trying to escape from North Africa to Sicily, some 70 miles away, in all manner of craft, including children's paddle boats, canoes, dinghies, rafts and rowing boats. *(G. Southern)*

Just after dawn *Zetland* was alerted to the plight of the destroyer HMS *Broke*, which was badly damaged and under fire from French 8 inch (200 mm) gun batteries situated on the cliffs of Cape Matafou, over-looking the Bay of Algiers. *Broke* had successfully carried out her task of landing fifty picked troops inside Algiers harbour, whose instructions were to take and hold key positions in the port area until the main body of invading troops arrived. As she withdrew from the harbour, she came under intense and accurate fire from the batteries and was hit several times, causing severe damage and casualties. One shell destroyed the bridge and another reduced the ship to a crawl. Lt Cdr J.V. Wilkinson, *Zetland*'s captain, immediately put his ship at full speed between the stricken destroyer and the batteries which were still targeting her. Laying a screen of smoke and pounding the batteries with her vastly outranged 4 inch (100 mm) guns, *Zetland* managed to silence the far superior fire power of the French gun batteries long enough to allow *Broke* time to reach the safety of the open sea.

Zetland received a signal to take the listing destroyer in tow and to make for Gibraltar. After securing tow lines we commenced the 400 mile (650 km) journey. Late that same night, taking in water and listing ever more, it became apparent that *Broke* was not going to make it to Gibraltar. In addition the sea conditions were worsening and conditions aboard were becoming untenable. It was therefore decided to abandon ship. All available hammocks and bedding were brought onto *Zetland*'s upper deck to cushion the sailors who had to jump on a given order, because one second *Zetland*'s bow would be 10 feet below the wallowing *Broke* and the next second 10 feet above. Hammocks were slung over the side to act as fenders and in a display of magnificent seamanship amid mounting seas, Lt Cdr Wilkinson kept *Zetland*'s bow within a foot or two of the sinking destroyer. Not one man was lost in the operation, which included transferring stretcher cases and severely wounded men. When the last man was aboard, *Zetland* steamed alongside the port side of the helpless *Broke* to drop two depth charges at shallow settings. After the ensuing underwater explosions, we watched as the gallant destroyer slid under the waves. The survivors were landed at Gibraltar and *Zetland* returned to Algiers to begin continuous convoy escort duties along the North African coast with sister ship HMS *Bicester*. In addition the two destroyers carried out night patrols in the Sicilian Narrows from the port of Bone in Algeria.

At the beginning of May, on the day before the Italian capitulation in North Africa, *Zetland* and *Bicester*, on patrol off Cape Bon, were mis-takenly attacked by a group of thirty Allied aircraft. Though no direct hits were recorded both ships suffered underwater damage from near misses and were recalled to the UK for extensive repairs and refitting, after which they returned to the Mediterranean to resume escort duties once again. At dawn on 1 December 1943 both ships sailed on escort duty from Augusta in Sicily, bound for Bari.

Shepherding the newly arrived convoy into Bari's outer harbour on that sunny morning of 2 December 1943 were the convoy escorts consisting of *Zetland* and *Bicester* and three minesweepers. Closed up at actions stations I noticed, as everyone on the upper deck did, a lone German reconnaissance plane high in the sky. It passed over the port in a north-westerly direction, evidently returning to a base in northern Italy.

Midday found the two destroyers tied up alongside one another at berth No. 26 on Nuovo Molo, bows facing the harbour entrance, *Bicester* taking the inside position next to the jetty. The long breakwater had been constructed in the shape of a crooked finger. It stretched from Bari's original small harbour and dockyard into the Adriatic sea to create a sheltered harbour where vessels waited before moving to discharging berths. Molo San Cataldo on the landward side of the harbour was a jetty where oil tankers discharged and where smaller coastal tankers loaded. The end of Nuovo Molo and the end of Molo San Cataldo, on which there was a lighthouse, formed the harbour entrance, a distance of approximately 300 yards. Strung between the two ends of the moles was a boom defence. Ahead of *Zetland*'s bows were fifteen merchant ships, all secured to the mole stern first, with anchors streamed to stabilise the bows. Because of overcrowding, the ships were moored closer together than was normal. These were temporary berths for the vessels, some of which were empty awaiting sailing orders and others awaiting discharging berths. Four American liberty ships were in the line of shipping. They were built to a revolutionary design: the parts of the ships were made all over the United States, dispatched to the shipyards and welded together in assembly-line fashion. From laying the keel to the finished product took only a matter of weeks, in many cases just six weeks.

In the berths nearest the end of Nuovo Molo were the Dutch ship SS *Odysseus* and the Italian SS *Frozinone.* Two American liberty ships filled the next berths, USS *John Bascom* with 8,000 tons of cargo including acid and high-test gasoline in 50 gal (225 litre) drums, and USS *John Motley*, which carried 5,231 tons of ammunition. The next four ships berthed in line were the British Coastal Forces tanker SS *Testbank,* classed as empty but with 50 tons of high octane aboard, the USS *Joseph Wheeler*, with a cargo of 8,037 tons of ammunition, the British vessel SS *Fort Athabaska,* waiting to sail for Algiers, and SS *Lars Kruse,* with a cargo of 1,400 tons of aviation spirit. Other ships in the line were the French diesel tanker SS

La Drome, three Norwegian ships, the naval coal ship SS *Vest*, SS *Bolsta*, which had several tons of benzine on board, and SS *Norlam* with a cargo of gas coal. At the end of the line was the British coastal tanker MV *Devon Coast*.

Between *John Motley* and *Testbank* lay the ship that was destined to create a horrifying situation never before encountered in the history of warfare – the USS *John Harvey* carrying a cargo of 5,037 tons of what were described as 'war supplies'.

John Harvey's keel was laid down on 6 December 1942 and she was christened by Mrs Margaret Grover on 19 January 1943. The ship cost $1 million and was built in forty-four days. She was 7,176 gross tonnage, had a top speed of 12 knots and was named after a member of the Continental Congress. She had made three trips before arriving in Bari, the first from Wilmington, North Carolina, to New York, the second to Oran and Bone in North Africa, the third from Norfolk, Virginia to Casablanca and back. The fourth and final voyage was from Baltimore, Maryland. Her master was Captain Knowles and the chief engineer was John White, who had served aboard the USS *Ozaka* before the United States had entered the war, when she took part in Atlantic convoys bringing much-needed supplies to Britain and Russia during the period of the lend-lease agreement. From Baltimore the *John Harvey* had sailed across the Atlantic for the last time, to Oran.

Meanwhile, in a room in Algiers, a small group of men made a routine decision that was to have far-reaching consequences, including 2,000 casualties, the sinking of seventeen ships, severe damage to many more and condemning hundreds of men and their families to years of illness and misery. So catastrophic was it that it had to be kept secret for more than thirty years and even today that secrecy is still maintained.

According to official accounts, Allied Headquarters Algiers gave instructions for 24,430 Bombs Chemical, HS (HS was the code description for mustard) to be loaded onto USS *John Harvey* at Oran. On 24 November, the Ordnance Officer HQ forwarded copies of the ship's manifests to Bari.

USS *John Harvey* sailed from Oran on 20 November 1943 in convoy KMS 32, arriving at Augusta on 24 November, and sailed to Bari in convoy AH10 on 27 November. There were nine merchants ships in this convoy and on arrival on 28 November, she was ordered the same day to berth 29 on the outer mole. The reason for berthing on the mole was that the unloading berths in the inner harbour were full, or not ready for unloading and it was unsafe to leave ships outside the harbour on account of U- and E-boat activities.

In an extract from the Official Account:

(a) The copies of the manifest referred to above were received and signed for by the Docks Superintendent at Bari on 25 November. What happened to those documents is obscure; there is no trace of them now and no evidence that they were distributed to anyone. Nor was a manifest received from the Master after the arrival of the ship.

(b) The 'breakdown' referred to above was received by the Ordnance Officer XII (ADV) on 28 November. It was distributed by the US transport, Adriatic Base, to his branches and to the Acting Port Commandant and the Docks Superintendent, who received their copies on 30 November.

(c) On the 28 or 29 November, a representative of the US Port Officer went on board the *John Harvey* and was told by the Security Officer that he had a cargo of mustard gas.

(d) There is some evidence that the presence of the cargo of mustard was discussed between the Docks Superintendent, the Acting Port Commandant, and the Sea Transport Officer, and it was considered, in view of her low priority and the berthing space available, that she was in as safe a place as could be found.

(e) Neither NOIC nor Comd No. 6 Base Sub Area were aware before the raid that the *John Harvey* contained toxic ammunition.

Though it is obvious that copies of manifests were distributed in Bari, it is also obvious that they went astray or persons having them in their possession feared to make the information available. In an account I received from Major Harry Wilkinson who at that time was Acting Port Commandant in the absence of Lt Col Marcus Sieff, it gives no indication he was aware of the presence of mustard gas aboard the USS *John Harvey*. Immediately after the end of the raid he was more concerned about a tanker unloading petrol on Molo San Cataldo. He also says that he believes the first indication of the presence of mustard gas was given by a doctor in the hospital who had some experience treating mustard gas patients during the 1914–18 war.

USS *John Bascom* arrived in Bari after a voyage in rough weather from New York as part of a convoy which arrived on the morning of 2 December. Making his first trip aboard her was Armed Guard Warren Brandenstein, a gunner. *John Motley* berthed between *John Harvey* and *John Bascom*. Another liberty ship, USS *Lyman Abbott*, arrived in the same convoy and because all the berths on the outer mole were taken up she had to anchor in the middle of the harbour about a ship's length away from the line of vessels. Armed Guards Stanley Wisniewski, and Leo Krause and Second Assistant Engineer George Maury were assigned to *Lyman Abbott* in May 1943. At that time her guns had not been fitted. She later made two trips to Britain, one to North Africa and the latest one to Bari with a shipment described as general cargo. Donald Meissner recalls that there were 28 armed guards manning the guns aboard the ship.

Also in the harbour were the British ships SS *Brittany Coast*, SS *Crista*, with a cargo of benzine, MV *Coxwold* and SS *Fort Le Joie*. SS *Dago*, a Polish naval ammunition ship, was also at anchor as was SS *Puck*, with a cargo of 770 tons of ammunition, another Polish ship, SS *Lwow*, and the Italian vessels SS *Casalla* and MV *Barletta*. Close to Molo San Cataldo were two small American coastal tankers, USS *Aristook* and USS *Pumper*.

SS *Vest* had sailed from South Wales, where she had taken on board a cargo of coal. It was intended that she would be used as a bunker ship for the minesweepers, many of which were converted coal-burning fishing trawlers. During the afternoon a minesweeper pulled alongside to take on coal. Second Engineer Robert Anderson, serving aboard *Vest*, noticed a great deal of activity aboard the liberty ship *John Bascom*, which had a deck cargo of petrol cans of the sturdy type carried on jeeps.

Fort Athabaska was a North Sands type coal-burning ship of 10,000 tons which had the distinction of being the hundredth ship to be built in the British Columbia yards of the gracious city of Vancouver. She had arrived in Bari on 19 November, discharged her cargo of bombs and ammunition and moved to the outer mole. On board were 76 tons of general cargo, 238 bags of ordinary mail destined for the UK and two German rocket bombs which had been captured intact and which were to be examined by weaponry experts in Algiers.

In the dockyard and inner harbour, and already discharging, were SS *John Schofield*, SS *Louis Hennepin* and SS *Spero*, a ship of the Ellerman-Wilson line which was unloading a cargo of frozen meat. She was a fully refrigerated ship employed in carrying frozen lamb and beef to troops in forward areas. The smaller vessels like *Spero* loaded up from larger and more valuable refrigerator ships which brought meat from Argentina, Brazil, Australia, New Zealand and the USA and which berthed in ports of comparative safety. *Spero* transported its cargo to ports as near the front line as possible where there was refrigeration storage capacity ashore. One such port was Bari. Second Engineer Don Beal was on *Spero*'s deck watching three men cleaning the Oerlikon gun.

During the afternoon of 2 December, the American liberty ship USS *Samuel J. Tilden* accompanied by SS *Lublin* and the converted trawler HMT *Mullet*, which had provided the escort for the two merchant ships, arrived outside the harbour and anchored, waiting for the opening of the boom defence. *Samuel J. Tilden* had sailed from New York in June 1943 where 17-year-old William W. Walters joined her after completing his training in Maryland. One of his fellow gunners was John Whitley, who joined the ship at the same time. Merchant ships that lay alongside discharged their cargo by means of harbour cranes and their own davits directly onto the moles and jetties, where they were stacked in huge piles awaiting transport.

On *Zetland*'s bridge as she lay alongside, Welshman Robert (Bob) Davies, a Leading Signalman who was a veteran of Atlantic, North Sea and English Channel convoys by the time he joined *Zetland* in May 1942, was looking forward to going off duty at the end of the second dog-watch (8 p.m.). Little did he know that twenty-four hours would pass before he was relieved. Afternoon and evening leave had been granted and many sailors has taken the opportunity to have a run ashore and look around the city.

Bob Davies in 1940. Bob was discharged from the Merchant Navy in 1938 because his health was considered too poor. He was immediately accepted into the Royal Navy when war broke out and served for six years, joining *Zetland* in May 1942. *(R. Davies)*

2

THE BUILD-UP

EARLY in the afternoon of 2 December, a fellow crew member, Albert Jones, and I left *Zetland* to spend a few hours looking around Bari, a city we had not visited before. Though we had escorted convoys to both Bari and Brindisi in the previous weeks, we had usually taken on board fuel at the small oiling port of Manfredonia, several miles further north, before carrying out night patrols off the coast of Yugoslavia.

As we walked along the outer mole we could see the tremendous amount of stores, munitions and supplies of every description piled high in every available space. Close to the sea wall stretched a long line of recently unloaded vehicles, presumably awaiting drivers. There were stacks of bombs, shells, boxes of small-arms ammunition, torpedoes, cans of petrol and other sealed crates and boxes. We had never seen, in any port we had visited, such an array of war supplies out in the open and in full view.

We strolled round the quaint streets and alleys of the old town and the newer city of Bari. There appeared to be little sign of the ravages of war; very little resistance had been offered by the retreating Axis forces when they evacuated the city and port, and Allied bombing had been minimal. Glancing in one shop window we saw displayed something we had never seen before: ball-point pens!

After a few modest purchases for our wives we decided to return to the destroyer. Retracing our steps we called at the forces canteen, had a snack and a cup of tea and carried on along the causeway of Porto Vecchio, the ancient port that divided the old city from the new. It was now a marina mainly used by pleasure craft, and was a focal point for servicemen as the Forces Club was nearby, as was the Teatro Margharita which was used for ENSA concerts and for showing films. Some time later, as the last rays of the winter sunshine disappeared we arrived at the dock gate to show our naval pay books to the military policeman on duty at the dockyard gates. Once inside we turned right to wend our way past the buildings commandeered by the Royal Navy which were now offices, base barracks, stores and warehouses.

There seemed to be the same amount of discharged supplies still out in the open as we walked along this part of the pier, which was wide enough for the discharging of vessels by crane. Two merchant ships, SS *Empire Sunbeam* and SS *Empire Meteor* were tied up alongside at berths 17 and 18. At the junction of the dockyard proper and the discharging pier lay the unseaworthy destroyer HMS *Quail* with her stern part missing. SS *John Schofield* lay in the next berth, No. 15.

On the evening of 21 December 1942, Gwladys Rees, a nurse in Queen Alexandra's Royal Army Nursing Corps (QARANC), found herself crammed into a lifeboat several miles off the coast of North Africa. She was one of the survivors from the troopship SS *Strathallan,* in peace time a P & O liner. The troopship had left Greenock in Scotland a week before and just north of Algiers had been struck by a torpedo fired from the German submarine *U 562.* The following day the abandoned ship had sunk while under tow to Oran.

Luckily there were few casualties and the nurses were landed at Algiers. After serving in military hospitals in North Africa, Gwladys and the medical unit she was part of embarked for the Italian port of Brindisi and then Bari. The nurses were on duty immediately as part of the 98th British General Base Hospital, which had been set up in what the Cardiff-born nurse says was 'a very large unfinished multi-building complex known as the Policlinic'.

Expropiated by the Allies, the complex housed laboratories, an X-ray department, a pharmacy, an officer's mess, a chapel, the quartermaster's stores and a few other buildings. Surrounding the complex was a huge ring of hut-like residences housing guards and sentries. The roadway ushering the ambulances from the battlefields led right into the midst of the hospital community. It was an ideal location, very near the harbour, railway and city. The flat roofs, which were easily accessible, commanded magnificent views of Bari harbour.

The clinic housed probably about five thousand people at a time, all transient except for the staff. South African, New Zealand and Indian units worked together here and up to the time of our arrival had been setting up the hospital. Like us, they had no idea where they would be going next, although they suspected they would be heading back to the Middle East. Despite our varied nationalities, we had one common concern, the treatment of the patients. We were on duty to receive survivors from a minesweeper which had been blown up by a mine in the harbour entrance. We nursed many of the wounded naval men back to health only to receive them back later as the result of a more ghastly disaster.

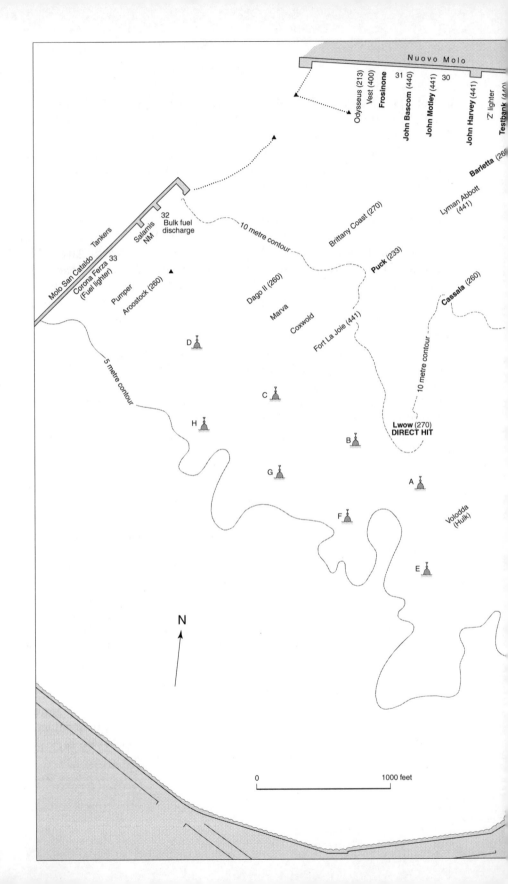

Nuovo Molo

Odysseus (213)
Vest (400)
Frosinone
31
John Bascom (440)
John Motley (441)
30
John Harvey (441)
'Z' lighter
Testbank (440)

Barletta (260)

Lyman Abbott (441)

Molo San Cataldo
Tankers
Salamis
NM
32
Bulk fuel
discharge

10 metre contour

Brittany Coast (270)

Puck (233)

Cassala (260)

Corona Ferza
33
(Fuel lighter)

Pumper
Aroostock (260)

Dago II (260)

Marva

Coxwold

Fort La Joie (441)

10 metre contour

5 metre contour

D

C

H

Lwow (270)
DIRECT HIT

B

G

A

Volodda
(Hulk)

F

E

N

0   1000 feet

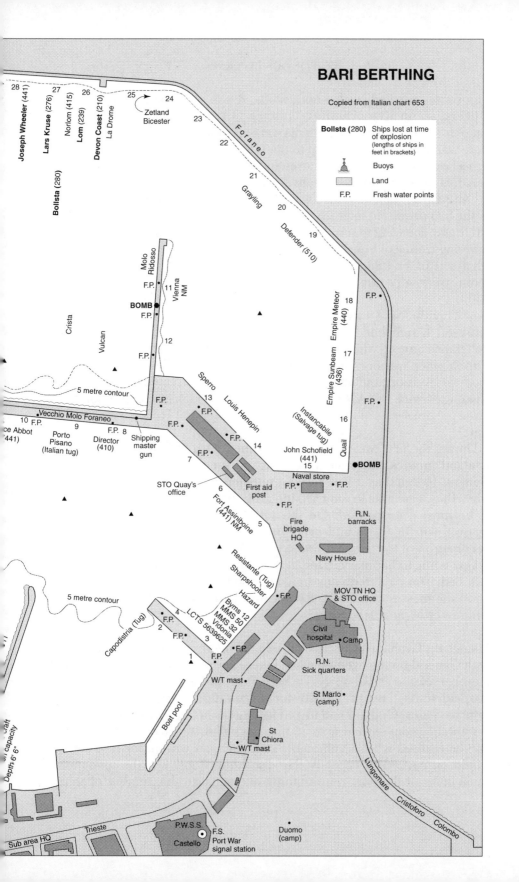

The nurses worked twelve-hour shifts, 8 a.m. to 8 p.m. Two medical officers, about five orderlies, another QA and Gwladys had ninety patients to look after. The patients were all more or less stable and many were waiting to return by ship to the UK or other Allied countries. 'Bari was a large city with a few theatres and myriad shops. We had minuscule personal property and it was always a treat to buy a little something.'

On 2 December, Gwladys was scheduled for night duty later on, but as she had promised to finish writing a letter for one of her patients to his girl friend, she went to see him before her shift began. The patient, a sailor suffering from eye injuries, had a tiny room to himself. 'We never knew what sort of buildings we would find to put patients into, but private rooms were very rare.'

Gay Trevithic was a nurse serving with the 3rd New Zealand General Hospital which had been allocated two blocks of buildings in the Policlinic, one of which had been used by the Italians as a hospital. Tripoli block was occupied by the surgical division, Beirut block by the medical division and the small building for the New Zealand Army Nursing Service (NZANS) was named Helmieh House, commemorating three previous sites of the 3rd New Zealand General Hospital during the war.

During the first two weeks of November, 64th NZANS and the New Zealand medical division were attached for duty to the 98th British General Hospital as it was without nursing staff. 'The nurses were glad when they were able to return to their own unit as we considered the 98th to be most disorganised. On the 1st December, Miss Chisholm [the matron] left for Cairo and everyone was sorry to see her go. She had beenmatron of the hospital since April 1941.'

Gay wrote in her diary: 'Dec. 2. I was off duty this afternoon but spent it in bed. Too cold to do anything and too tired to go out. Pictures were on in the mess room. Della, Robbie and I went muffled up to the neck and saw *A Night in the Tropics*.'

Lieutenant Graham Scott, RNVR was resting on his hospital bed in the 98th General on the evening when Gay was watching the film. He was a member of Bari's Royal Navy base staff and had been admitted to hospital some days previously for observation after suffering severe stomach pains. Graham had mixed feelings as he lay there, knowing that yet another convoy had arrived that day. With the arrival of the latest one he realised what a vulnerable state the port was in, for he knew it would be packed to capacity. He also understood that the unloading capabilities of the port were nothing like equal to the number of ships awaiting discharge. The daily visit of the German reconnaissance aircraft over the harbour also gave him an uneasy feeling, hardly the state of mind for a hospital patient to be in when awaiting examination results.

Watching the train arriving at the railway sidings on the Bari–Foggia line just outside of town was Bob Wills of the Royal Army Medical Corps (RAMC). Bob was a dental technician by profession and enlisted in theRoyal Navy on the outbreak of war. He then volunteered to join the Army and was drafted to the 98th General Hospital. He volunteered for overseas duty and landed in Algiers in early 1943. In late summer the unit embarked in the hospital ship *St David* (later to be sunk at Anzio) to disembark in Malta, embarked once more to land at Taranto and then travelled by train to reach their destination, Bari.

> The unit took over the Policlinic situated inland from the main railway station. The new hospital was built at the instigation of Mussolini, though by the time we arrived, the building was not completed. The British author-ities ordered the Italians to evacuate the premises, much to the indignation of the matron in charge. She was jumping up and down in anger, waving her arms about, shouting quotations from the Geneva Convention, but to no avail – they had to move.

On the afternoon of 2 December, the RAMC sergeant-major ordered four men of the dental department, Bob included, to board waiting ambulances to go to the railway sidings. They were to meet an ambu-lance train due in, which carried wounded servicemen evacuated from the 8th Army's front line in the north – the Sangro River area. As soon as the train ground to a halt Bob and his group set to transferring the patients to the ambulances, five to each vehicle, to begin a shuttle service to the hospital. During a break, Bob handed round cigarettes to the wounded men and offered the packet to a German soldier, one of a number of wounded prisoners of war. He sent the proffered packet flying out of Bob's hands as he refused the offer. All the others gratefully accepted.

Meanwhile, down at the docks, William (Bill) Moran was sitting in his 2 ton truck waiting for a ship to unload. Bill had been a boy soldier before the war and was now serving with No. 554 Bulk Petrol Company (Royal Army Service Corps – RASC) stationed in the small town of Trani, some 25 miles (40 km) from Bari. That morning he had been detailed off to collect a number of hand pumps from a ship in the harbour, but when he enquired at the port offices he learned that they had not been landed.

17

As he had an hour or two to spare, he had gone into town to the local Italian barber for a haircut, returned to the dockyard and was sitting in his truck waiting for news of the off-loading.

In the only part of Bari harbour which could be described as a beach, John Adams and his comrades had set up a mobile wireless station. John was serving in the Royal Corps of Signals and was attached to the 47th Light Anti-aircraft Regiment. The 30 cwt (1,500 kg) truck nicknamed by the signallers the 'Gin Palace' had been set up on the beach in late November. As it was manned night and day, a tarpaulin was erected at the rear and John and Robert (Mac) McFallon, his fellow operator, slept there. They had acquired two stout planks, which were painted in bright pink, and laid them across ammunition boxes to serve as the raised base of a rough wooden bed, albeit rather hard and narrow.

John and Mac watched the convoy enter the harbour and saw one of the ships berth a short distance from the station and immediately start unloading bombs. During the afternoon the soldiers had the wireless set operating but as they were not due to transmit for some time, they linked the set to a loudspeaker and listened to aircraft plots. John remembers seeing several seamen, soldiers and dockers gathered round the open hold of the ship. Standing behind the soldiers, which John thought were Basutos from the South African regiments, were three men dressed completely in green. Neither signaller had ever seen anyone dressed in that coloured uniform before and Mac cracked, 'The Martians are joining in.' Years later, John realised that they could have been members of a chemical warfare unit, but at that time he had no idea why they were wearing the strange-looking outfits.

Lieutenant Edwin Farnell of the Pioneer Corps left his sergeant in charge of the working party lined up on the dockside as he made his way to the port offices. Edwin was born into a musical family in Leeds, where his father was organist and choirmaster for over forty years at the city's Salem church. In the previous weeks, many of Edwin's brother officers had returned to the UK, but because he was proficient in Italian he had been retained in Bari to liaise with the Italian groups. There was already an Italian Army working party in the dockyard and the two parties, Italian and British, under the command of Lieutenant Farnell and an Italian officer who came from Sicily, worked well together loading and unloading ships.

At the offices Edwin was expecting to receive his usual evening orders, giving him the names and positions of the ships they were going to work on, the number of men needed for each vessel and what the cargoes consisted of. It was inevitable that there would be some confusion. In the office nobody seemed to be inclined to waste time answering questions, but at last he found out where his company was needed and thankfully returned to his men.

The officer commanding Transport Section RASC, Major Lumpton, was accompanied by two junior officers as he made his way back to his car, which he had parked outside the dockyard offices in the charge of his regular driver, Walter James Woodford. The RASC soldiers were billeted between Bari and Foggia and their depot was a disused municipal yard. On the other side of the road from the depot were the transport men's sleeping quarters in a five-storey building which had been a macaroni factory in peace time. Walter, who had joined the Royal Army Ordnance Corps in 1940 at Portsmouth, had arrived in Bari in October by way of Cape Town, Durban and Alexandria. He was now sitting in the driver's seat, looking forward to the evening off after taking the major back to his billet.

Working at berth 11 were a group of Royal Engineers (RE) unloading stores from the merchant ship SS *Empire Meteor*, Lance Corporal Edward (Ted) Fry was making out a convoy note for the driver of a lorry loaded with supplies. The driver needed the signed note to show to the military police on duty at the dock gate before being allowed to leave the area. Ted's job was the recognition, loading and despatch of RE stores, either to the RE dump in Bari or wherever directed. The lorries they used for the work were American 10 ton trucks and British 3 ton Bedford lorries, though horse and carts were still being used for transferring coal. Railway wagons ran as far as discharging berths 11 and 12. There were thirteen men in Edward's section, each man working a twelve-hour shift; the one Edward was working ran from 8 a.m. to 8 p.m. The only lighting was electric bulbs connected to the *Empire Meteor* by means of extra long leads trailed over the side of the ship. There was no permanent lighting on the quayside itself and Edward was writing out the note in the gathering gloom by the beam of the lorry's sidelight.

Near the harbour entrance, landing craft LCI *318* was waiting for a signal from Navy House granting permission to leave harbour. On board were 240 soldiers who were to be taken across the Adriatic Sea to be landed on the island of Vis, off the coast of Yugoslavia. Lieutenant Douglas Barnard, the captain of the landing craft, had joined the Merchant Navy in 1933 and received his mate's ticket four years later. On the outbreak of war, as a naval reservist, he became a naval officer serving aboard

19

several ships before volunteering for combined operations in 1942. He was drafted to New York to commission LCI *318*, which was being built at Brooklyn Navy Yard. After tests and trials the landing craft had arrived in Europe to take part in the landings in Sicily and Italy and for several weeks had been operating from Bari, ferrying servicemen, stores and equipment across the Adriatic.

Another peace-time merchant seaman in Bari that evening was Rowland Owen Roberts, who was serving aboard the small coastal tanker MV *Devon Coast.* He had been lucky to save himself from a watery grave when the small coaster he was serving aboard foundered off the south Devonshire coast. It was carrying a cargo of scrap iron and sank like a stone as the crew scrambled into lifeboats. Later Rowland joined *Devon Coast* during the North African campaign, where she supplied petrol to the forward ports of Bone and Bougie under constant harassment from the enemy. Now she was berthed on the outer mole awaiting a departing convoy which was due to sail the next day. Although the ship was considered empty, she carried in her bunkers 50 tons of high-octane petrol.

Anthony 'Paddy' Lindsey, an airman attached to the 1st Tactical Air Force based in Santo Spirito, some 5 miles (8 km) from Bari, was attending a friendly soccer match between a local team and a combined British services team; the venue was Bari's football stadium. As a pilot based in the south of England and part of a newly formed Royal Canadian Air Force (RCAF) squadron flying Handley-Page bombers, Paddy's first operational flight had been exceptional. He had been chasing and attacking the German battle cruisers *Scharnhorst* and *Gneisnau* during their dash from Brest to their home ports in Germany when, flying under cloud cover, he had seen a bright flash from the stern of the *Gneisnau* and promptly received a shell through the port wing. Some months later during training in four-engined bombers, Paddy had been grounded after receiving severe injuries in a crash. He recalls that during his time in Santo Spirito, Field Marshal Bernard Montgomery had a villa close by and during walks would frequently stop and chat to the airmen. From their elevated position in the stadium, Paddy and his companions could see the ships in the harbour.

During the afternoon, John Roberts of the Chaplain's Department arrived with some of his comrades to attend a fellowship meeting at the Italian church. John had arrived at Bari during September from Egypt, by way of Tobruk, Sicily and Taranto. He was the personal clerk to Colonel Hillbourne, the Assistant Chaplain General for No. 2 District, which covered the area of Bari and Taranto. The free churches had been made most welcome by the Italian Protestant Church (Waldensian Presbyterian) and had a very active Christian fellowship which John had enthusiastically joined. He recalls: 'How easy-going it all was when stationed in Bari – no air raid drills or precautions, no air raid shelters or at least I never noticed any, and ice cream on sale, something I had never seen for over two years.'

In the stokers' mess aboard HMS *Vienna*, Engine-room Artificer Keith Hedger was enjoying his tea after coming off afternoon watch. He recalls that in pre-war days the *Vienna* had been a cross-channel ferry peacefully plying between Harwich and the Hook of Holland. When war started she was converted to a Coastal Forces depot ship and was still coal fired. Keith says, 'I could write a book about the many problems we had trying to keep steam up.' The vessel was moored alongside the Molo Ridosso, the mole situated at right-angles to the main dock. Her role was to service and maintain the many small craft based in Bari. Standing sentry on her gangway was Able Seaman Francis Newman, who had arrived from training in the UK to join *Vienna* in Malta as a replacement for a sick rating.

Convoy Signalman Cyril James Simpson was serving aboard SS *Empire Meteor*, the ship that Ted Fry and his company were helping to discharge. Earlier in the war Cyril had been based at Liverpool, where his job was signalman on merchant ships which carried the Commodore. He eventually arrived at Augusta, where he was carrying out the same operation. The convoy, which numbered twenty-one ships with the Commodore aboard *Empire Meteor*, arrived at Bari on the morning of 2 December. Cyril and two other signallers arranged to go ashore in the evening, as once the ship had docked they were free of duties.

The American liberty ship USS *Samuel J. Tilden* arrived at Bari in the late afternoon of 2 December, accompanied by the Polish ship SS *Lublin*. Both had sailed from Taranto on the second leg of a voyage from Bizerte in North Africa. They were escorted by the trawler-minesweeper HMT *Mullet*. The American ship anchored just outside the harbour entrance. Captain Joseph Lumpkin Blair was the master of the vessel, which had on board a mixed cargo including five hospital units, two tractor-trailer units and 6,000 gal (27,275 litres) of high-octane petrol stored in Nos 4 and 5 holds. Besides a crew of sixty-nine, she had on board as passengers 186 American soldiers and twenty-three British Army personnel. One of the British soldiers was Anthony (Tony) Thacker, Royal Artillery, attached to the 1st Airborne Division. He and the rest of his group had embarked at Bizerte and as Bari hove into view, he was on deck surveying the scene.

The workhorses of the Royal Navy, the minesweepers, several of which were based in Bari, were kept busy sweeping the coastal shipping lanes and harbour entrances, as the enemy sowed large numbers of mines, mostly during the hours of darkness. HMS *Sharpshooter*, captained by Lt Cdr Omara, RN, had sailed from Glasgow to Malta in May 1943 to begin sweeping between Malta and Sicily in preparation for the mainland invasion. Since then she had been on constant sweeping operations and had arrived in Bari in early November. She was moored at berth 4 with her sister ship HMS *Hazard*, on board which Able Seaman Victor Webster was writing letters in the mess deck.

HMS *Hazard* had arrived in Bari after more than a year minesweeping in the freezing inhospitable waters of the Arctic Ocean, clearing the way for convoys to and from the approaches to the Russian port of Murmansk. Able Seaman Robert Forrest had joined the ship when she was undergoing a refit in Aberdeen in 1941. In the summer of 1943 she was recalled to the Clyde at short notice where she joined a convoy bound for North Africa, denying her crew any chance of leave.

Another small minesweeper in the harbour was the Royal Navy's BYMS *2012* which was built in Seattle on the west coast of the United States. In 1942 Hugh Hanley had crossed the Atlantic on the *Queen Mary* and then enjoyed a panoramic journey across the American continent by Pullman coach to join her. After commissioning, the ship had sailed through the Panama Canal to Brazil and crossed the Atlantic at its narrowest part to Dakar, on the west coast of Africa. She arrived at Bari via Gibraltar, Algiers and Malta. On the afternoon of 2 December, Hugh went ashore with two shipmates.

Three members of Coastal Forces who had not gone ashore were Peter Bickmore (MTB *234*), Jack Taylor (MTB *86*) and Arthur Styles (MTB *297*). The boats had returned to Bari that morning after carrying out night patrol operations off the coast of Albania and Yugoslavia. These motor torpedo boats were manned by a crew of twelve and MTB *297*, which was berthed adjacent to the base ship HMS *Vienna*, was captained by Lt John Woods, a Canadian.

Lt Cdr Morgan Giles MBE, GM, Staff Officer Special Operations at Bari, an officer with an outstanding war record, was in his quarters in the

Albergo Imperiale. The large hotel proved very convenient, not being a great distance from the harbour and dockyard.

That day, 2 December, signalled Captain 'Jock' Campbell's last day as Naval Officer in Charge (NOIC) Bari. In the evening he was at Navy House in the company of Captain Eustace Guinness, who was due to take over from him the following day.

The Polish vessel SS *Lwow* lay at anchor in the middle of the harbour about 300 yards from the end of Vecchio Molo and twice that distance from the end of Molo Pizzoli. David Williams and Arthur Spencer, two of the four naval gunners serving on board were below deck writing letters. In 1941 Arthur had spent an extremely cold, wet night in a lifeboat in mid-Atlantic after his ship had sunk under him. He was rescued and landed at the Azores on New Years Day. After survivor's leave he had been drafted to Barry docks, South Wales to join SS *Lwow*, one of six British men aboard. Little did he know that the letter he was writing would finish up at the bottom of the harbour.

Between berths 26 and 27 was the Norwegian ship SS *Norlom*. She had taken on board a full cargo of coal in October and arrived in Bari in the middle of November. Radio operator Frederick Ian Peyman, who at that time was twenty years old and serving on board, recalls, 'The Board of Trade in their wisdom had ordered 10,000 tons of coal to be despatched to Bari for use on the railways to supply the 8th Army, but when it arrived nobody in Bari had the slightest idea what to do with it.' Consequently while other ships were entering, discharging and leaving harbour *Norlom*, with her cargo of coal, stayed put for more than two weeks. Ian says the only excitement during that period was the evening practice alarms.

Riding at anchor in the middle of the outer harbour was the British motor torpedo depot ship HMS *Vulcan*. In a few hours this vessel which took its name from the mythical Roman god of fire and metal, was to be enveloped in a holocaust of those two elements plus explosions of poisonous liquid and fumes, the outcome of which was to affect Able Seaman Bertram (Bert) Stevens for the rest of his life.

Bert had joined the Royal Navy at Portsmouth in 1940 when he was seventeen years of age. He signed on for twelve years – seven in the colours and five in the reserve; at that time he had every intention of making a career in the Royal Navy. On completion of his basic training he had received a draft to the Mediterranean theatre of war. He had travelled by train to Glasgow where he was given a berth as a passenger on a troopship waiting in the Clyde. The ship had sailed round the Cape via Durban to arrive in Alexandria, Egypt, where he joined the naval draft pool. Two weeks later he had received his draft to HMS *Vulcan*, at that time based in the Egyptian port.

In the ensuing months *Vulcan* had operated in the Egyptian and Libyan ports as the 8th Army advanced and retreated during that critical period of the desert war. After the collapse of the Axis resistance and the Allied landings in Sicily, she had arrived in Bari in November 1943 and was anchored, waiting for an available berth. On the evening of 2 December, Bert was on quarterdeck duty, taking the last dog-watch, 6p.m. to 8p.m.

Five miles (8 km) from the harbour, on the road to Barletta, lay the small local airfield where two Royal Air Force men were waiting for a lift into town. The airfield was split into three sections: US Army Air Force, Russian Air Force and the Royal Air Force. The American section was sited at the top of the gently sloping airfield where on the opposite side of the road overlooking the airfield was a large Italian Army barracks. The USAAF carried out reconnaissance operations using Mosquito fighter bombers. On the opposite side of the airfield, adjacent to the railway line, 267 Squadron RAF had a flight of Dakotas which were used solely for transport purposes. The Russian sector, sited in the middle, had no operational role, although a squadron of Yak-90 long-range fighters was based there.

The two airmen waiting for a lift were Frank Saggers and Andy Carson. Both had seen service on the beleaguered island of Malta during the siege of 1941–3, and had then transferred to North Africa. After regrouping, the squadron had moved to Sicily and then to Bari in early November. On their evening off duty they were looking forward to the usual drink in the café-bar they had discovered soon after arriving in Bari. It was situated near to the old part of the city, on the main road, the Via Napoli, and a short distance from the garden square named after Italy's national hero, Garibaldi. It was also one block away from the buildings fronting the harbour.

The two airmen had soon made friends with the proprietor, Marcus, who, Frank recalls, 'kept a fine stock of wines'. In a very short time they were made to feel at home and in their spare time, when not playing or watching football matches, at the city's stadium to the south-west of Bari, they were usually to be found in the café. Another attraction was that the bar possessed a billiard table. Little did they know in no more than an hour or two the billiard table with its sturdy legs and thick slate bed would serve a very different purpose. The lorry picked the men up and after the short journey to town the driver dropped them off at their favourite watering hole. A few minutes later they were seated in the bar drinking a glass of the local wine.

One block away, in the next street, 13-year-old Alberto Lugli was playing cards with two British soldiers. Alberto lived with his mother and sisters in an apartment block on Corso Trieste, the main road skirting the harbour, one of seven blocks opposite the Molo Pizzoli, which was used as a berth for small craft. The seven buildings had been commandeered by the British war administration, though most of the families had been allowed to remain in their homes. The ground floors, which were occupied by servicemen, were designated by the men who worked and lived in them A Block, B Block, C Block etc.

The buildings were in the newer part of the city but not a great distance from the ancient Castella Federico di Evevia. The Lugli family, whose father was away serving in the Italian Army, lived in the middle block on the third floor and Alberto and his sisters attended a school in C Block. Over the last few weeks the British servicemen had made friends with the children who played in the adjoining streets with their friends.

Working with the 1007th British Port Authority Company at berth 17, where SS *Empire Sunbeam* was moored, was Dominico Iacabone. His job was the unloading and checking of stores and equipment discharged from ships. He worked alongside other units in the dockyard and on the

Football taking place in the Bari stadium. On the afternoon before the raid a football match took place between an Italian side and a Combined Services side. RAF man 'Paddy' Hanley was a spectator at the time. *(F. Saggers)*

evening of 2 December he was engaged in checking a number of American jeeps. The whole dockside was a hive of activity as every berthed vessel discharged its cargo in the glare of dockyard lights. He recalls, 'There were at least a thousand servicemen and civilians working on the dockside at any one time, twenty-four hours a day.'

Aboard the USS *John Bascom* the crew were delighted when Ensign Kay Vesole and Captain Otto Heitmann had returned to the ship with a bag of mail which was immediately distributed. In a short time Warren Brandenstein and the rest of the crew were reading their mail from home.

The master of the USS *Lyman Abbott*, Captain Dalstrom had also been ashore. With gunnery officer Lieutenant Walker he had left by motor boat to make the mile journey to the port office to receive orders and to draw money and dockyard passes for the crew. George Maury remembers that they returned in time for the evening meal and afterwards, 'We went to the purser's office to sign for our pay, his quarters being just the other side of the alley from mine. I don't know how it happened but they all finished up in my quarters discussing the queer-looking script that we were to use for money while we were in Italy.' Meanwhile Leo Krause had spent the afternoon relaxing after cleaning his gun and in the early evening he was writing letters in his cabin.

Stanley Wisniewski had spent part of the afternoon on the same task as Leo Krause and chatting to Donald Meissner, who was on watch at the stern of the vessel where the 3.5 inch (90 mm) gun he was cleaning was situated. Later in the evening he was getting ready for a friendly game of cards with his shipmates. Meanwhile Donald retired below to change from his foul-weather gear into more comfortable clothes.

3

THE DISASTER

IT was dark as Albert Jones and I reached the point on the outer mole where it narrowed. The wider part was Molo Foraneo; where it turned left at an angle of 45 degrees, it became Nuovo Molo, narrowed and ran for approximately 1,000 yards to the end. We were at the beginning of Nuovo Molo when we heard the sound of aircraft overhead. It was instantly followed by a single flare which illuminated the harbour and then several more. Both of us knew what that meant.

Many times previously, when escorting convoys off the North African coast, *Zetland* had been subjected to the deployment of flares, as the enemy dropped them in front of the convoy for hours on end. They lit up the scene for submarines and E-boats and, more importantly, kept convoy crews on constant watch the whole of the night, so that they would be tired and slow to react when the enemy attacks started. Here in Bari, however, as the flares slowly descended, the first bombs dropped. It signalled an outburst of activity. The scream of falling bombs rent the air and the crash and crump as they landed sent shock waves along the breakwater.

According to the British official report, written some days after the raid (and secret for thirty years):

> (b) Approach
> The enemy achieved a large measure of surprise by making a low approach to the point 20 to 25 miles North of Bari at which the climb to bombing height commenced. The raid was led in by two pathfinders who laid a screen of 'window' which effectively cluttered up the GCI screen and masked the approach of the main body of about 20 aircraft. This was the first occasion on which window had been used on the East Coast and, as a result, delay in recognition of the symptoms and their significance undoubtedly occurred at more than link in the chain of defence. The first pair circled about 10 miles off the port until joined by two more aircraft, when they came in and illuminated the target area with red and green flares.
>
> In short, the approach was well and carefully planned and most successfully executed. A very high proportion of the credit for the success must be given to the pathfinders who were drill perfection.

(c) The Attack

Planes came in at heights varying from 5,000 to 11,000 feet, except that at the end of the raid a single plane dived to 3,000 feet. Generally speaking bombing runs appeared to take the form of a shallow dive from East to West across the harbour, the majority directed at the San Caltado quay and the tanker at no. 32 berth. Sticks fell across the Eastern Basin, VIENNA being near missed ahead by one of them and astern by another, and the main quay, FORT ASSINIBOINE AT No. 6 being near missed. The hulk GOGGIAM, was hit and flooded, probably by the tag end of one of the latter, but the hulk VOLODDA, anchored off Molo Pizzoli, received individual attention and was hit by two of a stick of five.

Captain Campbell, in his report, has stated the Navy House was one of the main targets, but I consider this improbable in view of the fact that the only bomb on land anywhere in the vicinity fell just behind 15 Quay.

Even allowing for the degree of surprise achieved presented the enemy with his target 'on a plate' the attack was as well carried out and executed as the approach. RAF reported it as being the best planned and most skilfully executed raid in this theatre to date. Intelligence since the raid confirms the impression given by the performance itself, namely that the task was entrusted to a first class unit. It is probable that they came from a base North of the Alps, staging at an airfield in Eastern Lombardy probably RIMINI or RAVENNA.

Times

Time of occurrences during the night are difficult to report accurately as, in all reports received from Base Officers and from sources outside and authorities outside the Base, not one person has the same idea of the time of any given occurrences as any other person. The reasons for this are apparent. Such records as were kept in Navy House and probably in many other places were lost or destroyed during the night. Every man under conditions such as were prevailing that night has a mistaken conception of the passage of time, and, anyway for most people, time is immaterial and they neither look at their watch or ask the time. One which can be stated more accurately than any other is that of the first explosion which stopped many of the clocks in Navy house, thus leaving its own record.

In a mad scramble, lorries, half-tracks, jeeps, vans and motor bikes made a concerted dash along the mole, driving at breakneck speed, making for the dockyard entrance. Anyone walking, as we were, in the opposite direction of the mass of vehicles roaring by, took their life in their hands. Besides the heavy traffic we had to contend with a rush of servicemen and civilians running at top speed towards the exits and shelters. It was reminiscent of a capacity crowd leaving at the end of a football match. We struggled through the throng until we came to a concrete shelter built up against the wall of the breakwater. Standing guard just inside the entrance was a Sikh soldier, who called to us to take cover. The raid reached a crescendo, the tremendous noise pounding the eardrums as bomb after bomb struck in quick succession.

When we entered the shelter the noise was almost as deafening as outside. People were shouting and screaming at one another, some hysterical and scared out of their wits, others praying and singing hymns. After five minutes or so we decided to continue our journey back to *Zetland* and we thankfully came out of the shelter, leaving the seemingly unperturbed Sikh sentry still on guard. The raid was almost over – probably twenty minutes had passed since the start – but the noise was even more deafening now that the anti-aircraft guns had joined in. Vehicles were still passing, though not in the same numbers as before, and we could see in front of us that ships had been hit further along the mole. Fingers of flame and dense black smoke were belching into the night sky in the area of the line of shipping and as we hurried along we began to wonder what condition we would find our ship and silently prayed she was not one of the vessels on fire.

It was at this point that we came upon a most gruesome sight. In the fiery red glow, we could just make out, flattened to the concrete, the shape of a large body. Large because it had been rolled and stretched like pastry under a rolling-pin, arms and legs outstretched in the manner of a scarecrow or a small child's drawing, but unlike an inanimate scarecrow, only a few minutes before this had been one of us, a vibrant human being. The body had been run over time and time again by extremely heavy traffic so that when we approached it to examine it, there was nothing left but a vague human shape with no substance. There was no possibility of ascertaining what or who it had been as vehicles were still running over it, unseen by the unaware drivers.

Dragging our eyes away from the sickening sight, we continued along the mole and eventually reached the two destroyers which, to our relief, were still afloat and not on fire, though battered from near misses. We made our way over *Bicester*'s deck to board the *Zetland*. It was to be two days before I saw Albert again. Once on board I had a chance to see what the situation was and dashed to the forecastle, from whose raised vantage point I had a view, towards the harbour entrance, of some of the vessels moored stern first to the mole. Fires were raging on many of them, although the tremendous glare and smoke made it impossible to make out any individual ship in the middle of the line or see any sign of men on board any of them. I could, however, see ships' plates glowing red.

Bob Davies had been enjoying a pot of tea on *Zetland*'s bridge when the flares spread their penetrating glare over the harbour. When he heard the drone of aircraft he immediately hit the alarm button. The crash of bombs instantly followed as the enemy pilots targeted the line of packed shipping forward of *Zetland*. It seemed to Bob that the anti-aircraft guns took a long time to open fire, though he knew that the two destroyer's guns could not operate owing to the closeness of other ships moored nearby. As the rest of the bridge staff arrived, he noticed one of the burning flares gently floating down. It eventually came to rest in the mast of a ship just forward of *Zetland* and he believes it caused the fire which broke out on board. The fire soon became a raging inferno. Bob also believes the ship was the naval tanker *Devon Coast*.

For some time bombs fell all over the harbour, the men on the open bridge ducking and dodging flying shrapnel as successive near misses rocked the destroyer. Bob saw hits scored on the line of shipping and fires break out. The result was catastrophic. As the fires gained hold, preparations were under way on several vessels to abandon ship. Other ships at anchor in the harbour had received direct hits and the crews were already taking to lifeboats and rafts.

The sentry standing on guard at the foot of HMS *Vienna*'s gangway, Able Seaman Francis Newman, saw flares descending in the night sky, followed by the firing of tracer shells from a gun position in the city. He believed the firing of tracer was a prearranged warning signal of an imminent air attack. He did not see or hear any aircraft for a few seconds, then he heard a loud crash forward of the depot ship, immediately followed by another to stern. The two near misses caused considerable damage.

The first bomb exploded right at the edge of the narrow Molo Ridosso, where *Vienna* was moored at berth 11. It took out a large chunk of the mole and sent water cascading over the ship. Francis was knocked off his feet and sent reeling as the gangway behind him was carried away by the blast. Regaining his feet he looked towards the concrete pill-box which housed an anti-aircraft gun battery and was manned by soldiers with whom *Vienna*'s crew had become friendly. Only minutes before one of the soldiers had brought him a mug of tea. Francis could not believe his eyes. 'The pill-box had vanished and as there was no sign of the soldiers, I realised it must have been blasted into the water.'

*   *   *

John Adams and Mac, in the wireless truck, heard over the loudspeaker, 'One plane square one'. He does not remember the square number but knew that it was an area near Manfredonia, some 50 miles (80 km) up the coast. This was immediately followed by 'Two planes not showing IFF [radar response of friendly planes].' This soon became 'Three planes not showing IFF' in the same square but nearer. The floodlight on the discharging ammunition ship was still on as Mac, a veteran of Dunkirk, reached into the truck and without a word handed John his steel helmet and at the same time put his own on. Because of past experience, Mac had always impressed on John never to crawl under a truck to shelter, for he had seen too many soldiers crushed in that fashion, so they remained at the rear of the truck.

Suddenly they saw a stick of bombs coming down. John says:

> The bombs coming down passed the ones coming up out of the hold. The enemy bombs caused one of the most amazing sights imaginable. In a split second, the entire deck from stem to stern lifted with a thunderous flash and roar. The whole sky was illuminated as the complete deck section in one piece and still in a horizontal position, rose to a height of what I estimate was 1,000 feet. I can recall seeing the Basuto soldiers and the green uniformed men running across the deck and at that distance they were only quarter inch figures. The deck then disintegrated and flaming debris rained down over the whole harbour area. The hull of the ship was a mass of flame. I was amazed that the deck could have parted and gone up in one piece and afterwards I came to the conclusion that the ship must have been of welded construction.

Hugh Kerr and his shipmate 'Scouse', both gunners aboard the unseaworthy destroyer HMS *Quail*, heard the drone of planes and closed up at their 20 mm gun position. The *Quail* was used as part of the port defences and as flares began to descend the gunners opened fire. They had barely started when an officer demanded that they stop as no order had been given to open fire. No sooner had he departed than other guns opened up so Hugh and his pal carried on until the end of the raid. Later Hugh found himself as part of a scratch crew made up at short notice from members of the base staff, with the intention of manning an Italian tug moored in the inner harbour. He took over the job of helmsman in the small wheelhouse, but the stokers below in the engine room could not understand the controls, the descriptions of which were written in Italian. They had no option but to use the voice-pipe to relay orders to one another. Under way at last, the officer in charge ordered them to close up to the bows of a tanker in mid-harbour which had fires on her upper deck. As they approached, Hugh saw men flinging themselves overboard onto life-rafts and floats. Others were jumping into the water to escape the flames and still others scrambling down ropes and ladders to meet the approaching tug.

The tug had only taken a handful of men on board when the master of the tanker, the last man to board the rescue tug, shouted, 'Get away as fast as you can' as it was obvious he judged the tanker could not last much longer. The order 'Full speed astern' was given and the tug gathered speed but had only gone a short distance when the tanker blew up in an enormous sheet of flame.

The effect was devastating; the tanker disappeared in a spiralling ball of flame, leaving a mushrooming pall of smoke. Before the 20-year-old Scotsman lost consciousness he saw 'the tanker's sides ballooning outwards'. When he regained his senses, what remained of the tug was rapidly sinking beneath him. He was lying on what had been the deck with the shattered remains of the wheelhouse on top of him. Looking round, only one man was visible; all the rest had vanished, the rescued and rescuers alike. The other survivor, a shipmate of Hugh's aboard the *Quail* was lying besides him on the sinking wreck. He was strangely enough clad in a duffel coat which was to prove a disastrously lethal garment, but at that time Hugh never gave it a second thought. When Hugh had revived his shipmate he told him that their only chance was to swim for it before the wreck sank, so with the black greasy scum of water lapping round the remains of the tug, they lowered themselves into the water.

Besides the oil covering the surface, rubbish and debris from sunken and disintegrated ships added to the problem of swimming. As they struck out for the jetty, the filthy water got into their mouths and eyes and clung to their clothes, making progress painfully slow. Hugh saw in the distance a sheet of fire sweeping along the surface and he urged his companion to greater effort, but the other man, clad in his duffel coat, was beginning to falter. Both men had been too shocked and bewildered after the explosion to realise that he should have got rid of the coat before commencing to swim. As it became soaked, the woollen coat must have been a tremendous drag on him and it was obvious that he was tiring very quickly. However, it was now too late to attempt to take the coat off. After a few minutes he stopped swimming and began to cry out, 'Help me Jock, help me' time and time again. Their position became more serious as Hugh thought the flames on the surface seemed nearer than before. He exhorted his comrade once again to further effort, but to no avail; he had given up hope. Hugh felt his own strength slowly sapping away and at that moment realised that he would be lucky to make it to safety himself.

He concentrated on reaching the jetty, steeling himself against the pleading cries and screams behind him. He was still some distance away from the jetty when the cries ceased and after what seemed an eternity he at last reached the safety of the quayside. Grasping a dangling iron chain he stayed there for some time, unable to do more than hang on for grim death. Then inch by inch he dragged his weary, soaking body up the chain, every grasp of his swollen hands sending pains shooting up his arms. When at last he crawled over the edge and onto dry land he lay utterly exhausted on the wet concrete pier, completely unaware of the chaos and destruction around him. But his travails were not yet over for as he lay there a tremendous explosion occurred as one of the ships blew up and Hugh felt a terrific movement of air pass over him as the blast rocked the harbour. Some time later he gazed out over the water in the faint hope of seeing his comrade, but he soon realised he must have succumbed. The feeling of regret and the hopelessness of it all was to remain with Hugh for the rest of his life and was a recurring nightmare until his death in April 1993.

As the planes started to bomb the line of shipping, Leonard Walker, a Royal Navy gunner aboard the Danish ship SS *Lars Kruse* moored almost in the centre of the line of shipping, dashed to his gun position and commenced firing even though the gunners had not received orders from the bridge. They kept on firing until the ammunition on the gun platform had been expended and then dashed to the ready-use lockers on the main deck below for replenishment. At that point there was a huge explosion as the ship took a direct hit in Nos 2 and 4 holds, which contained high-octane petrol in cans.

Before he passed out, Leonard felt himself being lifted up. He came to on the deck near the bosun's ladder. As he staggered to his feet another blast hit him, this time carrying him over the side to land in the water yards from the ship. He came to the surface spluttering and choking, and trod water until his head cleared. He saw a section of wood floating on the surface substantial enough to be bearing the weight of a man spread-eagled across one end of it. He made for it and grabbed the other end. As he did so, the other man slid into the water and disappeared into the depths. Leonard expected him to surface but he never did. More than likely the man had died after pulling himself on to the makeshift raft. Minutes later the gunner heard cries and shouts, and through the smoke he saw a small group of men hanging onto a life-raft. He swam towards the survivors and found that one was a shipmate, an Army gunner. With great difficulty, paddling with their hands, they managed to bring the raft to the side of the mole, luckily at the bottom of a flight of stone steps.

Leonard dashed along the mole to join a queue of shivering, trembling, badly shocked men who were all in a filthy state as they waited their turn to board a destroyer moored alongside. It was at that moment that Leonard, also in a state of great shock, realised all his clothes had been blown away and he was standing there completely naked but covered head to foot in a black, greasy substance.

When the first flare came drifting down, Lieutenant Douglas Barnard was standing on the small bridge of the landing craft LCI *318*. He was surveying the peaceful though busy harbour scene as he waited for sailing orders from Navy House. Evenings in harbour were a special time for mariners. At sea dawn and sunset were the two most dangerous periods of the day and ships' crews closed up at action stations to cover those critical hours of semi-darkness. During most evenings in harbour sailors cherished the moments of peace, calm and quiet when there was time for letter writing or relaxing as Douglas was doing, thoughts wending their way over the miles to family and loved ones, thinking of what they would be doing at that very moment and hoping that fate would be kind enough to reunite them in the near future.

Little did Douglas know that for many of his fellow mariners and others, such thoughts were impossible dreams; at the moment the first flare left the aircraft, hundreds of lives were on the verge of extinction. He was suddenly awakened from his reveries when he heard the sound of aircraft overhead. Realising how vulnerable his human cargo was, he immediately took the decision to sail, for all the 240 soldiers on board were wearing full packs and equipment and were packed close together in the body of the landing craft. LCI *318* had reached the open sea and was on her way across the Adriatic before the raid was over.

One of the bombs landed on the naval tanker MV *Devon Coast*, where Rowland Owen Roberts had been ordered with the rest of the crew who were not needed on the bridge to take shelter in the alleyways astern. He heard a terrific whistling sound as the bomb struck. The explosion lifted him off his feet and carried him over the side to hit the water some 20 feet away, where he plunged into the blackness of the harbour depths. After what seemed an eternity, he rose to the surface, shocked and confused, his lungs bursting, not comprehending what had happened to him in those few short moments. He had the presence of mind to swim away from the tanker as he saw her rocking from side to side, as he feared being sucked under if she sank. Luckily he was a strong swimmer and kept his distance, from where he could see fires on the upper deck of *Devon Coast* and other ships on fire further along the mole. He made up his mind to make for the opposite end of the mole, nearer to the dockyard. He was fortunate to come across one of *Devon Coast*'s boats, which had been lowered earlier in the day for the use of the ship's company. The gunner's mate swam up alongside him as he reached the boat and both men struggled aboard to find that all the gear that should have been on board was missing or destroyed. It appeared that it was only the flotation tanks that were keeping it afloat.

Without oars or paddles but using bits of wood, they made their way towards other men in the water who were shouting and screaming for help. Both shipmates had an extremely difficult task hauling the men out of the water and into the boat, as most of them had little strength left. All were suffering from extreme shock, as were the two comrades themselves, and many of the survivors screamed with pain as they were dragged on board. When they had picked up as many as the boat would hold, they set off for the breakwater to land them on the far side of the two destroyers at berth 24. What happened to the survivors after he landed them, Rowland never knew, for when he and the gunner's mate climbed back down to the boat to resume rescuing, it sank beneath them some distance from where they had set off. The tanks must have been taking in water all the time since the explosion. For the second time that night Rowland found himself in the water and again had to swim for it. He thought he would never reach the breakwater, for his strength and endurance had been sorely tested, but eventually he pulled himself thankfully up onto dry land, although he saw no sign of his comrade.

The action stations alarm startled Warren Brandenstein as it reverberated round the USS *John Bascom*. He quickly threw on some clothes and dashed to his 3.5 in (90 mm) anti-aircraft gun situated on the bow of the ship.

> The sky was lit up by flares by the time I reached my battle station, put on my helmet and earphones and proceeded to take orders from Ensign Kay Vesole on the bridge. I was sight-setter on the gun. The ship next to us took a hit and the next thing I did was to go to the ammunition magazine on deck to re-set the explosive timers on the shells. At that time I had just got my head above the magazine as we were hit three times, on hold No. 2, the bridge and the after gun deck. My helmet and earphones were blown off my head and I fell down and crawled on the deck as all kinds of debris showered down. An officer gave the order to abandon ship. I was the last one off my gun position after trying to find my wristwatch which was blown away with my helmet and earphones. Crazy as it may seem, one of my shipmates, the radio operator, had to come and get me. Only one lifeboat

on the boat deck was serviceable when I finally reached there; many of the uninjured Armed Guard jumped overboard and swam to the breakwater only a short distance away and I was ready to go in the water when Ensign Vesole grabbed me and said 'Brandy [my nickname], get into the lifeboat – you are wounded.' I guess I did not realise that my face and left hand were a bloody mess. After reaching the breakwater in the boat, I could see there were many men from other ships retreating on to the end of it. Some of them, me included, got into the shelter, closed the door and prayed. Suddenly, a blast like nothing I had ever heard before blew the door in. We saw through the open door that the whole harbour was aflame, with burning oil on the surface of the water and ships were on fire and exploding. To make matters worse an off-shore wind was blowing the flames towards us on the breakwater.

Stanley Wisniewski never started his game of cards on board USS *Lyman Abbott*. Donald Meissner had just stripped off his foul-weather gear, George Maury was picking up from the deck the 'funny money' which the chief engineer had playfully tossed into the air and Leo Krause was sitting in the mess deck. Suddenly they heard a terrific bang as the bombing started. Leo rushed up on deck to his gun position as fast as he could as flares illuminated the night sky. When the rest of the gun crews arrived they immediately let go with all they had. At the end of the raid, *Lyman Abbott* suffered a near miss on the stern starboard side. Leo remembers: 'There occurred a terrific explosion which blew me off my feet and I landed on my back, where I lay dizzy for some time before I saw what had happened to me. There was blood all over, my right leg was twisted and I banged it to straighten it out. The wound was near my hip and the bone was sticking out.'

Donald Meissner stuffed cotton wool in his ears, put on his helmet and ran to his gun platform.

> I could not see anything above the flares but three bombs hit the water off our bow and the fourth hit just off the stern. It was so close the mud from the bottom of the harbour struck me in the face. I know the ship rose out of the water because I felt it slap the surface as it came down again. Suddenly there was a blinding flash as if night had turned to day, then a thunderous explosion sent all of us sprawling onto the deck, whose steel was vibrating as if to tear itself apart. It then began to rain shrapnel on the deck and I could tell the different sizes by the sound of impact. When all the fury of the explosion subsided, there was a deathly silence except for the moans and cries of the wounded and dying. A lot of blood was coming out of my nose and ears from the concussion, which had blown the shoes off my feet. One piece of shrapnel had entered my mouth, went

up through my upper left jaw, fracturing it and came out under my left eye. I had intense pain under my lower left rib and found I could not put any weight on my left leg. At that moment the coxswain arrived to tell me that the Captain had ordered 'Abandon ship'.

George Maury says that he was 'damn near trampled to death' as he bent to pick up his 'new' Italian money from the floor of his quarters, as all his shipmates made a concerted dash for their battle stations.

I was assigned to the 20 mm gun on the port bridge, my job was to wind up the spring feed of the magazine and pass them on to Lt Browne who was the loader and the gunner was a guy we called Ski for I never knew his name. The other loader was killed in the gun tub when a large piece of steel rolled up to about the size of a ten-quart pail landed on the deck, bounced up and hit him in the back of the neck, just underneath the rim of his helmet. I dived down behind the ready-use locker and my head was out over the coaming and I was looking down onto the hatches of No. 3 hold and thinking if that hold blew up, with my head out over the edge, it would take my head off; for there was 2,300 tons of fragmentation bombs down there. While this was going through my mind, debris and shrapnel began to fall and something hit and it hurt like hell. I thought, brother, you've had it. I felt around where it hurt, there were no holes or damage to my clothes or life-jacket so I checked some more. It appeared that a case of 45 calibre bullets had hit the rail around the flying bridge, burst open and a package of bullets had struck my life-jacket, round my hips.

The Captain called a meeting on the boat deck to assess the damage and the Third Mate, Rex Grodevant, came forward and reported that we had taken a hit aft and it had blown up the deck all the way up to the boat deck. He pointed to the spud locker and said that it had come out there. It looked as if the deck had been torn up during the blast, but what really had happened was that a huge chunk of steel from one of the exploded ships had landed on top of the spud locker. From the report given by the Mate, the Captain decided it was too dangerous to stay aboard.

When the alarm sounded, Stanley Wisniewski had a slight feeling of fear. He put on his steel helmet and his life-jacket and rushed to his station.

During the air raid I was at my gun position setting the sights for the gunner. Without warning an explosion occurred and I was knocked unconscious. I have no idea how long I lay there there on the deck, but when I came to I felt pain in my foot and in my buttocks. I also had a head wound and felt blood running down my face and I did not realise how badly my arms were burned. I limped forward, where I found my buddy, Paul Miller. He was standing holding a fire hose into the forward hold, only there was no water coming out of it. Today he does not know how or what he was doing at that time. I saw a pool of blood coming out of his thigh and I knew he was hurt for he had also been struck with a piece of metal the size of an orange. I said to him, 'Let's get out of here.'

At a site on the outskirts of Brindisi, John Dawson was the NCO in charge of a VHF/DF (Very High Frequency Direction Finder) station. It formed part of 286 Wing RAF and its task was to fix the position of our own aircraft forward of the station. On the evening of 2 December John recalls:

We were stood down, which meant that none of our aircraft were operational at that time. Although the station was still manned the sets were switched off and the operators were 'at ease', relaxing in the station mess hall. During the evening one of the operators called my attention to a glow in the sky interspaced with flashes that clearly spelt an air raid in progress. I was so convinced that enemy action was taking place that I felt constrained to contact 286 Wing Operations to enquire whether we should be stood down when there was obviously major action taking place to the north-west of us. I was assured that there was nothing on the board and therefore no need for our services.

At the air base of Foggia, some 130 miles (200 km) north-west of John Dawson's unit, and shortly before John had witnessed the glow in the sky, Aircraftsman Wireless Operator Fred Barlow picked up signals of a large group of planes. The aircraft were approaching from northern Italy heading in the direction of Naples. Fighter aircraft, including Fred's wing, were alerted and scrambled. Meanwhile, unknown to Fred, other enemy aircraft were approaching the port of Bari from the Adriatic Sea. These planes were detected too late to be intercepted. By the time the defending planes had been diverted, the damage had been done. To aid the deception, it transpired that enemy planes had flown down the west coast of Italy in what appeared to be a raid on Naples. The planes dropped large amounts of 'window', which was extremely effective in fooling the radar defence screen into believing that the port of Naples was the intended target.

The ambulance train in the sidings was almost empty as Bob Wills leaned against the railway coach, enjoying a cigarette while waiting for the ambulance to return from the hospital to pick up the few remaining patients. He was gazing up at the hundreds of stars, resplendent in a cloudless sky, when without warning the area was illuminated by flares. Bofors and Oerlikon guns sited nearby opened fire at low angle as the American smoke machines went into action, churning out clouds of black impenetrable smoke, and in a matter of minutes visibility was down to a minimum. Unknown to Bob while this was taking place the last ambulance had come, loaded up and departed leaving him stranded in the middle of a dense blanket of fog, not knowing which way to move and completely disorientated as his field of view was about 2 inches from his nose.

Adding to his terror was the tremendous noise. Bombs shook the ground under his feet as explosions sent him reeling. Shrapnel was clattering down all around him and his only thought of shelter was underneath the train – if he could find it. He got down on his hands and knees and crept in ever widening circles until his fingers came into contact with the edge of the platform. He scrambled over the lip and lay tight up against the wall. It gave him some protection, though his heart was in his mouth at the thought of the train moving off under orders to remove it from danger. It might have saved the train but would have in all probability crushed Bob to death. In the event it did not happen and he had to decide on his next move.

Outside the harbour entrance, the liberty ship USS *Samuel J. Tilden* lay at anchor bathed in the beam of a searchlight. The reason for the searchlight was that for some time German E-boats had been sowing mines in the entrance and approaches to the harbour during the hours of darkness. During November, two British warships had been put out of action after striking mines, and to counter the mine-laying, the Port Authority had decided to illuminate the entrance.

As the planes roared in they passed over the American ship and the gun crews, realising that an attack was imminent, closed up at action stations. It was not long before the vessel became a target, and she sustained two near misses before the searchlight was switched off. Some minutes later one of the planes came in very low, little above mast-height to strafe the bridge and forward gun position with cannon fire without causing any damage. The plane wheeled away to make a turn and commenced another attack. This time the pilot made no mistake. The bomb struck *Samuel J. Tilden* amidships on the boat deck, starboard side. It caused tremendous damage as it went through the deck to the engine room, where it exploded in a sheet of flame. It set fire to the whole midships section, demolished the saloon, the crews' mess-deck and all the officers' quarters, and put out of action the 5 in (125 mm) gun.

Immediately another bomb struck, this time an incendiary which landed forward of the bridge.

The fire quickly took hold and spread along the length of the ship to the stern. Captain Blair ordered the evacuation of the bridge as falling debris made the position untenable. Meanwhile, below deck Royal Engineer Tony Thacker, on his way to the upper deck, felt a thud that reverberated through the ship, followed by another explosion which knocked him unconscious. He remembers:

> From below me there was a terrific glare and something flew up into my face and on to my hands and arms. It is almost impossible to describe the next few moments as I finally came to. I struggled to my feet and as I tried to walk forward I realised that I could hardly see and that there seemed to be something stretching the skin on my face, arms and hands.

He managed to stand but because of the damage to the ship he dared not move. 'Luckily for me, I heard footsteps moving about. I called to the unknown man and he led me to the upper deck.'

Gunner John Whitley recalls: 'The bombs killed and wounded several Army personnel and seamen. Most of the Armed Guard gunners received shrapnel wounds and burns from incendiary bombs and it seemed that the personnel at stations above deck fared the best.' In a very short time it became obvious that the fires were out of control and Captain Blair gave the order to abandon ship.

The signalman serving aboard HMT *Mullet*, David Smith remembers attempting to communicate with the shore signalling station before the raid began. 'Planes dropped white flares, which by coincidence was the correct recognition signal for that time of the day. Consequently, I reported the planes were friendly.' When *Mullet*'s captain saw the fires break out on *Samuel J. Tilden* he immediately ordered lifeboats to be lowered to pick up survivors. Captain Blair had ordered 'Abandon ship' because he realised that the explosions had cut off steam, rendering the hoses useless. He decided to stay with his ship as long as possible and ordered all available men to get the injured out of the dangerous areas and into the lifeboats. But another problem presented itself: some of the lifeboats had been destroyed. The remaining ones were lowered without mishap, however, and the more seriously injured were taken aboard them. Luckily the sea was fairly calm. The master ordered the anchor cable to be parted, all the remaining rafts to be thrown overboard and the ship to be abandoned in an orderly fashion.

John Whitley saw many men were in the water, who had either been blown overboard or had jumped. 'I remember tossing a life-ring to a soldier who was struggling in the water and I was able to grab hold of a life-raft and later was picked up by a British motor launch.' Captain Blair and the ensign stayed with the stricken ship until all personnel still alive were in the boats and rafts and only then did both of them go over the side. Captain Blair carried with him a perforated metal canister containing the ship's confidential codes, which he ditched over the side in 30 fathoms. William Walters managed to get into a lifeboat and 'we rowed away from the blazing ship and some time later a British boat picked us up and landed us at the jetty where we waited for transport to hospital'.

Blind and helpless, Tony Thacker had been led away to the upper deck where 'I realised the ship was well and truly on fire and listing badly and it seemed inevitable that we would have to abandon ship at any moment.' He has only a hazy recollection 'of a lifeboat being dropped, as distinct from launched, into the sea and a member of the crew diving overboard to steady it in the sea. I was helped over the side on to rope netting and after hesitant progress, jumped into the lifeboat. As soon as I was seated in the boat, I realised I was blind.' Shortly afterwards those who were able took to the oars and began to pull for shore. They had not gone far when Tony heard instructions coming from a loud-hailer asking the boat to hove-to in order to facilitate the picking up of survivors. When it was his turn, 'because I could not see, I was stood up on the lifeboat seat supported by two other survivors, with my arms aloft. As the swell lifted the lifeboat somebody aboard the rescue vessel clasped me under the armpits, lifted me clear and hauled me aboard.'

The other survivors in the boats and rafts saw the magazine on the *Samuel J. Tilden*'s poop deck explode in a sheet of flame. No distress signals were sent but forty-five minutes later MTB *297* and MTB *697*, which had been picking up survivors in the harbour, arrived on the scene. Motor launches ML *240* and ML *1273*, on patrol in the Adriatic, were immediately recalled to assist. HMT *Mullet*'s lifeboat approached the abandoned ship to pick up survivors and David Smith remembers seeing six men hauled from a raft. 'Two of the survivors were burnt to a cinder.' One of the blackened men, screaming in agony, was taken below, placed on the mess-deck table and sedated to ease the pain. He died shortly afterwards. Charles Murphy, on board *Mullet*, says the reason the ships did not enter harbour when they arrived at Bari was because the boom defence was in place. He believes *Mullet* picked up about seventy survivors.

As Arthur Spencer dashed to his station aboard the SS *Lwow*, he was joined by two other Royal Navy gunners, Harry Cross and John Hayes, and Josep, a Polish gunner whom Arthur had befriended. At the very moment the four men closed up, the *Lwow* received a direct hit. A gaping hole was created between Nos 1 and 2 holds and wreckage was strewn all over the battered ship. Shrapnel and larger pieces of metal ripped through the bridge and cabins, causing frightful injuries to the crew on the upper decks. The shipmates regained their feet to return to the gun position to commence firing. It was then that *Lwow* received her death blow: another direct hit. Arthur heard 'the scream of the approaching bomb, followed by a tremendous roar, a brilliant blinding flash, a red-hot blast and then silence as I passed out'. When he regained his senses he saw John Hayes lying on the deck a few feet away. There was no sign of Harry Cross but Josep was already on his feet and groggily made his way along to help Arthur. John was still alive but lying inert and quiet. Most of his clothes had been blown off him and what remained hung in tatters.

The vessel had now become a raging hulk as fire swept along her full length and, as some sort of protection, Josep wrapped his woollen jersey around John. They discovered a raft secured to the gun platform which they threw overboard. The next problem was how to get their badly injured shipmate onto the raft; the listing ship was making it difficult to keep a foothold. They lashed a rope round John and lowered him down to the raft. The rest of the crew were abandoning ship any way they could. David Williams, another gunner, recalls seeing 'several men so shocked, they were attempting to swing out a lifeboat even though the sinking vessel was listing badly on the other side'. It was now a case of every man for himself as the list became more pronounced. Arthur and Josep appeared to have obtained the only serviceable raft left on the vessel. As hundreds of tons of water rushed into the ruptured holds most of the crew who were able, dived overboard. Arthur also dived over to secure the raft before John was lowered down, after which Josep slithered down the rope to join his comrades on the raft. They made John as comfortable as they could though there was nothing they could do to protect him from the shrapnel falling all around. They were shivering with cold and shock, for Arthur was clad only in underpants and Josep in a pair of overalls.

They set off for the nearest jetty, Vecchio Molo, about 300 yards away – a very long way in the prevailing conditions. At once another problem faced them: there were no paddles among the gear.

At the very end of the outer mole, Captain Ruig, aboard the Dutch ship SS *Odysseus*, was playing cards with fellow officers when the watch look-out on the bridge pressed the alarm button. The ship's gunners closed up and commenced firing. The vessel suffered several near misses before a bomb burst on the port side with shattering effect. *Odysseus* listed heavily to starboard and Captain Ruig had a blurred impression of the devastated upper deck. A quick check showed that no one had been killed, although several men had sustained injuries from blast and splinters. These men were attended to by Second Mate E. de Blauw. During this period the Mate and the Bosun reported that there was no damage below and all was water-tight. But where the funnel should have been was now only a space revealing a crimson red sky. As *Odysseus* depended on the funnel for the natural draught to maintain the furnace head which was the main source of her steam power, it was a cause of great concern to Captain Ruig. The starboard lifeboat had been damaged in the near miss so the motor boat was lowered to ferry the wounded across to the mole. The crew rigged the hatch covers to form a substitute funnel, the boilers were stoked, the makeshift funnel survived, steam was raised and the vessel made the short journey out to sea.

The ship in the next berth to *Odysseus* was the Norwegian vessel SS *Vest.* Some minutes previously a minesweeper had just finished the grimy task of taking on coal and had departed to berth in the inner harbour. Almost immediately the raid began and *Vest* was one of the first ships to be hit. The bomb landed in the hold, which was full of hundreds of tons of coal which cushioned the explosion. All the crew felt was a dull thud. At the time radio officer Bob Anderson was rushing from his cabin. 'Little did we know when loading up with a cargo of coal in South Wales and grumbling about all the attendant dust and grime, that we would have to thank that cargo of best Welsh slag for saving our lives. Had our cargo been anything else we surely would have perished.' Standing on deck, Bob watched the scene on board the American ship *John Bascom*, two berths away.

> The crew were desperately trying to quell the flames consuming the ship, but the hoses could not cope. An explosion occurred and instantly the water all round together with what was left of the liberty ship was engulfed in blazing petrol and oil. Above the pandemonium I could hear the screams of men caught in the lethal inferno.

On board *Vest* the order was given to abandon ship, the lifeboats were lowered and in orderly fashion the whole crew took to them, reaching the harbour side in comparative safety. One memory has remained with Bob: 'The skipper was not the last man off the doomed ship but the first – his reason being he was going for help for the rest of the crew.'

*   *   *

At the Italian Protestant church, John Roberts and several other servicemen were chatting and passing the time of day with some of the parishioners before the service started. Without warning they heard the most frightening, ear-piercing roar. The bomb caused havoc. The front wall of the church, the windows protected by metal shutters and grilles, blew out into the street with an enormous crash and all the lights went out and came on again. Inside the church John surveyed a scene of devastation. It was as if a hurricane had swept through. He recalls, 'The pulpit had crashed to the floor. The blast carried the wreckage of it full tilt through double doors, making what had been two rooms into one and created an archway where the doors had been.' Every window had been smashed and the flying shards caused cuts and bruises to many parishioners. All the pews, tables and chairs and other furniture were as matchwood and the only object that John noticed was 'a plain wooden cross fastened to the wall above where the archway had been formed'.

Ian Peyman, who was blown into the water from SS *Norlom* and was washed from a raft with Norwegian radio officer Halvor Stensrud. Ian survived to spend many weeks in hospital but Halvor was never seen again. *(I. Peyman)*

The soldiers dashed up a nearby alley, from where they heard screaming coming from behind a locked door. They kicked down the door to enter a living room, where John found an elderly Italian woman lying on what remained of her bed, with most of the ceiling on top of her. The most incongruous part of the scene was a large religious picture in an ornate frame which had broken loose from its fastening on the wall at the head of the bed. It had crashed down and finished up round the woman's neck as she lay in the bed. Luckily, though badly shocked she suffered no cuts or bruises. The soldiers helped the lady up and together, British and Italians sheltered underneath a staircase until the raid was over. At this juncture, they began singing hymns, one of which John remembers had the lines 'If this be it, dear Lord, we will come to you singing'. He says, 'I will never forget singing "O God our help in ages past" and ever since it has meant a great deal to me.'

The gunners aboard the Norwegian ship SS *Norlom* were seated round the mess-deck table playing cards when the raid began. They all made a rush to the upper deck and radio officer Ian Peyman followed them at a more leisurely pace. As he reached the upper deck he heard the guns banging away. He says, 'Everything went blank and the next thing I remembered was coming round after being knocked unconscious. As I regained my senses I realised I was soaking wet and lying on a small raft with my cabin mate Halvor Stensrud, the Norwegian radio officer, beside me.' The crew of a motor launch had pulled both men onto the raft with the intention of towing it to safety. Ian asked Halvor if he was all right and he replied that he was, 'although we were in too much shock to know how injured we might be'. Of those moments he says, 'All hell was going on in the harbour, fires on the water and shrapnel falling all over, and when the launch started up to take the raft in tow, perhaps a shade too quickly, both of us having nothing to hold on to, when the raft tipped we were both thrown into the water again.' The young radio officer was not a strong swimmer but managed to keep afloat until the launch turned back to pick him up once more. 'I must have passed out again for I do not remember being hauled into either the boat or the raft.' His shipmate Halvor Stensrud was never seen again.

As Lieutenant Edwin Farnell came out of the port offices to rejoin his company of Pioneers, flames appeared overhead, much to his surprise, and immediately bombs started to fall. He was surprised because usually he was given notification of any impending air attack – but not this time. The lights illuminating the dockyard were switched off as the bombing became more intense. At this juncture one of his men went into a fit and collapsed. His comrades took him into a dockside warehouse where he was attended to. Having seen him safely inside, Edwin realised that it was possible to get all his men under cover while the attack was continuing. The 150 soldiers trooped into the warehouse leaving Edwin and his senior NCO outside to keep an eye on events.

They watched the fiery scene which was mostly taking place at the other side of the harbour, the bombing and gunfire now at its most intense. In the midst of the bombardment they looked upwards and were transfixed with horror as they quite clearly saw a bomb hurtling down towards them. 'This is ours,' shouted Edwin as both men instinctively grabbed one another, not wanting to leave this world alone and realising that these were their last moments on earth. But miracles do happen and Edwin remembers, 'The bomb landed about four or five yards away from us, right on the very edge of the dockside, the middle part of the bomb, between the nose and tail-fin, hitting the dock at an angle without exploding. It then glanced off and entered the water of the dock where it sank to the bottom.' A million-to-one chance indeed!

The magnitude of his escape made Edwin decide to take his men away to a safer position, but also to keep them available for any tasks they may be called upon to carry out. Fifty yards away was the outer wall of the old town and he had the men sit under it with their backs to the wall, able to watch the sky above and across the road to the harbour and to take evasive action if necessary. A young Italian girl of about sixteen years of age, clearly in shock and dazed, came meandering along the road. Separated from her family she was crying for help, nursing a shrapnel wound on her right arm. Edwin calmed the hysterical girl down and sent her with one of his men to a first-aid post further along the road.

Awaiting the unloading of ammunition on the quayside was Dunkirk veteran Eric Foxford, RASC, attached to 396 General Transport. He was the driver of a large 10 ton lorry which was being loaded with shells directly from the ship by means of a crane. The lorry was half loaded when the air raid began. Immediately, the Italian working parties evac-uated the vessels on which they were working and flung themselves underneath the trucks for shelter, as did Eric and the other soldiers. In an instant as Eric dived underneath, he realised he had made a mistake. 'The vehicle was a massive combined tank transporter and trailer loaded with steel girders and when I glanced to the rear I saw an array of huge wheels across the full width. Luckily I did not stay for more than a few seconds, as without any warning, the transporter moved off.' Several soldiers and Italian workers were still underneath and Eric learned later that one man was crushed to death under the wheels. (The gruesome scene of the squashed body that Albert Jones and I had witnessed could well have been the horrifying result.)

Eric started up his truck and with the half load of ammunition drove out of the dockyard and unloaded at a dump out of town. Later he returned to his billet to find that some of his fellow drivers had come across sailors on afternoon and evening shore leave wandering around in Bari, and as they were not inclined to return to the harbour, they had brought them back to their billets for the night. On examining his vehicle the next morning, Eric discovered a hole in the fuel tank about the size of a tennis ball. It had been caused by a lump of shrapnel, but luckily, with the fuel being diesel oil, there was no combustion. Later when talking to some of his comrades who helped to clear up in the dockyard, he learned that they had filled up many lorries with the dead and transported them to the mortuary.

Within a few days Eric and his company moved further north and he never returned.

Another man serving aboard the disabled destroyer HMS *Quail* was Leading Seaman Douglas Moore. During the afternoon he opened up the beef screen to hang up a frozen hind-quarter of beef to thaw out for use on the following day. These screens were wire mesh cabinets usually situated on destroyers between the bridgeworks and the funnel. The mesh allowed fresh air to circulate and at the same time kept out the many flies and insects. This was not his usual job, but with the depletion of the destroyer's company after it struck the mine, Douglas volunteered to take over the task. Later in the afternoon he washed and changed and went ashore with a shipmate. He recalls that up to that time Bari had been quiet and peaceful, with plenty of entertainment and well-lit shops and no black-out. The two sailors wanted to see a film and queued in the foyer, waiting for the second house. The first Douglas knew of the raid was when suddenly, after an enormous blast, the glass dome which formed part of the ceiling of the foyer crashed down on top of the waiting queue. He and his companion were thrown to the floor and when he struggled to his feet he discovered that he had been cut on the head by a piece of flying glass. They made their way to the top of the stairs, where Douglas remembers looking out towards the harbour and seeing 'a raging inferno'. When he and his comrade reached the street they were surprised to see, waiting outside, the car belonging to *Quail*'s captain, Lt Cdr Jenks, who had taken over as Port Officer. The driver called to the two sailors to hop in and immediately set off into the darkness, not in the direction of the harbour but heading out of town.

Douglas recalls that as they approached the top of a steep hill, they were halted by a soldier of the Italian Alpine Brigade, who threatened to shoot the three sailors if they refused to turn back. They had no alternative but to turn round and travel some way back to Bari, where they spent a freezing night in the car. When they arrived back on board, the hindquarter of beef was covered in a black, greasy substance and had to be ditched. Two days later Douglas formed part of a team assigned to retrieve bodies from the harbour. The corpses began to rise to the surface at that time, and did so for some weeks. He was not issued with any special protective clothing, though he believes British soldiers wore anti-gas capes. One year later he reported sick with chest trouble and was diagnosed as having bronchitis, from which he has suffered ever since.

The Assistant Port Commandant, Major Harry Wilkinson, was at the wheel of his jeep in the centre of Bari when he heard the sound of gunfire, which appeared to be coming from the direction of the harbour. He immediately headed in that direction, which took some time as the streets were full of people fleeing to shelter or to outlying districts. By the time he reached his office in the dockyard, the raid was over, although he could see that there had been a great deal of damage. As Assistant Port Commandant he knew full well the overcrowded state of the harbour and at that time his responsibilities were increased as his superior, Lt Col Marcus Sieff (later to become Managing Director of Marks and Spencer and later still Lord Sieff) was away attending a conference in Cairo. Harry dashed to his office on the first floor of the building, which gave him a fine view of the harbour.

It was a grim scene spread before him. He saw that the line of shipping on the outer mole had received the heaviest attack, and several vessels were on fire. Thick, black smoke was beginning to roll over the harbour, making things difficult to see. At that moment he saw and heard the most tremendous explosion. Brilliant lights, fire and sparks shot skywards at terrific speed. He had no time to take in any more before the shock wave swept over the port towards the dockyard. An enormous blast of hot air hit the building. 'It picked me up like a feather, hurling me across the full length of the office, to finish up on the floor at the other side of the building, which itself seemed to be in an imminent state of collapsing beneath me.'

Amazingly, although every pane of glass and every loose object was destroyed, the building – or shell as it now was – appeared to be intact. If the scene that had greeted the major when he looked out previously was chaotic, he could hardly take in what he beheld when he staggered back to the space where the window had been. The whole window frame had disappeared and all the buildings as far as he could see had suffered the same fate. Walls had been completely demolished and small boats thrown up onto the harbour wall, together with all manner of debris. He saw men on the jetty, all in a shocked state, some lying where they had fallen in the wake of the blast and others wandering aimlessly around.

He decided to visit the oil discharge dock on Molo San Cataldo, where he knew a tanker was discharging high-octane petrol. Descending the battered staircase he breathed a sigh of relief when he found that his jeep, which he had parked at the rear of the building, was still serviceable. He set off for the other side of the harbour amidst pandemonium and chaos. The roads were chock-a-block with all types of vehicles, some being driven away from danger areas, some arriving for vital stores and others to give assistance. Meanwhile, machines were churning out smoke to add to the billows of smoke rising from the burning ships, and the fog-like situation made driving more of a gamble. After many stops and starts, Harry eventually reached the discharging dock to find to his relief that although there had been a near miss on the edge of the mole, the tanker was intact. After satisfying himself that everything on the mole appeared to be in order, he turned to his jeep to drive off. He had only taken a few steps when 'a brilliant white light lit up the night sky, followed by a massive explosion. At anchor a half-unloaded ship, carrying a cargo of petrol in cans, blew up. Though the vessel was some way off the mole the roar was deafening.' For the second time that night he was caught in an explosion. 'The blast of hot air lifted me willy-nilly off my feet and deposited me on top of a barbed wire security barrier.'

After gathering his wits and extricating himself from the barbed wire, he made for his jeep which, like Harry himself, seemed to have a charmed life, for once again it had weathered the upheavals. It started up at once but after half a mile his luck ran out as it stuttered to a halt. He discovered that the radiator had been pierced by shrapnel and he had no alternative but to continue the long walk on foot.

With a tremendous roar one of the ships on the outer mole blew up – it may have been two blowing up together; there were no witnesses near enough to be certain. *Zetland*'s bows and bridge, which were facing the line of shipping on Nuovo Molo, caught the full force of the gigantic eruption. Standing on the forecastle I just had time to see the massive upheaval before it engulfed me in a terrific movement of searing hot wind. The excruciating hot air filled my lungs and body until I felt as if I was bursting and burning inside, and at the same time as if my whole body was being held in a huge vice. The last thing I faintly remember was my feet leaving the deck.

Zetland's bridge staff were sent reeling and flying in a tangle of arms and legs in the confined space of the open bridge as the destroyer lifted bodily out of the water. Lying on his back, Bob Davies regained his senses just as a heavy shower of water soaked him to the skin. He says, 'Even in a bemused and shocked state I was surprised to be wet through for I had never expected rain that night.' Lt Cdr John Wilkinson, *Zetland*'s captain was lying alongside him on the deck and when Bob struggled to his feet to assist his skipper he saw that he had been struck in the face by a large chunk of flying metal. The captain was in severe pain when he was lifted to his feet, although he insisted on carrying out his duties. The Navigating Officer was slumped over the port side bridge-wing groaning in agony, the Yeoman of Signals was sitting in the corner on the starboard side saying he could not see and the Sub-Lieutenant was appealing for someone to help him. He had been hurled into the bunting locker at the rear of the bridge and was almost compressed into it and could not move. By dint of moving his arms and legs a little at a time they managed to release him and though he appeared to have suffered from no more than cuts and bruises, he was in pain.

We all discovered that we were not soaked with rain but with a thick, greasy liquid which was as black as pitch and gave off a foul stench. The upper decks and bridge were covered with the same substance, together with shrapnel and debris, including small-calibre shells and cartridges which landed at the same time as the torrent of water. Unknown to the destroyer's crew, who were all flat on their backs when it occurred, the eruption carried the water over 1,000 feet (300 metres) into the sky to cascade down onto the entire harbour area. Some days later the crew discovered that the bridge had been moved two feet backwards during the blast.

The explosion had dumped me underneath the starboard side bridge-wing some 20 feet from where I had been standing. I came to, feeling shocked but more than pleased to realise that I was still in one piece and appeared to have no broken bones. How long I had lain there I do not know but when I moved along the deck and went below, survivors from other ships, covered head to foot in what at that time we thought was fuel oil, were being hosed down in the heads (washrooms).

Chief Petty Officer Robert Isles remembers HMS *Bicester* being boxed in between the mole and her sister ship, *Zetland*, on her port side. In that position she was unable to move, her boilers were shut down and in the cramped conditions, her 4 in (100 mm) guns were out of action. Petty Officer 'Buck' Taylor received orders to move the vessel manually. He mustered as many men as possible, mooring lines were cast off and *Zetland* fended off to allow *Bicester* to move. The party secured lines to

Bicester's stern and with some men fending the ship from the mole, the rest heaved on the towing rope. During training and exercises and on sports days tug-of-war was a regular feature, but none of the sailors could have imagined such a one-sided event as they were now taking part in: tugging an inert 1,000 ton ship. All the time they were straining and pulling, shrapnel was raining down, peppering the ship and the mole.

Slowly *Bicester* began to move and once under way it became easier for Buck and his party to tow her another three berths away from the raging fires to a position where she could move once steam was raised. After securing the destroyer to the mole, it was found that several of the men were suffering from shrapnel wounds and that Buck was in severe pain, having been struck more than once. His shipmates carried him aboard to the sick-bay, where Gunner Bill Rickerby was already being attended to. Bill had been on deck when the explosion occurred and felt a terrific blow on the side of his body, instantly passing out. When he came to after what he thought was a few minutes, he realised that he could not see. He attempted to regain his feet but found his legs would not support him. He started to crawl towards where he judged the bridge to be, for he could make out voices above the din. John McAteer, one of his shipmates, saw him crawling on the deck, picked him bodily up and took him below, where the ship's surgeon gave him a shot of morphine and took a lump of shrapnel out of his side. Bill was strapped to a stretcher and fastened to a mess-deck table as the doctor was called away to deal with *Bicester*'s many wounded and the large numbers of survivors arriving on the gangway after swimming ashore.

Meanwhile in the hospital, to Nurse Gwladys Rees, writing the dictated letter for the young blinded sailor, everything appeared to be quiet. It was a period of calm, she says, not too busy, although an ambulance train was due in during the afternoon and preparations for its reception had been completed. There was also an air evacuation from the hospital due at about the same time. The young man for whom Gwladys was writing the letter had been blinded when his ship had struck a mine. He should have been going on the morning flight to the UK, but the medical officers were worried about a secondary injury he had suffered, and decided he was not fit to travel. While she was writing, Gwladys heard gunfire in the distance. Curious, she and another nurse decided to see what was going on and, informing her patient she would be back shortly, both nurses donned steel helmets and capes and ventured up onto the flat roof.

They could see immediately something unusual was happening; the anti-aircraft barrage was becoming more intense over the harbour and within a short space of time the whole area was a blazing inferno.

Gwladys says, 'Some of our staff were down on the waterfront arranging the evacuation of patients to the UK by ship and we hoped they would be all right.' As they lay flat on their stomachs peering over at the sight below, a powerful explosion suddenly shattered every window in the building. They decided it was time to return downstairs, and as they moved they brushed shards of glass off their clothing and crunched broken glass underfoot. The electric power was off, but it appeared nobody had been injured by flying glass.

It was not long before the influx of patients began and Gwladys never finished the letter for her naval patient.

The rumours circulating were all the same. A lone bomber had managed to score a direct hit. The terrific vibration of an ammunition ship blowing up was what had turned our hospital into a glass shambles, but at least it was still standing. We worked by the dim glow of hurricane lamps and I recall fixing an intravenous drip by the light of a single match held by the orderly in front of a heavy screen to prevent the draught blowing out the flame. Though the winter wind forced its way through the makeshift window coverings, we found we had hot running water for the first time – nothing short of a miracle. We worked long into the night and early morning. Intravenous bottles were dripping from every third bed and corridors were crammed with patients for whom we could find no accommodation. We were soon receiving patients via the operating theatre, patients with bilateral amputations of legs still wearing their lifebelts.

The work of the often overlooked Royal Army Medical Corps orderlies and stretcher bearers was admirable. They were marvellous, carrying patients in, transferring them to different wards, making hot drinks and keeping us in cups of tea for the next two days and nights. They worked alongside us, keeping up a cheerful banter, helping us to maintain sanity. The whole staff worked in complete harmony and co-operation, even though each ward had, for two days, double its usual number of patients. The ward I was on had one hundred and sixty, but with many orderlies working with nurses on shift, we handled the workload.

The aftermath of the explosion was almost too pathetic and grim to describe. Only a few hours before dawn following the raid we began to realise that most of our patients had been contaminated by something beyond all imagination. I first noticed it when one or two of my patients went to the sink looking for a drink of water. This was odd because drinks had been taken round as usual and we could hardly control them. They were complaining of intense heat and began stripping off their clothes, and patients confined to bed were desperately trying to rip their dressings and bandages off. What little knowledge we had, our first thought was that these boys were suffering from mustard gas burns for there were blisters as big as balloons and heavy with fluid on these young bodies. We were not sure whether the staff was at risk as we did not know what the fluid contained. Although we tried to get tests done, we were never informed of the results. We did everything humanly possible – draining the blisters, constant intravenous and eventually mild sedatives, but it was no good. It was horrible to see these boys, so young and in such obvious pain. We could not give them stronger sedatives, since we were not quite sure how they would react with whatever had poisoned them.

The medical officers tried to get through to the War Office in London for information, advice and an antidote, but none was forthcoming. We were all furious and yet, if the War Office could not release the information, it must be a military secret and if that was the case we were certain we were witnessing the effects of poison gas. Although we did not know it at the time, there was indeed the very worst kind of poison involved. Both day and night staff were now on duty. Despite our ministrations, we were at a loss to battle this poison and we couldn't save the majority of the wounded. Almost one thousand men died in one night and just as many in the aftermath. I think they knew we were doing our best to save them. We tried to make their last hours as painless as possible. Most of them were conscious throughout their ordeal and were so confused about their injuries. Their eyes asked us questions we could not answer.

The explosion and subsequent tidal wave flooded the harbour smashing HMS *Vulcan* against the jetty and covering her with water and crude oil. The broken mooring lines allowed the ship to drift away from the jetty without power. The main steam pipes had been fractured and the ship could not raise steam. Another explosion rocked her, now drifting out of control and moving ever closer to the dangerous lines of shipping on the outer mole. Bert Stevens recalls, 'It was a scene from hell, ships were blowing up, others burning and out of control. The surface of the water was alight, debris crashing all around and when I looked over the side of the ship both port and starboard, there seemed to be hundreds of chaps desperately swimming and floundering, screaming and shouting for help.'

Francis Newman, who had been on sentry duty, was carried aboard HMS *Vienna* by way of a plank acting as a substitute gangway after the explosion had knocked him out. He was taken below to his mess-deck. His shipmates had found him on the quayside dazed, dripping wet and covered in a black, oily substance. Shortly afterwards he attempted to eat his supper, but as soon as the food hit his stomach he had to struggle out to the upper deck to be sick. He returned to the mess-deck, crawled underneath the table and fell asleep expecting to be called on watch in an hour or two.

Sheltering under the ambulance train in the Park Nord sidings, Bob Wills decided it was time to make his way back to the 98th General Hospital. As the bombing had ceased he crawled out from underneath the train and, judging in which direction the hospital lay, he began to run. After crossing several railway tracks the smoke became less dense and he came to a field of cabbages in which there was a stone shed. He sheltered there as a shower of shrapnel descended and then vaulted over a wall surrounding the field. To his surprise he found himself falling about eight feet at the other side, tearing his shin on a roll of wire. Continuing to run he thought he had arrived at a driveway to a large house which he could not see but imagined was behind him. At the end of the driveway were two imposing stone pillars. His heart was pumping with exertion when the loudest noise he had ever heard blasted his ear-drums. Then the blast caught up with him. Bob describes 'feeling I was running up a slope which, if I had continued, would have taken me right over the top of the pillars, and being cocooned in a pleasant feeling of warmth and comfort, so much so that I smiled to myself at the pleasure of it all.' But that was all he remembered of the rest of the night.

At the 98th General Hospital, New Zealander Gay Trevithic was watching the display over the harbour when 'there was a sudden blinding flash and a terrific explosion. We were thrown to the floor as the windows came in, glass falling everywhere. Except for a few scratches, no one in the room was hurt.' Gay entered in her diary:

> A convoy of patients had just arrived and were lying on the floor. I think nearly every window in the building was broken . . . Place was really congested . . . Went up to our quarters and found that our beds were covered in debris and the whole window frame had been knocked in . . . Fires burning in the town, whole city lit up . . . An hour later another blinding flash followed by an explosion . . . Up goes another ship . . . The sky was a magnificent sight . . . Bombs dropped in town and near us.

Royal Navy Lieutenant Graham Scott was out and about in the hospital and chatting to other patients when one of the nurses watching at the window with a group of walking patients called excitedly to him to come and see what was happening. He dashed to the window, expecting to see something unusual happening among the newly arrived patients from the ambulance train, who were still being carried in on stretchers and into the wards. Little did the staff of the 98th General Hospital realise that in the next few hours and days they were to face one of the greatest tests of any military hospital during the war, yet something of which more than half a century later, the Royal Medical Corps admit to having no records. It would begin in the harbour, where the USS *John Harvey* was minutes away from destruction.

Graham gazed upon a display of colour and unexpected beauty, brilliant darts of fire climbing higher into the sky, like rockets on bonfire nights in those seemingly far off days before the war. In a state of apprehension, he watched the tragedy unfolding before him. He realised that the ships in the harbour must have suffered grievous damage and at that point he decided that, as he was mobile, he must do something to help his comrades. As he hurriedly changed his clothes his attention was drawn once more to the window by cries and shouts from the watching group. He was just in time to see 'the most colossal fountain of pink sparks shooting upwards and outwards into the night sky. The effect was of a huge Roman candle, surpassingly brilliant and beautiful, silent and remorseless as it fanned upwards, shedding its rosy radiance over the whole city.' Five seconds later they were all flat on their backs wondering what had hit them, as a roar and blast tore at them, pounding and stunning the senses. As they stumbled away from the window, broken glass could be heard tinkling all over the hospital as the building shook.

Recovering themselves, the nurses and other staff dashed off to console the shocked and bewildered patients, many of them in a state of panic, not knowing what had happened. Graham wondered what could have caused an explosion powerful enough to wreak large-scale damage at a distance of 2 miles (3 km) from its eruption.

At almost the same time, Captain Ray Bennett of the Royal Engineers realised that a raid on Bari was in progress. He immediately left his billet to join his sergeant in the unit's compound. They both stood in front of the stores depot watching the tracer weaving patterns in the sky, with the sound of bombs to be heard quite plainly. They were enthralled by the colourful display, but at the same time apprehensive and worried. For some time after the raid was over the two men continued to watch as numerous large and small explosions took place. A short time later they were surprised to see a massive eruption far larger than any so far. Ray recalls: 'The sky was lit up as this mammoth display of every colour imaginable shot skywards, soaring hundreds of feet into the air scattering outwards and downwards, to be followed later by another one even more spectacular than the first.' In astonishment they watched a huge mushroom of flame, colours and smoke lighting up the whole area as if it was daylight. Before the two soldiers had recovered from the surprise and shock of this latest demonstration of power, they heard 'a noise which could only be described as the roar of an express train approaching at full speed, followed almost immediately by a blast of very hot air which sent both of us staggering'. When they recovered from the shock, they discovered that the depot doors behind them, which had been fastened top and bottom, had been blasted inwards. The depot was situated in the coastal village of San Spirito, some 5 miles (8 km) from Bari.

Bert Staniforth and his fellow 8th Army soldiers were strolling towards the harbour when they saw the explosion. 'Without warning the whole area seemed to erupt. Flames of every colour shot into the sky, hundreds of feet across and rising to a thousand feet or more. It was like a solid wall of gold and silver without a break in it. If it had not been so serious, a magnificent sight. It then tapered off with flecks of red, green, orange and white.' But before the soldiers could take in any more they were hit by the blast, which lifted them off their feet and sent them flying back down the road, arms and legs tumbling helplessly. Bert says, 'My head and ears seemed to be at bursting point.' Dazed and unsteady, and trembling with shock, they staggered to their feet, took a roll call to see if anyone was hurt, decided enough was enough, turned round and made their way back to barracks.

In his billets in Bari, James Seal, a driver in the RASC heard the air raid take place. When it was over he received orders, with the rest of his group of six, to move their lorries down to the harbour to render whatever assistance they could. The journey took longer than normal because of the exodus from the harbour and city. Hundreds of fleeing citizens were making their way out of town to the outlying countryside, and vehicles from the harbour crammed the roads. When at last they reached the dockyard they were stopped by the military police on guard at the gate, who were only allowing rescue personnel through. 'A scene of absolute chaos greeted us, smoke and flames hung over the harbour and ships were blazing fiercely on the far breakwater. All the while explosions constantly rent the air.'

Halting their trucks on the jetty, four of the six drivers dismounted and boarded a ship berthed alongside, leaving James and the other driver to keep an eye on the vehicles. As the four did not return immediately, he decided to see what was happening. He had just dismounted from the lorry when an ear-shattering and blinding explosion occurred. He never saw how or where it happened, he only knew he had his hand on the door handle in the act of closing it behind him and seconds later he was sent hurtling along the jetty as the blast struck him. Some minutes later he picked himself up and discovered that he was still clutching in his hand – which was extremely painful – the door handle. The truck had disappeared. The pain in his hand, he realised, was from a broken thumb, but he had hardly time to take in any of the startling events before another catastrophe enveloped him. A huge tidal wave swept up to and over the jetty, taking him with it. He recalls that he was unable to stop himself being carried along as the wall of water struck him. He felt himself going over the jetty before passing out. The next thing he knew he was coming found to find himself spreadeagled on the jetty once again. He never knew how it happened, whether somebody had pulled him out and left him or whether some freak backwash had deposited him there.

Some distance away he could see his comrade still sitting in his badly damaged lorry. James wrenched open the door to get him, but recoiled in horror as he saw that the front seat was covered in blood. His dead mate was sitting in the driver's seat and had both of his legs sliced off below the knee. Feeling sick to his stomach, James left the tragic scene and approached another soldier, who was sitting upright on the jetty with his back to him, which made him hope that he was not too badly injured. On reaching him, he was horrified to find him covered in blood and gore, attempting to push his insides back into his body. James was so shocked that the only thing he could think of was to light up a cigarette and place it in the dying man's lips and run along the quay for help. Of the remaining four lorries and drivers there was no sign.

In the water, the three survivors from SS *Lwow* were attempting to reach safety, John Hayes was lying still on the raft which they discovered was without paddles, as Arthur Spencer and Josep used bits of driftwood and their hands to propel the raft along. It was slow going; they had little control over the direction they were going and Arthur kept slipping into the water to pull the unstable raft on to course for the mole. A massive explosion occurred as one of the outer lying ships blew up and seconds later the raft was rocked by a huge wave. One bit of good fortune was that the mole they were heading for, which formed part of the inner harbour, gave them some measure of protection and though the raft was sent rocking and spinning, they managed to keep it afloat. They were aware of shouting and screaming, and of small boats some distance away, but as dense smoke rolled over the water, visibility was reduced to a few yards. Eventually the three shipmates reached the quayside, where they rested for some time before hauling John onto the concrete, where he lay inert and quiet.

*   *   *

Bari Città Vecchia (old city) taken from the roof of Jim Proud's billets, showing the narrow streets of the old city and the place where children played. *(J. Proud)*

Jim Proud (middle) with two fellow soldiers in front of an engine in Bari dockyard. *(J. Proud)*

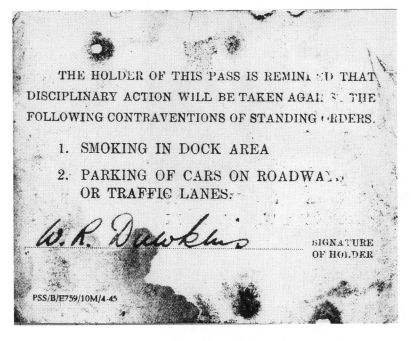

THE HOLDER OF THIS PASS IS REMINDED THAT
DISCIPLINARY ACTION WILL BE TAKEN AGAINST THE
FOLLOWING CONTRAVENTIONS OF STANDING ORDERS.

1. SMOKING IN DOCK AREA

2. PARKING OF CARS ON ROADWAYS
   OR TRAFFIC LANES.

SIGNATURE
OF HOLDER

PSS/B/E759/10M/4-45

Bari dock pass made out in the name of W. Dawkins. Passes were needed to gain entry to the dockyard. *(Mrs Collier)*

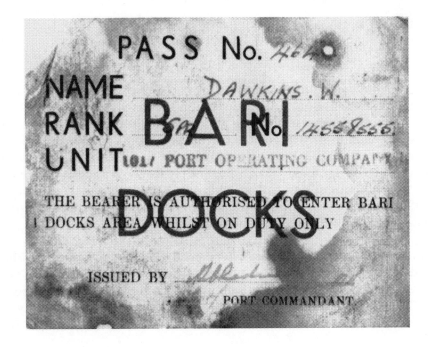

PASS No.

NAME   DAWKINS. W.

RANK BARI No 14558556

UNIT 1017 PORT OPERATING COMPANY

THE BEARER IS AUTHORISED TO ENTER BARI
DOCKS AREA WHILST ON DUTY ONLY

DOCKS

ISSUED BY

PORT COMMANDANT

W. Dawkins (centre).
(Mrs Collier)

The engine pulling the empty wagons had halted during the raid and when it was over, British Army driver Jim Proud, who was in charge on the footplate, decided to continue his journey to the docks. The train had crossed the Bari–Barletta road to reach a point some 500 yards from his destination when there was an explosion. He was thrown out of his cab to land at the edge of the track, where he lay for some minutes before he regained his senses. He was deafened and shocked, but appeared to have suffered no more than bruises. He looked round for his Italian co-driver but he had vanished from the footplate.

On her way to enter harbour at Bari was the SS *Empire Copperfield*. She had sailed to Augusta, missed the last convoy and was ordered to sail unescorted to Bari. One person who was looking forward to going ashore in Bari was 16-year-old William Hall. He had joined the ship at his home town, Hull (where he still lives today), and during the voyage from there the convoy of which *Empire Copperfield* was part was attacked by German aircraft. During the attack William and another 16-year-old manned a gun and commenced firing. The planes were driven off, causing no damage. As *Empire Copperfield* approached Bari, William heard crackling sounds coming from the direction of the port, followed by what he described as 'fireworks shooting into the sky'. Other members of the crew joined him at the ship's guard-rail to watch what they realised was an air raid taking place. The captain reduced speed as he saw there was no chance of entering harbour for some time. At that moment he received a signal ordering him to avoid Bari and to turn and make for Brindisi. The raid had finished and some time later, as the ship started to make her way back down the coast, William saw 'a mass of orange, red and black, reaching upwards, lighting up the whole of the coastline and surrounding sea for miles'. The huge mixture of thousands of gallons of water, high-octane petrol, high explosives and disintegrating ships reached its pinnacle. It cascaded outwards taking the shape of a massive fan, a wide semicircle of white-hot venom, a rainbow-coloured parasol of destruction poised above the harbour, ready to envelope it in shrapnel and steel.

William Hall has never forgotten that voyage to Italy. 'Perhaps *Empire Copperfield* and her crew escaped destruction by an hour or two; had not the engines broken down, she would have been berthed in the harbour with the rest of the convoy.'

In the forces cinema on the Porto Vecchio, where the film *Sergeant Yorke*, starring Gary Cooper, was showing, William Ellis and his two fellow officers felt the building tremble as they were thrown to the floor. They and the audience quickly evacuated the building. They had well over a mile to walk to return to their ship and were shocked on arrival to find that the only part of SS *Fort Athabaska* visible was a steel stanchion sticking up out of the water. All the forty-two men who had stayed on board perished as she blew up and only two bodies were recovered: the master, Captain Cook, and the ship's carpenter, John Sherwood.

How thin is the knife-edge between life and death. In the afternoon prior to the raid, William Ellis, writing at his table in his cabin, had been called on by three companions who invited him to join them on a visit to the cinema. He declined, saying he had seen the film before. They went off but after a while he changed his mind and hurried after them. He caught up with them on the mole and they had not walked more than 50 yards before one of the others had a change of mind, and decided to return to the ship. William's change of mind, though reluctant at the time, saved his life; his fellow officer's decision to return sealed his fate.

There were no witnesses to *Fort Athabaska*'s fate. It was later learned that *Joseph Wheeler* was struck by a bomb and blew up, causing *Fort Athabaska* to catch fire and blow up too, sinking within five minutes. It is possible that the two German rockets stowed in No. 2 hold may have exploded at the same time. All confidential codes were lost with the ship.

Bill Moran never collected the consignment of hand pumps he had been patiently waiting for. He remained underneath the lorry for the duration of the raid and later stood listening to the struggles of the men in the water, shouting and pleading for help. He remembered that he had a spare tyre in the back of his truck. He fastened it to a length of rope, making a makeshift life-belt and threw it towards the struggling swimmers. By this method he pulled a number of survivors to the dockside and dry land.

The Pioneer company, with Edwin Farnell in charge, were still sitting against the wall when Major Baxter arrived on the scene to see how many of his men had been lost or injured. He was amazed and relieved to discover that none had been hurt and even the man who had experienced the fit was back on duty and none the worse for it. The major had brought some lists that needed checking and he and Edwin walked over the road to a concrete structure situated to the side of the dockyard entrance. The building had an overhanging apron that ran round three sides in order to give full views of the harbour entrance and to check vehicles in and out of the dockyard. They were standing on the apron, checking the lists when an explosion occurred. Edwin says, 'Another great mass of multi-coloured fireworks soared into the sky and slowly descended. The next thing we knew, the concrete construction on which we had been standing had collapsed, all four walls falling inwards, and yet both of us were unhurt, not even sustaining a scratch.' The officer and his men returned to barracks after enduring what Edwin says, were 'the longest hours I have ever lived through and a night that anyone who lived through it, could never adequately describe.'

One lump of metal crashed onto SS *Dago*'s deck with a shuddering force accompanied by the screeching sound of steel tearing through steel. On inspection, John Kirkwood discovered that part of a ship's derrick, blown from a disintegrated ship, had landed on the after well-deck. It had carved its way through like a knife through butter and finished up on the lower deck. As the ship had a cargo of ammunition and bombs on board, it was lucky that nothing more serious occurred.

*   *   *

After seeing the complete hull of a ship lifted skywards in the wake of an explosion, Cyril Simpson, the Commodore's Signalman serving aboard SS *Empire Meteor* moored at berth 18, dashed from the ship to a shelter on the mole. In the thickness of the wall were huge compartments used for storing equipment such as ropes, pallets and the like. 'As we approached the entrance to one of the cavities, there was another great explosion. The blast rushed headlong along the wall, blowing us about twenty feet to the rear of the cavern where we lay shocked and bemused.' The only injury they received was 90 per cent deafness that lasted for some days. Cyril says, 'Today I still suffer with screaming tinnitus and loss of hearing inflicted at the time, but the War Pension people will not accept it.'

After watching the football match in Bari's stadium, 'Paddy' Lindsey and his two fellow airmen went to an ENSA show in the forces canteen but came out when the air raid started. Making their way back to their billets they were knocked off their feet by a blast. They picked themselves up and carried on, passing a crowd of Italian people sheltering under a large stone archway. One of the Italians called to them that there was room for them under cover. Before they reached it, however, part of a ship's superstructure, blown out of the water, crashed down onto and destroyed part of the archway together with most of the people sheltering beneath it.

Many sailors were killed or drowned in the bombings and resulting fires. Mooring ropes and anchors were destroyed, allowing ships already on fire to drift dangerously close to other vessels. It was not long before the whole line of shipping became a raging inferno. With all the vessels being moored stern-first to the mole, there was no direct escape route to the mole except by boat, and many of the boats were away at the time, while others had been destroyed or damaged during the explosions. Almost without exception the crews abandoned ship, most of them leaping overboard in the hope of finding a raft or other means of support, or of swimming to the mole. The bomb which struck Molo San Cataldo ruptured a petrol supply line, causing gallons of petrol to leak into the harbour. It settled on the surface and in a short time ignited; the breeze swept it across to where the men were attempting to escape.

That was not the end of their nightmare. When the mighty explosion took place, sucking the water up like an enormous geyser, it created a huge tidal wave that rolled the full length of the harbour and into the dockyard area. It tossed ships and boats about, breaking mooring lines and gangways. Second Engineer Don Beal, aboard SS *Spero*, recalls the scene:

As the raid ended, the whole harbour appeared to be one huge inferno. Fires raged on several ships as flames leaped across the space between vessels which before the raid started had been too narrow for my peace of mind. Now with mooring lines parted the ships drifted closer than ever and some started to drift into the middle of the harbour. I saw many seamen diving over the sides of their stricken ships as they realised time was running out for them. Luckily for us on *Spero*, the wind was blowing away from the ship.

Some time later Don saw a massive explosion across the other side of the harbour. A tanker with a cargo of aviation spirit erupted in a blinding flash, followed by a torrent of water raining down like a cloudburst. Don heard large chunks of metal crashing down onto the ship's decks as he watched the tidal wave sweeping across and he grabbed and clung tightly to a steel stanchion. As the wall of water arrived, it lifted *Spero* up several feet and dashed her against the jetty, smashing the gangway and parting all mooring lines and ropes as she reeled back on to an even keel. The quayside was littered with shell cases and the gangway scattered like matchwood. On the vessel astern of *Spero* he saw the imprint of his vessel's anchor fluke. It was way above his head, showing that the *Spero*, with the heavy anchor secured to the ship's bow, must have been lifted several feet to smash against the other ship's side.

In the coastal village of San Spirito, about a mile away from where Ray Bennett and his sergeant had been standing, John Hutchinson was sitting on a chair in a wooden recreation hut, watching a film. An American unit of the 15th Army was based in the small enclosure and John had been attached to them. Thursday night was film night, and when the show started at about 6 p.m., the hut was quite full. The film was *Pearl Harbor* and John thought how realistic it was: the noise of the dive-bombing Japanese planes, the crash of bombs and the crump of anti-aircraft fire. Then amazingly the wooden hut started to shake. Somebody dashed outside to discover that the shuddering of the hut was caused by the explosions which they saw over Bari. The film was stopped as the entire audience came out to watch. After some time they all trooped back in to see the finish of the film. When they returned to barracks they discovered that every window had been blasted in.

Aboard SS *Empire Meteor*, Robert Thompson was getting ready to meet two shipmates in Bari later in the evening. The two men had gone ashore just after midday but Robert had been on duty at the time. He was down below when he heard a high-pitched scream and a thud, and felt the ship keel over and then back again. He dashed along the companionway and up the steel ladder, arriving on the upper deck just as two red-hot pieces of shrapnel landed on the fore-deck, instantly setting fire to the wood-work. The crew attacked the fire with buckets of sand (most ships carried these for this very purpose). As they were doing so, there was another explosion, this time more intense than before – Robert believes it was a tanker blowing up. He received that information some time later, for when the explosion happened he had no time to think about anything. He was knocked helter-skelter along the upper deck, arms and legs flailing uncontrollably, and crashed against the iron bridgeworks. He felt a searing pain in his leg when he tried to regain his feet; though he did not realise it at the time, his knee-cap had been smashed. He was in extreme pain as he tried to shelter but luckily, even though most of the ship's company was ashore, two shipmates helped to drag him below deck. He was lifted into a bunk and left there, lying on his back. When he turned on his side he discovered that his eyes were level with a port and when he looked out of the small aperture, he recalls, 'it was the most amazing sight I have ever seen. My whole field of view seemed to be one huge conflagration of flame and fire.'

When he looked to his right, from approximately berth 25 to the far end of the outer mole, every ship appeared to be ablaze. All the time large and small explosions were taking place. Straight ahead he had a view down the length of the outer harbour to the entrance, though huge clouds of dense smoke obliterated it as the night wore on. Robert admits that he was not feeling very brave, much less so when he imagined the flames creeping along the surface of the water and *Empire Meteor* carrying a mixed cargo of munitions. He says, 'It was not an ideal set of circum-stances I found myself in as I lay there all night, helpless in the bunk, shivering and shaking with pain and shock.' During that endless night, as he prayed for dawn to break, he had an enforced bird's eye view of the horror of Bari.

Next morning a jeep arrived to take him to the dockyard entrance, where he was placed on a stretcher, awaiting an ambulance. 'There were hundreds of wounded men waiting with me. I had only a scratch compared with the injuries most of the others had.' When he finally arrived at the hospital, he was told by a nurse that he would have to wait for some time before his knee could be looked at. She said there were too many far more seriously injured patients to be treated and he would have to wait his turn. Robert was eventually attended to and stayed in hospital for ten days. On discharge he was admitted to hospital in Sicily and from there went by hospital ship to Algiers.

*   *   *

Robert's shipmate Cyril Simpson emerged with his two comrades from the wall cavity on the mole in time to see an incident which, in other circumstances, could have been amusing.

> A group of about twenty Americans were making their way along the quayside towards the dock gate. They were stopped by military police who asked them where they were going. Many voices spoke up, they were taking an injured seaman ashore for medical treatment. The injured man was buried in the centre of the throng, quite capable of making his own way. After much arguing two men were allowed to accompany him and the rest were turned back – to what I often wondered. Certainly that inferno was no place to be turned back to.

The three sailors returned to *Empire Meteor* and rested as best they could until morning. Only then could the extent of the damage be seen. 'All around the harbour, fires were blazing and on the deck of our ship were lumps of steel and hatch covers from other ships and debris that would be hard to describe. I wondered how it was nobody was cut to ribbons.'

In the middle of the harbour a lifeboat was launched as preparations were in progress aboard *Lyman Abbott* to abandon ship. Leo Krause was strapped into a stretcher and taken by his shipmates down the gangway and placed in the lifeboat, and when the boat was full it headed for the dock. When the lifeboat reached the quayside, planks were lowered into the boat and reared against the concrete wall in order to slide the stretchers up out of the boat. As Leo lay on the stretcher on the dock there was another explosion as a ship blew up with a deafening roar. Also in the same lifeboat, Donald Meissner recalls 'seeing ships exploding and fire everywhere. One of the ships was riding high in the water and coming straight at our lifeboat but somehow we managed to get round it and I never knew how we got to shore.' Two British soldiers picked him up and took him to a jeep.

> One of them looked at me and said, 'We had a bit of a bloody time, didn't we sailor?' They drove me to a British Army hospital and helped me into bed. Some time later a British nurse came to help me and was wrapping my feet in a blanket when another explosion happened. She said, 'That was a bit close, sailor, wasn't it?' She then brought me a small dish of porridge and a 'spot of tea'.

Leo was also lifted by two soldiers and taken into an ambulance which had just arrived on the jetty and was quickly taken to hospital.

The injured Paul Miller was helped down into one of *Lyman Abbott*'s lifeboats by Stanley Wisniewski, who recalls:

> That is when I saw the boatswain's mate dive into the water to secure another lifeboat that was heading towards a burning freighter. As for seeing what happened to other ships around us, all I can remember is seeing men running for their lives. Ships were on fire all over the harbour and we were told later by the merchant crew that a whole gun was caught in one of our torpedo nets. When we reached the dockside I was taken to hospital with some of my shipmates. George Maury helped me lower the lifeboats and rafts and gather the wounded and the dead to be placed in the boat. We had lost the chief mate, the chief steward, the first and second cooks and two navy gunners. The second mate was injured and later died. The lifeboat had holes punched in the bottom and it soon filled up with water up to the thwarts so that we were sitting in water. We did not know at the time that there was anything in the water that might have been dangerous and a few of us received gas burns in sensitive places. Afterwards I discovered I had a beautiful brown backside, but some men were badly burned.

The lifeboat landed at a quay, alongside a liberty ship which George noticed was called *Grace Abbott*, which he thought was a coincidence. (SS *Grace Abbott* was berthed at the very end of Vecchio Molo, one of the inner moles.) The survivors went aboard the ship for she was not damaged, although she had been littered with debris. They had not been on board very long when another ship blew up, and with an enormous crash a complete winch riven from it landed on the deck. They immediately left the vessel and took refuge in a concrete shelter and from that moment George says he does not remember anything until early morning when he found himself in hospital.

> At that time nobody knew about the gas in the water, though it was beginning to show up on survivors. I had brown lines across my forehead and down the side of my face where the straps of helmet had touched my skin. The straps had previously got soaked in the lifeboat when I had passed it to someone who used it for bailing out the water in the boat. I had been sitting in the boat with water sloshing right over the seats. My right forearm was the worst for I had been wearing a heavy woollen sweater and somehow my arm got soaked and the wool held the water; the prolonged exposure gave the gas time to work on my arm and it burned a hole in it about the size of a dollar. I started to be aware of it when I took off my sweater after we went back aboard the *Lyman Abbott* the next day.

67

When the lifeboat left *Lyman Abbott* an oiler by the name of Chason dived overboard and took a line over to a raft which was barely moving, in order to take it in tow. George says, 'Looking back now, it seems sense-less, when we could have rowed over to the raft with the line. When we left Bari some days later, Chason was still in hospital, lying underneath a wire cage, nude, his body covered in large blisters. I did hear afterwards that he recovered.'

Both William Walters and John Whitley, survivors from USS *Samuel J. Tilden*, were waiting for transport to hospital. They had been landed at the jetty after being picked up by the British MTBs. John recalls:

> Before we were landed, the crew of the boat gave me a tot of rum. [It would appear the jetty they landed at was Molo San Cataldo.] While on the jetty I dived flat on my stomach as a mighty blast hit us and I felt the heat passing over me. After some time we were taken to hospital by lorry where we got as far as the entrance lobby where the floors were lined with injured civil-ians and military personnel. In the lobby I was surprised to see a German pilot still wearing sidearms and I realised it was obvious the hospital could not take any more patients so two men and myself decided to be taken to a British field hospital.

William remembers:

> An ambulance arrived to take me to hospital and it was so crowded that I bummed a ride back to the waterfront in the same ambulance that had brought me and which was going back for another load. The rest of the night I, along with my captain and the gunnery officer and three or four other crew members stayed in an open shed and watched our ship and the whole harbour burn.

After being rescued from *Samuel J. Tilden*, Tony Thacker knew he must have presented a sight when he heard gasps from the men who hauled him aboard *Mullet*. He was taken below to the mess-deck and given tea, and a member of the crew was detailed off to look after him. In due course *Mullet* completed her rescue operations and headed for the port of Brindisi, arriving, so Tony was told, at 8 o'clock next morning. He was stretchered off to the 84th British General Hospital. Some of his clothing had to be cut off, his left arm dressed, and at about 10 p.m. he was taken to the operating theatre for what proved to be the first of five visits.

On the breakwater, Warren Brandenstein and the rest of the survivors from *John Bascom* were still marooned on the end of the outer mole. He says the wind had changed direction, otherwise their only option would have been to jump into the sea on the other side of the breakwater.

> About this time our signalman, Bob Kelly, somehow had kept hold of his signal lamp and kept signalling to anyone who could read his signal. Some time later a boat approached us and we were taken off the mole. As the boat left to head for safety, I can still remember thinking while looking back at what was happening in the harbour – this must be what Hell is like.

Ted Fry, in charge of the unloading of the SS *Empire Meteor*, found shelter on the mole during the air raid and as the smoke defences commenced to churn out the dense smoke he decided to stay where he was until it cleared a little. He also realised that his relief was not going to turn up. When at last he made his way towards the dockyard exit he came upon a party of Royal Navy personnel. They were running at the double in the direction of the line of shipping on the outer mole. He noticed that some of the sailors carried bags of tools and one man was carrying a very large wrench. He wondered what they were up to, for 'most of the ships on the mole appeared to be well ablaze and I could see flames reaching over the sterns of vessels and enveloping the width of the mole, making passage impossible.'

Ted passed through the dock gates and into his office in a narrow alley. He mentioned to the office sergeant that he had seen a naval party dashing along the mole. The sergeant said the sailors had orders to try to scuttle a ship that obviously had something highly dangerous on board. Ted remarked, 'They haven't got a cat in hell's chance of getting anywhere near.' He left the office to return to his billets about a mile away and was given orders 'to get some sleep as you will be on duty at the harbour at 8 a.m. tomorrow.'

Not all the tragedies occurred in the harbour. Thirteen-year-old Paolo Pizzati and his family lived on Via Murat and his father worked as a barber in his shop on Via Piccinni. At the time of the raid he was about to close his shop when a bomb fell close by. The explosion rocked the street and the subsequent blast blew the shop front in, which caused a great deal of damage to mirrors, chairs and fittings, but he was lucky to escape without injury. Next morning Paolo was told by his father that as soon as the raid started, people rushed to the shelters. Many of them crammed into one shelter until it was so packed that the occupants could hardly move and some time later a passing fire engine crew heard a shout of '*Aqua*'. Thinking that some of the people inside needed a drink of water, one of the firemen turned the hose on and poured it into an opening.

It was not until the next morning that the horror was unfolded. The first refugees who entered the shelter were pushed up to the end by a great heaving mass of people behind and within minutes were packed like sardines, unable to move if they wanted to. What none of them realised was that an underground water main had burst underneath the floor and was beginning to flood the shelter. It caused panic as people who could see what was happening tried to get out but were unable to move and yet others near the entrance were still pushing to get in, unaware of the rising water. This was the moment when the cries of '*Aqua*' were heard. The onrush of water from the fire hoses sealed their fate. When the rescue workers took out the bodies next morning they found only one survivor – a youth agile, strong and quick-witted enough to cling to a light fitting fastened to the ceiling. Paolo says, 'Amazingly I discovered the youth was my cousin.'

On Corso Trieste, the road flanking the harbour, in the apartment block in which he lived with his mother and two sisters, Alberto Lugli was startled to hear gunfire. A minute later the air-raid warning sounded. Immediately the two British soldiers he was playing cards with threw down their cards and made a dash downstairs and across the road to their base in the dockyard. The four members of the Lugli family made their way downstairs, decided it was too risky to go outdoors and settled for refuge in the basement, where they joined many of their friends and neighbours.

Some time later a violent explosion rocked the building. Alberto thought the block had received a direct hit, but a little later a friend came into the basement to inform them that 'something terrible had happened in the harbour'. When the all-clear sounded the family climbed back up the stairs to their apartment, which they found in a shamble. The windows and frames were broken, glass lay all over the floor and furniture had been tossed across the room to lie broken in the middle of shattered ornaments and crockery. Even so, in the midst of the chaos, curiosity got the better of the young lad and he stepped out onto the balcony, which he found covered with bits of steel. He had magnificent views over the harbour. Today, 70-year-old Alberto Lugli says, 'As a 13-year-old boy I saw and heard at that moment something that has remained with me all of my life. The harbour was one mass of flame and from somewhere in the midst of it all I could distinctly hear shouting and screaming and the word "help" over and over again.'

Alberto's mother was aghast to see her son standing on the shattered balcony and dashed forward to pull him away from the tragic scene and take him back with his sisters into the basement shelter. As they reached it a huge explosion occurred, followed by others during the night. Many of the shelters on the seafront were destroyed, causing great loss of life. Alberto remembers 'the whistling shriek of the falling bombs and an apocalyptic fire covering the harbour for days and days.'

Alongside the *Empire Sunbeam*, where he had been working unloading and checking the jeeps which formed part of the cargo, Dominico Iacabone was knocked unconscious. After some time he regained his senses and believes it was a doctor who was attending to him when he did so. All he remembers of the moments before he was knocked out was 'a deafening roar and nothing else'. He then experienced 'one of the most vivid memories of my life – an appalling scene'.

> I had just staggered to my feet and, looking around, I saw a negro soldier running for shelter who, without any warning, stumbled and fell sprawling on the quayside. I was horrified to see the soldier's head had been completely sliced from his body. I never knew what the cause was but imagined it must have been a sharp piece of flying metal among the shrapnel.

Dominico and his companion had no time to stand and stare for they were ordered aboard a vessel that lay alongside the mole. The officer who gave the order was limping badly and had received an injury to his arm. 'Though it looked mangled and he must have been in intense pain, his only concern was to issue orders to his crew to clear the harbour as soon as possible.' The ship cast off and left harbour for the open sea, where she stayed for several hours before returning to dock.

Leaving the heads aboard *Zetland*, where the shocked and shivering naked survivors were being hosed down, and making my way midships, I was in time to hear that the captain had decided to launch the ship's boat. This was not to abandon ship but to carry out rescue operations. The destroyer was fended off to allow the boat to be lowered from the davits and five ratings, myself included, clambered aboard. The engine fired and we turned our backs on *Zetland* and slowly made our way out through an impenetrable pall of black smoke. It was not without apprehension and a sense of foreboding on my part and I am sure, though it was unspoken, my shipmates were feeling the same.

In a few minutes we broke through the smoke to head in the direction of the harbour entrance, where the line of shipping on the outer mole was on our starboard side. Almost immediately we saw two struggling swimmers heading for the mole astern of *Zetland*. We pulled the choking, spluttering, half-drowned men into the boat and headed back to the mole. The two survivors scrambled up onto dry land as we turned round and once again set off to continue our rescue mission. We sailed through the dense blanket of black smoke and as we came out of it, in the slightly clearer visibility, we had a view of the whole line of shipping berthed along the length of the outer mole. Never in my life could I have imagined the scene spread before us.

We beheld a sight of such magnitude we could hardly believe our eyes. In the line of fifteen or so ships, several were blazing furiously, spewing forth shrapnel and red-hot sparks. Reaching upwards and upwards, high into the sky, the long tongues of red and yellow flames gave off huge clouds of black smoke which billowed and spread above and along the mole. The many fires raging on the vessels reflected on the undersides of the clouds to light up the ghastly, nightmarish scene, the crimson glow spreading to form a Hades-like backdrop to the line of doomed ships. During the day, the southerly breeze had gradually swept rubbish and dunnage towards the outer mole and in addition there was the debris that had been created since the raid began, all of which at that time formed an almost solid barrier on the surface of the water. To it was added fuel oil, high-octane petrol and far more deadly, though we did not know it, liquid mustard gas. The combination formed a sinister chemical cocktail; the catalyst that created the holocaust. Subsequent explosions caused the petrol on the surface to ignite and the breeze rapidly fanned the flames from one patch to another until the spaces between the closely moored ships were a wall of fire, in effect creating several roofless wind tunnels. On the surface of the water between the ships, the hungry flames devoured the inflammable and toxic mixture and amidst a noise like a hundred blast furnaces the flames rushed along the spaces between the vessels up to the mole and spread out along it. Of that very long night and the many hours I spent in the middle of the harbour, one memory has stayed with me. It was the tremendous overpowering, ear-shattering noise, relentless, never-ending and intimidating. Had we not been so engrossed in what we were attempting, we surely would have been quaking with fear.

Slowly we made our way towards the maelstrom and to our amazement and horror, as the flames and smoke momentarily cleared we saw in the opening between two blazing ships silhouetted in the horrific crimson backdrop, a man on the mole. He was dancing up and down, moving about and madly waving his arms to attract our attention. Turning the boat in his direction we slowly neared the bows of the blazing ships until suddenly the boat was pulled up short by a clogged propeller. The engine was stopped while two of my shipmates tried to clear the screw, which was completely fouled up with rubbish, making the shaft immovable. As it was impossible to move any nearer to him, we began to shout and scream at the top of our voices to the luckless man to swim for it and jump for it, but whether he heard us or not, or whether he found some other means of escape we shall never know. The smoke and flames obscured him from view and when it cleared again, he was no longer there.

As we still had not cleared the propeller, the man would have had time to reach us if he could swim. The obstacles he would had to overcome to reach us were formidable, the rubbish was so thick there seemed to be no clear water between our boat and the mole and fires were raging on the surface of the water from side to side of both burning ships. But the only means of escape on the mole itself appeared to be through a wall of fire on both sides, with possibly more fire beyond. We knew for sure that if he had not moved he would have been roasted alive for to us in the boat, some 100 yards away, the heat was intense and ever-increasing. Sweating profusely, with foreheads burning and bodies lathered in sweat, we became hotter and hotter. The steel plates of the ships only a short distance away were glowing red from the heat within and without and it must have been only a matter of time before one or both of them blew up. I firmly believe that if the fouled propeller had not stopped us going further, we would have found it physically impossible to reach the doomed man.

The intense heat generated from the two blazing vessels would surely have overpowered us and our small boat, made of wood, would have been in grave danger of bursting into flame. To the best of my knowledge, not one person ventured as near to the shipping on the outer mole as our small party did in *Zetland*'s boat. The only survivors rescued from the mole were the crew of *John Bascom* and others who had abandoned ship previously and with their captain, Otto Heitmann, had landed on the mole before it became a conflagration. By running along the top of the sea wall they had gained shelter at the extreme end of the mole. They were rescued by Captain Williams of the Royal Engineers, who commandeered a steel lifeboat manned by two American sailors serving aboard one of the two American tankers moored at the Molo San Cataldo. He took charge and, realising it was impossible to approach the mole from the harbour side, he took the lifeboat outside the harbour and rescued the survivors from over the sea wall.

Having failed in our rescue attempt, our own situation was far from ideal and we would soon be in need of rescue ourselves. We were

exposed to the many explosions large and small which were still occurring, showering the water around us and sending our vulnerable boat
rocking. We were helpless without power and in imminent danger of
being blasted out of the water by a heavier explosion or being run down
by drifting ships and boats. Another thought kept returning to nag me:
would the *Luftwaffe* return for a follow-up raid?

4

THE RESCUE

AWAKENED by somebody shaking him vigorously, Francis Newman was in time to hear a roll call being taken by one of HMS *Vienna*'s petty officers. When he was spotted underneath the table, the petty officer asked a shipmate, 'Who is he?' Francis did not realise what a picture he presented, lying on the floor, covered head to foot in a black substance, even his hands and face the same colour. After explaining to the petty officer that he had been sick, he was escorted by two shipmates to the wash place where they stripped him of his filthy gear, soaped him all over and dressed him in clean clothes. They turned him into his hammock with orders to stay, as his sentry duty had been taken over by a relief. His hammock had been slung in the ship-wright's workshop, which was being used as a makeshift ward, and the dead were taken into the torpedo workshop which became a temporary morgue.

One of the small boats carrying out rescue operations was MTB *243*, which tied up to a buoy close to its base ship *Vienna*. Three officers and five ratings were on board (the rest were on shore leave) as the small craft commenced its dangerous task of rescue. One of the ratings was wireless operator Peter Bickmore. Their first call was to a damaged British ship in which a crew member had been struck by a large piece of flying metal. The razor-sharp projectile, travelling at the speed of a bullet, had hit the unfortunate seaman on his ankle, severing his foot. The disabled man was taken aboard with other members of the merchant ship's crew and brought back to *Vienna*.

From then until the early hours of the morning, Peter and his shipmates picked survivor after survivor out of the water, pulling them onto the MTB after the wretched men had dragged themselves up the scrambling nets. Peter remembers: 'They were in a terrible state, covered in black oil and in severe shock, shivering and shaking. There were times during those hours of rescue when I was sure that the small 70 foot boat was going to capsize with the weight of survivors we dragged out of the harbour.' He has another memory, a vivid one that haunts him to this day. He saw a group of survivors from a tanker. 'They were swimming

MTB *243*, the boat aboard which
Peter Bickmore served. *(P. Bickmore)*

Peter Bickmore, aged nineteen at
the time, who carried out rescue
operations from MTB *243*. He
described fearing the MTB would
sink with the numbers of survivors
picked up. He was contaminated
and admitted to hospital and later
awarded the BEM for his actions.
(P. Bickmore)

Crew of MTB *86* at speed with Lieutenant Edward Young in command. Jack Taylor carried out rescue operations from MTB *86* and is convinced he escaped contamination by having a shower after discharging survivors to HMS *Vienna*. *(J. Taylor)*

Crew of MTB *86* having 'five minutes' alongside in Bari harbour. *(J. Taylor)*

in the harbour, surrounded by burning petrol, screaming and shouting for help amid enveloping flames, and nobody able to assist them.'

Another mission was to a vessel in the fairway that was well down by the stern. The master refused to leave until one of the crew on the upper deck, who had his legs trapped between the bridge structure and a vent pipe, was released. Peter and a shipmate climbed aboard to join Sub-Lieutenant Collins who had previously boarded the ship and shouted for assistance. They helped to free the hapless sailor. It took some time as pieces of metal had to be cut away bit by bit with a small hacksaw until he could extricate his foot. Once free, the rescued man and his skipper abandoned the sinking ship, boarded the MTB and returned to *Vienna*. The rescue work carried on for hours until about 2 a.m., when Peter and his fellow rescuers were overcome with exhaustion. Large blisters had broken out on his arms, face and the back of his neck and he was partially blinded. Eventually the small party made the last journey back to *Vienna*.

Three shipmates serving aboard SS *Fort Assiniboine*, who had been ashore, hurried back to the harbour to witness with amazement the immense amount of damage. They had not walked very far before they were pulled up by an Army officer who asked them for assistance. A group of about ten soldiers were frantically loading heavy boxes of small-arms ammunition onto a truck as Jack Manning and his two comrades joined them. He saw the reason for the haste. Further along the wharf, less than 20 yards away from the ammunition stack, was a huge pile of petrol in 5 gallon (23 litre) cans, nicknamed 'flimsies' because they often leaked. Through and beyond the swirling smoke Jack saw a wall of fire on the water. It was a race against time. After working some time at top speed with the rest of the party, he mentioned to the officer that they should have reported back on board, for they did not know what state they would find *Fort Assiniboine* in. The officer agreed, thanked the mariners and wished them luck.

When they reached the ship, they discovered that the gangway had disappeared and a ladder had been roughly lashed together as a means of boarding. *Fort Assiniboine* had received orders to clear the port with her volatile cargo of 'block-buster' bombs. Steam was raised and after a tortuous passage through the harbour she eventually reached the open sea. She was to return to Bari some days later.

The Royal Navy's small boats carried out most of the rescue operations in the harbour and it was fortunate that the four or five MTBs that did so were not patrolling off Albania that evening as they had been doing for some weeks. The crew of MTB *86* stayed below decks until the air raid

MTB *270* with Lieutenant Woods, a Canadian, in command, was the MTB ordered to break off rescue operations and to sink the abandoned, blazing USS *Samuel J. Tilden* which was drifting dangerously outside the harbour. *(A. Styles)*

Arthur Styles, who carried out rescue operations aboard MTB *270*, and was aboard when she sank *Samuel J. Tilden* with two torpedoes. *(A. Styles)*

was over and immediately afterwards were called out to commence rescue operations. Able Seaman Jack Taylor was one of the crew. 'We worked from our small boat, picking up survivors out of the water. Some were seriously injured, others too late to save, but they were all pulled aboard, the living and the dead together.' Jack and his shipmates ferried them to the base ship *Vienna*.

The crews dedicatedly carried on with the extremely dangerous work and Jack recalls the boat being subjected to torrents of water and shrapnel, the explosions rocking the boat alarmingly, soaking rescued and rescuers alike. 'One vessel loaded with a cargo of petrol blew up with a mighty roar, drenching us all with a thick, greasy liquid slime. The slippery oily mixture made it difficult to manhandle the survivors and in some cases impossible to keep a hold on the half-dead men, who had little strength left to help themselves.'

It did not deter the Coastal Forces men from sticking manfully to their humane task, though making way in the boat became increasingly difficult as every explosion created more rubbish, driftwood and debris to float on the surface. Jack says:

> It also created a more sinister situation as the petrol-impregnated rubbish burst into flame. The swimmers found themselves not only having to contend with filthy harbour water but with fire as well. We, the boat's crew, were in a sorry mess, covered head to foot in thick grease and wet through to the skin as time and time again we made that journey out into the hell that the harbour had become, to bring back more survivors.

Unknown to any of them the water was contaminated with liquid mustard gas.

During one of the return journeys to *Vienna* Jack took the opportunity to grab a towel and have a quick shower and change of clothes. The rescue work commenced again and carried on until the early hours of morning when at last no more survivors could be seen.

The next morning MTB *86* in company with another boat set sail for the port of Brindisi, having to keep a sharp look-out for underwater obstructions as they left harbour. During the voyage, the skipper called the crew together and explained, to their great surprise, that the burns and blisters they were suffering from were the result of exposure to mustard gas which one of the sunken ships had been carrying. He said it had been released after an explosion. He also informed them that decontamination units were being set up for their arrival in Brindisi and by the time the boat arrived, because of the painful sores and blisters which had begun to appear on hands, faces and in some cases lower parts of the body, only three men were fit enough to take the boat into harbour.

The burns the crew suffered were extensive and severe. The motor mechanic was blinded and the coxswain burnt from his waist down to his knees, including burns to his genitals, and was in constant pain. Jack Taylor firmly holds the view that 'I was lucky not to have been more seriously burnt. The fact of me managing to shower and change during the night saved me from extensive burns and contamination.'

After carrying out rescue operations from one of the MTBs of the 20th Flotilla which had refuelled in Bari, Able Seaman Denis Johns and a shipmate came across one of the flotilla's boats. On boarding her they were surprised to discover, below deck, the skipper and first lieutenant still aboard. Both officers were in a bad state: one was blinded and the other was suffering from blisters on exposed parts and in extreme pain from burned and blistered genitals. After making the two men as comfortable as they could, they set to work cleaning the boat. They fitted a jury rig and made her reasonably seaworthy. Some time later they sailed from the harbour and slowly made the journey to Brindisi. On arrival, the two officers were taken ashore to hospital by ambulance and an armed guard was posted on the gangway to prevent Denis and his shipmate from leaving the boat or speaking to anyone. All the boat's gear and bedding was taken away and stacked on the jetty. In its place they were issued with army gear and bedding.

The Polish gunner Josep and his comrade Arthur Spencer took it in turns to carry their shipmate John Hayes along the mole until near the end of it they came across a group of soldiers and army trucks. From there they were transported to hospital together with other survivors. The two mariners staggered into the hospital, but would not rest until, by pestering and imploring a doctor, they got him to agree to take a look at John, who was lying still, covered in black filth as they themselves were. They were stuck dumb when the doctor quickly examined John and said, 'Sorry lads, he is dead.' He told them that one of John's arms was almost severed and he had a large wound in his side, and that it was likely that he had died before they left the ship. Arthur and Josep were ordered to strip off all their clothing, were given injections and doses of medicine and admitted to hospital.

Shortly after I left *Zetland* with my shipmates in the boat to carry out rescue operations, Commander Bennets, the captain of HMS *Bicester* detailed one of his junior officers, a lieutenant, together with Bob Davies of *Zetland*, to contact Navy House for orders and instructions, the reason being that because of the dense smoke and fire, visibility was nil and communication with the shore base and station was non-existent. The two men left the destroyers, which were still taking on board survivors seeking refuge and treatment. As they commenced their dash along the mole, which was littered with debris, a gruesome sight of carnage greeted them. Spread over the mole, lying in grotesque positions, were bodies, mostly soldiers and civilian port workers caught by the blast and hurled against the high protecting sea wall. Streaming along was a crush of people, many injured and wounded, some rushing, others just managing to stagger along towards the dockyard exits and first-aid posts and centres.

As they picked their way through the masses of rubbish, the two navy men came upon a mortally wounded sailor lying on the concrete. Bob Davies recalls:

> He was in a serious condition, the bottom half of his body was badly muti-lated and blood was spurting from a gash in his neck. Realising he was dying, I called to my comrade to carry on and I would catch up with him. I knelt on the mole and cradled the dying man in my arms to give him what little comfort I could amongst the ghastly nightmare around us. I whispered a few words of comfort to the young seaman and within a few minutes he died in my arms.

Taking the dead man's identity disc, Bob lowered him to the ground and dashed after the lieutenant. He had not gone far before he caught up with the officer, who had been halted by sentries cordoning off a suspected unexploded bomb on the breakwater. No one was allowed to pass, but after explaining the urgency of their mission, the two men were allowed through.

At last they came to the shattered Navy House which, though bombed out, still had a skeleton staff and an officer with some authority to give orders. The instructions were for the two destroyers to leave harbour if at all possible and to make for the port of Taranto. Through the black fog of smoke, Bob and the lieutenant retraced their steps back to their respective ships. At that point Bob remembers feeling very sick. When he arrived back on board *Zetland*, the survivors were still being hosed down in the heads. The crew manning the hoses at that time thought they were swilling fuel oil from the men – they had no reason to think otherwise. How many lives were saved by the sluicing down we shall never know. Once cleaned and dried, the survivors were given what clothes could be spared, even if it was only a pair of overalls. Mugs of tea were dished out by *Zetland*'s sailors, who looked after them until some time later the train of evacuation to the hospitals was organised and under way.

Bob was instructed to gather all signal books ready for dumping overboard, for it was apparent that *Zetland* was severely damaged, though no inspection was possible at that time. Lt Cdr Wilkinson, though in great pain and discomfort, had remained on the bridge. He decided to attempt to take in tow the Coastal Forces petrol tanker MV *Devon Coast* which had broken loose from her moorings. The crew had abandoned her and she was on fire, drifting dangerously towards the middle of the harbour. He ordered Lieutenant Nicholas Twigge to take four men and board her and secure a tow-line. Lt Cdr Eric Locket remembers: 'The *Zetland*'s hoses were played onto *Devon Coast* to keep the fires at bay from the boarding party attempting to secure the line. Some time later, realising that the fires raging aboard were out of control, the captain ordered the boarding party to return to *Zetland*.'

After abandoning the tow, Lt Cdr Wilkinson saw through the swirling black smoke another vessel in distress. It was the Admiralty diesel tanker SS *La Drome*. She was the most easterly of the ships in the line of vessels tied stern first to the breakwater and though damaged by blast, she was not on fire. She was, however, in imminent danger from the burning, drifting *Devon Coast*. *Zetland*'s skipper put his ship alongside *La Drome*, the tow line was taken by one of the tanker's crew, none of whom had abandoned ship, and when secured, the destroyer proceeded to tow the tanker to a safer berth nearer the dockyard. Lt Cdr Wilkinson had remained on the bridge, battling against the pain of his injuries while directing these activities, but when he received the order to make for Taranto, he made what was to be his final decision as captain of *Zetland*. He informed Commander Bennets, captain of flotilla leader *Bicester*, that Lt Cdr Eric Locket, RNVR was appointed in command of *Zetland*. The wounded skipper was taken down to his cabin, put in his bunk and attended to by the sick-bay staff as the destroyer's surgeon had gone ashore during the afternoon and was not to rejoin the ship for two days.

Now in temporary command, Lt Cdr Locket received an order from Commander Bennets, instructing him to lead the way out of harbour and he would follow because *Bicester* had suffered damage affecting her navigational efficiency. The mooring lines were released and *Zetland*, followed by her sister ship, made her way out to the fairway. Lt Cdr Locket ordered a jury chart table to be rigged on the coming bridge and Sub-Lieutenant Norman Smith took over the chart-work duties. The two destroyers began their tortuous and dangerous journey out to sea and to the Italian naval base of Taranto. Not knowing what obstacles could be in their path, and with visibility down to a few yards, it was only possible for *Zetland* to move with extreme caution. To facilitate the operation, Petty Officer Robinson, armed with a long bearing-off spar, was lowered over and secured to the bow. He prodded and felt his way round drifting ships on fire, stretches of water where the surface was aflame, unseen underwater wreckage and obstructions. His directions from the bow were relayed to the shattered bridge by a 'runner' as all manoeuvres were carried out to the accompaniment of overpowering and deafening noise.

Eric Locket recalls:

> The entire ship's company had worked magnificently throughout the oper-
> ation and I was particularly impressed by the marvels of Yeoman of Signals
> John Farmer and Leading Signalman Bob Davies, who kept an eagle eye
> on all developments in the harbour and maintained visual communica-
> tions in such atrocious conditions.

During the slow passage towards the harbour mouth, through the crimson haze of flame and swirling smoke, Bob Davies caught a glimpse of men in the water.

> They were trying to pull themselves up on to the extreme end of the mole.
> They kept slipping back into the slimy water, time and time again. The
> mole was covered, as were the men, in greasy scum which made it impos-
> sible for them to get any hand-hold or purchase. It was much like the greasy
> pole at a fairground, only in this horrific instance, success meant survival,
> failure meant certain death.

George Skuse aboard *Bicester*, following *Zetland* some yards astern, recalls, 'It was touch and go whether we would be able to get out of the harbour because burning ships were drifting dangerously in the fairway and when on one occasion we did squeeze between two of them the heat was so intense, it scorched *Bicester*'s paintwork.' In the harbour entrance and just outside, *Bicester* stopped to pick up survivors, many of them from USS *Samuel J. Tilden*. Once out into the Adriatic, Lt Cdr Locket set course for the port of Taranto by dead reckoning, with *Bicester* following astern. Because of the explosions, the magnetic and giro compasses had acquired large errors and at daybreak it was discovered that the two destroyers were nearer the enemy coast than the Italian. Immediately, Lt Cdr Locket got *Zetland* back on course.

Aboard both ships, symptoms of mustard gas poisoning began to appear. They were the usual burns and blisters to all exposed parts and Bob Davies discovered that he had lost tufts of hair from the front and back of his head, where the vile liquid had stuck. He also found it diffi-

84

Below:
HMS *Zetland* on her way to
Taranto showing huge
chunks of metal thrown
aboard during and after the
explosions (port side).
(G. Southern)

Above:
Another photo of damage
aboard *Zetland* (starboard
side) *(G. Southern)*

cult to use his telescope because of painful blisters which had formed round his eyes. In daylight the damage sustained aboard *Zetland* could be assessed. The funnel was squashed and leaning over drunkenly, the mast had broken off, and the aerials and radar were missing. Huge chunks of twisted metal had been tossed on deck, some of it too heavy to be manhandled overboard. It had to be left where it had landed until the ship reached port. When the ships arrived in the bay of Taranto, *Bicester* took over the lead through the swept channel but it was discovered that none of her officers had enough sight to negotiate the entry to the port and a signal was made to the shore base to request assistance. Some time later pilots were sent out to guide the destroyers safely in.

After docking, all *Bicester*'s crew were lined up for medical inspection. Doctors, both naval and Army, checked the men and dabbed the blisters with various coloured creams, which some of the men applied for more than a week before the sores began to clear up. Bill Rickerby was examined and transferred to hospital. Commander Bennets requested that Hurts certificates (a Report of Wound or Hurt document, signed by a doctor signifying the bearer had sustained wounds in the course of duty) should be issued to all crew members as he surmised that the blisters and burns had been caused through contact with a chemical agent of some kind. However, he was informed by his superiors ashore that no such thing had happened. Bob Davies was sent to hospital, where he received treatment from doctors and afterwards, back on board, from the sick-berth attendant.

Bill Rickerby, suffering from fractured ribs, was transferred to the 70th Field Hospital situated on a hill overlooking the harbour. Some days later a nurse washed his matted hair and was worried enough to call a doctor to have a look at his scalp. The doctor ordered all his hair to be cut off to facilitate the treatment against what he thought to be oil contamination. He also told him his hair loss would be permanent. That did not do much for Bill's state of mind, though his sight was beginning to return and three weeks later he was discharged back to *Bicester*.

When the explosion hit HMS *Vulcan*, drifting out of control, Engine Room Artificer (ERA) Jack Burnell was on deck. 'It immediately caused the ship to heel over to port, the angle so acute that water poured in through the scuppers before she rolled back again.' The ship's dynamo had ceased to function, resulting in a complete loss of power. Chief ERA Harry Isham and Jack went down to the engine room to find it full of steam. The steam pipe to the dynamo had fractured and water was pouring into the bilge, where the general service pump had broken away from the sea-water inlet. Fortunately the flow stopped when the two engineers managed to shut off the undamaged inlet valve. The petrol-drive auxiliary dynamo was on the upper deck in the after deck-house. They started it up and returned to the engine room, which was now filled with steam, to change over the lighting panel switches to restore lighting to the ship. By the time it came on, burning oil and petrol on the surface of the water, fanned by the breeze, was approaching *Vulcan*. Captain Samuel Grice gave the order to move the ship away from the flames to a less dangerous position alongside one of the inner harbour jetties.

Meanwhile up on deck, *Vulcan's* crew pulled survivors aboard as fast as they could. The ones they could not reach, they had to leave. Bert Stevens recalls 'a group of seamen sitting and holding onto an upturned ship's propeller waiting for help. When they realised we could not reach them, they just waved and cheered us on, poor devils.' The survivors they did pull aboard lay sprawled exhausted on the upper deck, coughing and choking. Jack and his chief encountered problems in getting the triple expansion engine moving owing to condensed steam hydraulically locking the piston movement. The Hotwell pump was shattered and the stem drains were unable to cope with the flow of condensate from the cylinders. At the risk of fracturing the cylinder heads they gently applied pressure and eventually they were able to obey the telegraph commands and get the ship under way.

Shortly after berthing, Jack noticed an Army ambulance coming to a stop on the jetty and the medical team coming aboard to attend to the survivors and injured crew members. Jack was one of them; his face was covered in blood which he had been unaware of until it was drawn to his attention, so he went ashore with the rest and was taken by ambulance to the 98th General Hospital in Bari. Bert Stevens also saw the ambulance arrive and watched it depart, carrying some of his injured shipmates. 'The rest of the crew left on board were also in severe shock and as things turned out, the ones who were taken to hospital were the lucky ones. Those remaining behind on the ship were far more badly affected by extended exposure.'

None of *Vienna's* crew had slung hammocks on the mess-deck, which became crowded with survivors, most of them nursing injuries sustained during the raid and subsequent explosions. At first many of the injured made their own way to the mess-deck and those too badly injured were carried aboard. The vessel took over the role as the main reception and first-aid post, and in a short time survivors picked up by the rescue boats began to arrive, sodden to the skin and covered in slime.

One of these was Rowland Roberts from the tanker *Devon Coast*. He had been found wandering along the jetty in a semi-conscious state by a sailor who took him to a small boat tied to the outer mole and brought him across the harbour to *Vienna.* Rowland thought at that moment that his trials were over; little did he know that they were not. He can only remember going on board through double doors in the side of the ship. Once inside he had the impression of a large shed full of casualties. Some patients were lying on stretchers on the mess-deck, others were spread out on greatcoats and other survivors, bandaged but on their feet, were standing around talking to one another. Even in his bemused state he recalls the impression made on him of the hysterical din in that confined space. All the while, members of *Vienna's* crew dished out mugs of tea while medical staff dealt with scores of patients.

To add to the confusion, and making matters far worse than they already were, they heard a loud explosion which battered the ship, sending her rocking from side to side. The sound inside the steel hold was ear-splitting and to add to the terror the lights went out. The utter darkness created panic among the survivors, whose nerves were already at breaking point, but after some time calm was almost restored when the lights came on again.

The crews of the small boats risked life and limb in the search for survivors. When dragged into the boats many of the injured who had been caught by fire had huge patches of skin hanging from their bodies and were in agony, screaming with pain as they were helped over the sides of the boats, teeth chattering, shivering uncontrollably from the effects of cold and shock. They were transferred from the boats to *Vienna* and then to the hospital. Sadly many of the inert bodies picked up by the gallant rescuers had succumbed to the effects of the explosions and fire. Other boats landed survivors on Molo Ridosso, some of the men found their own way to *Vienna* and others boarded ambulances and other vehicles which were arriving at the quayside.

5

THE SURVIVORS

Bob Wills, who was knocked unconscious after he had left the ambulance train, was picked up later in the night by two American soldiers driving a truck full of ammunition. 'They sat me in the back propped up against a huge shell and in that fashion I was transported to the 98th General Hospital, about a mile away.' He arrived to see the hospital a hive of activity and immediately joined in as a stretcher bearer taking patients to the operating theatres and also to the cellars, where the dead were taken. He met up with the rest of his unit. Of the hospital Bob says:

> There were dead servicemen lying in the corridors because nobody had time to move them and I remember a staff nurse shouting at a passing soldier to 'Cover that man's face up.' Many of the wounded were covered in black oil, completely unaware, as I and everybody else was, of the presence of mustard gas in the filthy mixture.

What happened next was the most harrowing sight of his whole wartime service.

> So badly injured were some of the men, mainly sailors, that though still alive there was nothing possible that could be done for them. With hundreds of patients needing more urgent attention, those unfortunate men were taken to a special ward which we referred to as 'the death ward' where the wounded with no hope of recovery were taken and left to die. There were about twenty of these hopeless men laid on stretchers.

On one of his journeys to 'the death ward', Bob could hardly believe his eyes. 'Some of the dying were restless and moving about and although I should not have been there, and would have been in trouble if caught, I held the hand of the most active to give what little comfort I could and told him he would be all right.' In the ward a merchant navy cadet kept shooting upright in his bed and shouting in a loud voice, 'Did you hear that bloody bang?' He had to have injections to calm him down.

The influx of patients resembled an anthill as stretcher bearers rushed

89

Bob Wills (left) with colleagues of the operating theatre staff of the 98th General Hospital enjoying an afternoon off on the Molo de Bari. Taken before the raid. *(B. Wills)*

A donkey race in the compound of the 98th General Hospital (Policlinic). Bob Wills is on the left *(B. Wills)*

Group photograph of medical orderlies on the steps of the hospital (Bob Wills with dog). Standing at the top is a Panzer corporal (POW) who slept in the 'other ranks bar', guarding the beer. *(B. Wills)*

around with injured servicemen in all directions, giving the impression of complete confusion. The normal procedure for admitting patients was abandoned. They were brought in by any means of transport that could carry them – ambulances, lorries, vans and old Italian Army trucks left over when the Germans had retreated. Anyone on hand helped to bring the patients into hospital including German prisoners of war who were usually engaged in cooking and looking after stores.

In her diary, nurse Gay Trevithic wrote:

> What a night followed, ambulances screamed into hospital all night long with casualties from the raid. The majority of them were either burnt and covered in oil or had limbs blown off . . . Twelve inches of oil lay on the

water [in the harbour] . . . We were all on duty and cases just poured in. Many died long before reaching hospital . . . The cries and groaning were heartbreaking, all night long it went on and no one slept . . . 98th admitted to overflowing and we had over two hundred, it was a nightmare of a night. Soap and water would not bring off the oil, it had to be scraped off with kerosene . . . Blankets, coats and life jackets lying about in all corners of the hospital told their own story . . . It was so bad that when the boys came in we did not know whether they were Italians, Indians or British . . . I only hope I never live to experience another night like this.

In the harbour, a platoon of soldiers of the Leicestershire Regiment helped men of the Medical Corps, who were quickly on the scene, to pull survivors out of the water. Corporal Ernest McCartney was in charge; he and his men had been marching out of the docks after a full day's work and were looking forward to a night of relaxation. They were old campaigners of India, France, Dunkirk and North Africa and had taken shelter behind a high wall until the raid was over. Ernest vividly remembers, 'The men we pulled out of the water were covered in black, greasy filth. To me it looked and smelt like oil. The badly wounded were taken to hospital, some minus arms and legs; what a night.'

The platoon accompanied some of the wounded to hospital and on arrival assisted the medics in any way they could. Ernest says, 'There were not enough beds in the wards. It was a shambles, most of the patients had to be left on stretchers placed anywhere on the floor between the beds and down the gangways. They were crying and calling out in pain, waiting to be attended to, but the small number of doctors were overwhelmed.' In the course of the following week during which the platoon remained, things became better as more medical staff arrived.

Having decided to discharge himself from hospital, if only temporarily, Lieutenant Graham Scott passed the bewildered stretcher cases as he hurried from the building. He hitched a lift in one of the returning ambulances, which dropped him off at the harbour. The driver informed him that almost every building in the harbour was minus a roof and that every pane of glass lay shattered in the streets. Graham made his way to Navy House, only to find that the building had been swept clean of every stick of furniture. All the windows and doors were hanging from shattered frames. He heard later that the staff had abandoned the building for the time being for a safer billet out of town, taking what was left of the confidential papers with them. He commandeered a roadworthy lorry, climbed into the driver's seat and headed for the central pier of Molo

Faraneo, where he knew HMS *Vienna* was berthed. At that time the survivors were being taken aboard the depot ship and with pleasure he recognised among a group of men standing on the mole the face of Petty Officer Harry Winter, a member of base staff who had arrived a few minutes before Graham. The two sailors commenced picking up those of the wounded who could be moved, placed them in the back of the truck and slowly drove out of the crowded dockyard. All manner of vehicles were moving around, making driving extremely difficult.

Once outside, Graham had to cope with a mad exodus of people fleeing the city in droves. On arrival at the 98th General Hospital, the survivors were met by nursing staff and taken inside. Harry and Graham made their way back to the devastated harbour to continue their self-imposed task. During one of the journeys, Harry recounted what he knew of the events of the night and of the situation in the harbour. He gathered that the explosions had been caused by tankers and ammunition ships catching fire and blowing up. The explosions set fire to other ships carrying deck cargoes of petrol, which either burnt or leaked into the harbour, and he said one ship that blew up 'just evaporated'.

As they drove along the harbourside Graham saw one wrecked ship which had been tossed onto the jetty, its bows out of the water and the after part of the vessel under water. He tried to visualise the power that could toss a ship out of the water like a piece of driftwood. At that moment, a massive explosion ripped through the air. A blinding light and overpowering noise beat at them as a high wall on their left hand side was reduced to a few inches in height and a pile of scrap iron in front of it was blown away like chaff in the wind at harvest time. Graham could not understand how the lorry remained on its four wheels during the huge blast but he had no time to muse over the strangeness of it all as more and more wounded began to appear through the smoke and dust. The truck soon filled to capacity and Harry took over the driving.

The rescue work went on and on, torn bodies loaded one after another onto the lorry, many near to death, accompanied all the while by a most deafening and awesome cacophony of sound: the crackle of flame, explosions of small-arms and larger shells, ambulances and trucks, horns and sirens blaring, tyres screeching on the tarmac as the vehicles made their way through the dense smoke. But above all, beyond the curtain of smoke and fire, could be heard the agonised cries and calls from unseen desperate men struggling to stay alive in the water. Hours later the makeshift ambulance reached the 98th General with the last group of survivors. The wounded lay quiet in a state of shock and Graham recalls one of them whispering to the two sailors, 'Thank you, sorry to be such a nuisance.'

*   *   *

When Rowland Roberts of MV *Devon Coast* was admitted to the 98th General, he noticed patients stretched out in every conceivable space, all the aisles and passages taken up by wounded men. They were on bunks, camp-beds, mattresses, groundsheets and in some cases on the floor on coats and blankets. The vast number of patients filled the wards and still they came. All hospital staff had been recalled to help in the enormous task of dealing with the overwhelming numbers, and so great was the backlog that it was not until the next morning that Rowland was attended to. He spent all night covered in the thick black mixture and by the time he was examined he thought he had gone blind, for he could not see at all. His eyes felt as if they were full of broken glass, his right hand had shrapnel embedded in it. His wrist was broken and he had numerous cuts, bruises and blisters on his face. He was completely stripped of his filthy clothing, decontaminated and smothered with ointment, his injuries were attended to and in the following days he began to make a slow recovery.

Donald Cook of the Royal Engineers was put into a ward with four other patients, two of whom Donald believed were crewmen on torpedo boats who had been contaminated by fuel oil. He remembers how horrific their wounds were: 'Their blisters would burst, the puss running down leaving ugly streaks, and settling into creases in the flesh. The unfortunate sailors were stripped naked and then underwent the added humiliation of being photographed for the benefit of the hospital staff.' Donald never knew his room-mate's names. 'They sounded like north country men and were aware that they were soon to return to the UK.'

By daybreak the hospital resembled a refugee camp. Every non-urgent patient was moved out to make way for the influx of injured and wounded from the harbour. All those capable of speaking complained of sore throats, eyes and faces. They were given the usual treatment for shock: warm tea, a shot of morphine and left to rest and keep warm. One patient who was not moved was William Mason of the 2nd Battalion of the Lancashire Fusiliers. He had been seriously wounded in both legs during fierce fighting as the 8th Army attempted to cross the heavily defended Sangro River line. After emergency treatment in hospital in the town of Vasto, he had arrived in Bari in late November. He remembers how speedily the wards were cleared to prepare for the survivors. All the walking wounded and others, even some confined to bed, were taken out of the ward, leaving him on his own for some time. The nurses covered him over with as many blankets as could be spared and left him on his own, feeling scared and apprehensive.

The noise and shuddering of the foundations combined with the clatter of hurried footfalls as medical staff ran to and fro bringing more and more wounded, pain-wracked men to fill the ward. The survivors were suffering burns and blisters and doctors were constantly administering injections of morphine to alleviate the pain. Afterwards one doctor told me he had worked non-stop for five days without sleep.

One of the wounded soldiers admitted to the 98th General from the ambulance train was paratrooper John Meek. He did not arrive in comfort but on a stretcher. He had been evacuated from the front line near the village of Guardragnelle in the mountains 70 miles (110 km) north of Foggia. He was part of a night patrol caught in murderous cross-fire. They were carrying phospherus hand grenades in their belt pouches, many of which exploded into flame, creating human torches. Only John and another man survived. They were brought down the mountainside strapped to a mule.

When he was lifted into the ambulance at the sidings, he almost imagined he was back in the front line as he heard and felt terrific bangs and crashes from bombs falling a short distance away. On arrival at the 98th General, the stretcher cases were carried into the hospital, but much to his surprise not to a ward, but into a corridor, where they were lined up close to the wall. He soon realised why as patients were carried in screaming and shouting in agony as they were taken into the empty wards.

It was difficult to get any information from anyone, but I did manage to learn that most of the wounded from the harbour were seamen of the Royal and Merchant Navies, many with serious burns. The doctors and staff were trying to cope with the vast numbers but were hopelessly overwhelmed. The patients from the hospital train together with patients who had been admitted previously were completely ignored. The medical staff continued to treat the new influx which they assumed were suffering from the effects of exposure and fuel oil contamination.

A retired CID officer now living in Liverpool, John says, 'Since 1943, whenever I have mentioned the incident in Bari to anyone, I have not only been disbelieved but told I was making the story up.'

Joe Collin, a member of the RAMC remembers: 'We handled hundreds of casualties from the disaster, with our theatres working full steam for about five days, a period when we never saw bed.' Nurse Gay Trevithic wrote in her diary: 'My word, I am fed up seeing so many mangled humans. It's simply heart-breaking. The sisters of the 98th are suffering from laryngitis and sore eyes as a result of the mustard gas on the clothes of the patients admitted on the 2nd December.'

When Peter Bickmore of MTB *243* returned to HMS *Vienna* after his night's rescue operations he was sent to the 98th General to have his blisters and burns attended to and had to wait hours to receive attention. He was kept in hospital for two weeks and was transferred by air to Luqa hospital in Malta. The events of that night have remained in Peter's memory and many times since he has asked himself, 'Could Bari have been better protected that fateful night and need the number of casualties have been so high?' For his part in the rescue operations, Peter was awarded the British Empire Medal (Military Division) and Sub-Lieutenant Collins received the Order of the British Empire.

Supper had been cleared away and radio operator Arthur Styles was stripped off washing himself in the heads aboard MTB *297*. The boat had arrived back in Bari that morning after taking part in a night patrol off the coast of Yugoslavia. She was manned by a crew of twelve and commanded by Lieutenant John Woods, a Canadian. The boat was moored adjacent to the base ship *Vienna* when the raid started. Of the following hours Arthur can recall little of the sequence of events except the boat sailing through the fire and smoke, then dragging men out of the water to land them ashore and continuing to search for more. Just before midnight, Lieutenant Woods received an order to break off rescue work, proceed to sea and to sink the abandoned USS *Samuel J. Tilden*, which was drifting and on fire outside the harbour. Just after 1 a.m. on 3 December MTB *297* lined up her torpedo tubes on the stricken liberty ship and fired two torpedoes. According to the official report, 'USS *Samuel J. Tilden* sank in deep water.'

On night of Friday, 13 November one of the Royal Air Force boats attached to the 253 Air Sea Rescue Unit was sunk while carrying out rescue operations off the coast of Albania. Senior Wireless Operator Cliff Llewellyn was a survivor and while waiting for a new boat to arrive, he and the other survivors lived in a flat in Bari. When the raid began, Cliff remembers, 'There was chaos in the streets. The Italian people in the same block seemed very afraid and we did our best to calm the younger children, and our rations of sweets and chocolate just vanished.' After the raid, one of the unit's boats under the command of Flight Lieutenant Jack Wall, took part in rescue operations, saving many men. Cliff says that in some cases, however, the airmen had difficulty in persuading some of the crews to leave their damaged vessel. The next morning he was stopped at the dock gate by a military policemen who would not allow him through because he was not wearing a hat. Cliff recalls with amusement: 'When I was shipwrecked I abandoned the boat with nothing but what I was wearing and yet the MP was more concerned with the fact that I hadn't a hat than all the carnage around him.' He was eventually let through and was amazed to see in daylight, the tremendous damage. He remembers seeing 'a chunk of a ship's side about the size of a house lying twisted and torn like a piece of crumpled paper that had missed the waste paper basket, and it was a quarter of a mile from the nearest water.'

Not all the survivors were taken to the 98th General in Bari. When Francis Newman reached the port of Brindisi aboard HMS *Vienna*, he learned later from some of his shipmates, his body developed a deep brown colour with large pink blisters on his face, arms and legs and the back of his head and neck. He was admitted to hospital – a building he believes had been a church at one time. Fifty beds lined the walls and a large stained glass window filled one of the end walls. Most of the crew of *Vienna* were under treatment and Francis had all his hair cut off and his blisters lathered in ointment. All the patients were issued with eye-shades to wear during daylight as the brightness caused extreme discomfort. Beside his bed, each man had a bowl of hot water into which friar's balsam had been added. The patient placed a towel over his head to inhale the steam. Francis remembers:

> A shipmate of mine had been wearing nothing but a pair of overalls at the time of the raid and consequently was soaked to the skin. One night as the pain became unbearable, in a frenzy he tore off all his dressings and the ward was in uproar until he could be sedated. For days afterwards the unfortunate man spent all his time lying on his stomach. It was the only way he could find some relief from the burning pain.

Francis spent several weeks in the hospital before he was discharged, with his legs heavily bandaged, back to *Vienna*.

After the injured crew and survivors had left HMS *Vulcan* to be admitted to hospital, the captain received orders to sail to Taranto at 'best rate of knots' – six if possible. During the passage Bert Stevens recalls a curious odour beginning to permeate the ship, mixed with the smell of crude oil. He says, 'It reminded me of Old English Pear Drop sweets, though most of my shipmates said it smelt like garlic.' He felt his eyes smarting and running and his throat and tongue felt like two sheets of sandpaper rubbing together. He began to itch all over so he went below for a wash, but his skin was so tender by that time that when he ran the water on his blackened hands he cried out in agony. Most of the crew were having the same problem and did not attempt to wash themselves. Blisters were forming on all exposed parts of the body, and eyes were beginning to close.

Bert says, 'It took about three days to reach the Bay of Taranto, living and sleeping in our clothing and eating and drinking with that peculiar smell clinging to everything.' When they reached the harbour entrance they received a signal to turn round and make for Brindisi, where preparations were in hand to attend to the crew. On arrival they had to anchor outside the port and wait for a tug to tow them in. When it arrived, it towed *Vulcan* to the most secluded part of the harbour, well out of the way of prying eyes, where the ship was ordered to drop anchor. A motor launch arrived with Army personnel on board and the order was given to clear the lower deck. *Vulcan*'s crew formed a line and the soldiers walked along and picked out the worst cases, including Bert, led them to the launch and ordered the remaining crew to close down the ship ready for fumigation. They were also told to be ready to be picked up in twenty minutes. There was still not a word of explanation about their condition.

At the military base they were ordered to strip off, as all the discarded clothing had to be burnt. From that moment things became vague – Bert supposes it was because he was in good hands and was at last receiving treatment. Some of his blisters were the size of an old penny, and they were now beginning to appear on his private parts. The next thing he remembers was waking up in a tented hospital, his eyes covered, his hands sore but bandaged and still unaware of why he was in that condition. A few days later the doctor removed the bandages from his eyes and told Bert that his vision would improve in time. He said the soreness had been caused by dust and smoke, the blisters were clearing up and he apologised for having to cut clumps of hair off his head in order to treat the blisters.

A week later he was discharged to an Army camp and issued with Army clothes. While he was there he asked the Army barber to complete the job on his hair and shave it all off. He never returned to HMS *Vulcan*. He received a draft to the UK two days after Christmas and says 'I never realised that thirty-nine years would pass before I knew the truth.'

Bert's shipmate, Jack Burrel, who had been admitted to the 98th General in Bari, and was described by Bert as one of 'the lucky ones', learned that there had 'been some sort of contamination' in the harbour. As he says, 'There was plenty of evidence of that on many of the patients, some being unbelievably blistered. I was lucky in that respect, only suffering from a cut forehead, temporary loss of sight and burns on the top of my head.' On discharge he was sent by road to Brindisi to join the rest of the crew in an Army transit camp. He returned to *Vulcan* to help repair the bridge, which had almost been blasted away.

Much to his surprise, he did not go to sea again aboard *Vulcan*, for he was drafted back to the UK via Naples. After a spell of leave, he returned to his home base of Chatham, only to be admitted to hospital with a suspected patch on his lung. He was eventually discharged from the Royal Navy in March 1945 as unfit. He says, 'No doubt the thirty-year censorship applied in this instance, the truth being too politically sensitive to reveal.' Jack is now in his late seventies, living in Tring, Hertfordshire, and enjoying retirement to the full.

From his home in New York, Warren Brandenstein recalls that on the morning of 3 December 1943 he found himself in the 98th General Hospital in Bari where he was very well looked after.

> I heard later that Ensign Vesole had died from his wounds. He received the US Navy Cross and a destroyer was named after him. He did a great deal of rescue work out on that breakwater and if he hadn't ordered me to get into the lifeboat I might have died. Most of the men who went into the water instead of the lifeboat were critically burned inside and outside of their bodies, mustard mixed with oil-slick.

In the shattered, empty gymnasium on Bari's seafront which had all its windows blown out, William Walters and John Whitley, two of the survivors from USS *Samuel J. Tilden*, shared the quarters with a group of British soldiers. 'I stayed for two days,' William recalls.

> The British shared with me what little food they had. When I had dashed to my duty station before we abandoned ship, I had not had time to put any shoes on, so I was bare-footed. One of the soldiers told me if I would help him unload bodies and parts of bodies retrieved from the harbour onto trucks, he would give me a nice pair of English boots. Besides the gift of the boots, I stole a pair of woollen socks off the clothes line on a British ship.

Both men received a pair of boots from a British soldier on guard duty.

After leaving the 98th General, John Whitley had spent a few hours in the field hospital to which he had fled, and was then transferred to the gymnasium where he spent the next two days sleeping on the floor. During his stay, 'A doctor went from man to man asking "are your eyes bothering you?" It seemed the day after the raid, some men had difficulty

USS *Lyman Abbott* at sea (taken from a US Navy dirigible). *Lyman Abbott* was the abandoned ship that the author and four shipmates from HMS *Zetland* boarded in order to fight fires. Though the Official British Account described her sinking during the night, she was still afloat at the end of the war. *(John Hill Collection)*

Wrecked ship laid on its port side. *(John Hill Collection)*

Sunken ships USS *John Bascom* (right) and USS *John Motley* (left). *(John Hill Collection)*

USS *Joseph Wheeler* resting on the bottom of the harbour. *(John Hill Collection)*

British soldiers playing water onto a wrecked ship which has collapsed midships.
(*J. Risbridger*)

seeing.' During this period, German planes came over to observe the damage.

> This caused air-raid alarms and sharing an underground air-raid shelter with the local people crying and praying while standing in water was an experience in itself. One of my navy friends [William] had to leave the ship without his shoes. I lost mine while I was sleeping in the gymnasium, making the mistake of taking them off. We walked bare-footed down to the docks where a British soldier on guard gave us both a pair of combat boots.

Gunner's Mate Humphries persuaded the British doctor to release the American sailors from the walking wounded, saying he would take care of his men. The US Air Force based in Foggia furnished them with a truck and driver and the next day they were transported to the port of Taranto.

> Our quarters in Taranto were in a public school building and before I had conquered the Italian lavatory system we were aboard a landing craft, LST *359*, bound for Bizerte, North Africa, where we arrived on December 9th. We spent a pleasant four days in an olive orchard and were transferred to the local air base for a flight to Catania in Sicily. When we asked for information on how to use a parachute, the Air Force officer advised us to

use them for sitting on because it was much safer to ride the plane down. Catania air strip seemed to be an abandoned German air field. All the hangars and other buildings had been shot up. From there we were taken the few miles along the coast and put aboard the USS *Lyman Abbott*, which had arrived in the bay on December 4th after leaving Bari on the previous day.

Lyman Abbott needed seven men to replace those she had lost and William remembers:

> It was decided that seven men out of the twenty survivors of *Samuel J. Tilden* would be transferred to make up the numbers. We were told to draw numbers and those drawing the seven lowest would stay on board and the rest would return to the States for further orders. I drew No. 13 but swapped it with a married man who had drawn No. 6. He wanted to return home and I wanted to stay.

John Whitley was one of the men who was to return home and he was transferred with the others as passengers aboard USS *John Shires*, which landed them at Oran. They were transported to Casablanca by train where the accommodation was on the floor of a box car, three hot days and three freezing nights. USS *General W.A. Mann* left Casablanca and landed the survivors in Norfolk, Virginia, on 17 January 1944. John survived the war and now lives in Delmare, Delaware.

William Walters stayed aboard *Lyman Abbott*, which remained in Augusta for almost two weeks before returning to Bari to discharge her original cargo. She arrived on Christmas Eve and after several days discharging, she left Bari, crossed the Atlantic and arrived in New York on 13 March 1944. From there he went on survivor's leave. He says, 'Both the *Samuel J. Tilden* and the *Lyman Abbott* had a deck load of mustard gas. It was in metal canisters and very plainly marked MUSTARD GAS on the side of the containers.' William served twenty-three years in the US Navy and twenty-two years as a deck officer in the Merchant Marine. He retired in 1988 and now lives in Boston.

A British patrol boat took George Maury with the captain, the chief engineer and the rest of the engineers to the *Lyman Abbott* on the morning after the raid, 3 December. 'What a mess, pieces of ship's steel and other parts all over the deck. There were small pieces one or two inches in size to large chunks of metal I should guess weighed a ton or more.' The rest of the crew came aboard to start cleaning up the mess while the engineers went below to check the damage there.

Everything appeared to be all right, one boiler still had enough pressure that we could light it off and raise pressure we could use. The port boiler had lost all pressure because the concussion had whipped the steam line to the whistle and due to our money-hungry shipbuilders using ⅝ [16 mm] bolts when they should have used ¾ in [19 mm] bolts, it had allowed the flanges in the line to move out and grind out the gasket which gave the steam a way of escape. The boilers being the responsibility of the Second Engineer, it fell to me to repair the steam line. I replaced the gasket and rebolted the flange with ¾ in bolts as it should have been done in the first place, when the ship was built.

Orders were received that a convoy was leaving Bari during the afternoon and if possible *Lyman Abbott* was to be ready to join it. 'Nobody wanted to stay in Bari and we all worked hard at making the ship seaworthy.' The vessel was ready in time and left harbour to join the convoy. Two British destroyers recalled from Adriatic patrol formed part of the escorts. During the raid, *Lyman Abbott* had suffered a near miss on her port stern quarter.

> We did not know it at the time but it had twisted the rudder post 17 degrees to starboard. It was quite exciting for a while trying to manoeuvre among the other ships of the convoy, so we had to steer by the emergency wheel aft. The chief engineer almost lost a finger when he was releasing the collar on the shaft just as the helmsman decided to correct the course. They found that if they steered with a 17 degree to port, they could handle the ship.

After some difficulty the convoy arrived back in Augusta. Those men that were still having problems with their injuries were taken ashore to a field hospital for treatment. Some of the men were sent to the British military hospital in Syracuse for further treatment. 'Nick [Frank Nichols, Third Assistant Engineer] and I were sent there as they did not know for sure what had caused the burns and were concerned that we might have eye trouble and in consequence we were examined frequently. At one time the hospital had been a mental institution and the ward doors only had knobs on the outside.'

During their stay in Syracuse both men took the opportunity to see some of the sights of the ancient city.

> We saw the Temple of Minerva, now a Catholic cathedral. The tombs where John the Baptist was supposed to have been held, and the ropemaker's grotto where the ropes were used to raise the massive columns

of which the Temple of Minerva were made. Also the amphitheatre where they held the contests and the grotto where the prisoners were held. The accoustics were so good that you could hear a whisper anywhere in there.

Towards the end of December, the captain and chief came to see how the two men were going on and to inform that that *Lyman Abbott* had received sailing orders; to return to Bari in convoy the very next morning and unload the cargo.

I very near burst a gasket thinking she might sail without us and that we would remain in the hospital. Nick and I hustled up the doctor to discharge us, which he agreed with on condition that we both sign release forms absolving him from any blame for anything that might happen to us. The reason being that he thought our burns were not healing as fast as he thought they should. We didn't hesitate long and left with the captain and chief to board *Lyman Abbott*.

My arm was still giving me a lot of pain and the doctors had been treating it with gentian violet. Back on board, the gunnery officer was treating some of the crew with sulphur drugs; we tried it and it improved the healing process so that the pain was less severe in a couple of days and the hole in my arm scabbed over and started to heal though all these years later I still have an indentation where it was.

When we arrived in Bari, the harbour was a mess of sunken ships and all kinds of debris. I was able to get ashore to see the damage the city had suffered. It had taken some bombs and there were a few buildings damaged. We had to visit the hospital to be checked out and okayed. We had our Christmas dinner there and went to a show at the Royal Navy club. I don't remember the date we left Bari but we sailed to Taranto to the ship-yard. We were there for two weeks, the time it took the Italians to straighten out the rudder problem. I remember the interpreter asking the Italian boss how long it would take to fix it. He said at least ten days. We reminded him it only took ten days to build the ship – the boss replied, 'That was America, not Italy.'

Lyman Abbott left Taranto for Augusta to await a convoy destined for Oran and some time later entered the Erie Basin in New York for a complete overhaul and general repairs which took six weeks. Today George Maury lives with his family in Vineyard Haven, Massachusetts.

Leo Krause was carried into the hospital in Bari where the two British soldiers laid the stretcher down on the floor of the hallway. He was able to see that the whole place was packed with wounded. About fifteen minutes later a doctor came and looked him over and gave him a shot of morphine to ease the pain. He returned in half an hour to give him another shot and that was all that Leo remembered until he awoke next day in the afternoon, where he found himself in a room with four English sailors. His leg was in a 'Thomas' splint (used for fractured femurs and injuries to lower limbs) and his other wounds were bandaged.

> The third day Lt Walker came to see me and told me he was trying to find the rest of the gun crews. He told me that Lt Brown, the Armed Guard Officer, one of the gunners and two of the merchant seamen had been killed. Most of the others were only slightly wounded. They moved the ship away from Bari and made some repairs. I was holding my own in hospital, where I stayed until Christmas Eve when I was flown with other wounded men to a US dispensary in Palermo, Sicily. There I was operated on and placed in a 'Spiker body cast' [a molded cast extending from chest to groin to immobilize the spine]. I was in that until about the third week in March 1944. Another operation followed in which the doctors took some pieces of bone, dungaree and shrapnel out of my leg, afterwards putting a smaller cast on my leg. I stayed in Palermo for another month and was then flown to Oran to be admitted to another hospital in which I stayed until the 6th May. I finally left Oran to land in Charleston, South Carolina on May 24th. I still could not walk and my leg was still draining.
>
> On September 1st I was sent home for one month's leave after which I reported to St Alban's, New York, to the Naval Hospital. I firmly believe if I hadn't been a big strong man, I don't think I would have made it back. I was six foot three and weighed 195 pounds [almost fourteen stone].

Today Leo says, 'I now weigh slightly more at 200 pounds but suffered a stroke in 1998.' He is seventy-nine years of age and lives in Pine Grove, Pennsylvania.

Stanley Wisniewski was admitted with some of his shipmates to the 98th General and put in a bed in what seemed a tented area. He was there for about a week and then moved into the main part of the hospital. Some days afterwards he was transferred to Palermo to recuperate. His wounds consisted of burns to both arms and the right side of his face. He had shrapnel wounds above his right eye and in his right foot above his ankle. 'The burns on my arms and right side of my face were treated as if they were oil burns.' Stanley survived the war, but died on 19 April 1999. His daughter, Cathy Pack wrote to me that in November 1998 she had the most wonderful opportunity to sit with her father for an afternoon while he told her his story about *Lyman Abbott* in Bari. Cathy says, 'His story is something I will cherish for ever. When you are a young child growing up you never think of your parents so young and frightened. That day was most enlightening for me. To think of my dad at eighteen years of age and what he went through, I can only pray that my son never sees anything like that.'

The nurse who brought Donald Meissner his plate of porridge and a 'spot of tea' later brought him a set of fresh clothes and a pair of size 12 combat boots. He recalls that they were three sizes too big.

> The nurse said my feet were so swollen she thought size 12 would be best. The doctor told me I had a fractured jaw, a ruptured spleen and a slight fracture of the left leg. He went on to say that with luck my spleen would heal (it later had to be removed). They wired my jaw and put a brace on my left leg. The doctor said to watch my lungs because the harbour was full of mustard gas and that he was amazed that I got out of the harbour alive.

Donald was taken in a British Army truck to a location the Army had taken over. They had control of the area and had commandeered some residential homes. About eight of his shipmates from the gun crews were there and the British turned one of the homes over to them.

> It was comfortable apart from there being no heating and lights. We were issued with a blanket each but there were no beds or mattresses. Next door was an Italian cemetery. The Germans had bombed it and there were corpses everywhere. The British did not fight on their stomachs as bread, jam and tea was about all they had. On special days they had spam. They shared everything with us but they had very little to start with. Trying to sleep on a cold concrete floor wasn't easy and putting my head on it was the hardest part of all. It was so cold that some nights we went out on the edge of the cemetery and built a fire. One night some Italians saw us making a fire and took pity on us. They brought us some 'home brew vino' and at two in the morning we were all sitting there drinking vino and trying to keep warm. We were billetted there for about three weeks before a British soldier said he had orders to take us out. In an Army truck we headed for the hills. Most of the roads we travelled on were like pastures and a good part of the time we were travelling up mountains.

It took four hours before the steep road levelled off at what Donald describes as 'the top of the world'. Another four hours later they came to a US Army Air Force base (probably the Foggia complex), which had previously been bombed and strafed. Pulled to one side at the end of the airfield was a wrecked German dive-bomber which had been shot down.

The group of men finally boarded a plane to Catania. They were met by a US soldier who took them by truck along the coast to Augusta at the base of Mount Etna.

Anchored in the bay was the *Lyman Abbott*. None of us had an idea she was still afloat. A small boat took us out to board the ship, which we found in a mess, her decks blanketed in shrapnel. There were complete cases of small-arms ammunition littered all over and a huge plate of steel weighing over a ton, had landed amidships. An army truck secured to the deck had a large shell in the passenger seat. The nose of the shell projected out of the window and the base was against the front seat.

There were not many seamen aboard ship and only about ten gunners to man the guns. The food had deteriorated badly and the flour was full of weavils and large ants. Most of the meat was spoiled but we had lots of coffee for which I was grateful. During the next two weeks more of the original crew turned up and at last we set sail for Bari. We had problems with the rudder, which did not respond to the helm but eventually we arrived at our destination to find the harbour was a graveyard of sunken ships. We had to negotiate very carefully between the wrecks and at last we secured to the dock and immediately started discharging. We were all relieved to see the cargo unloaded at last, even if it was a month later than originally planned.

Donald recalls the voyage home.

My jaw and spleen had been giving me a lot of pain and I would go below to wrap a towel round a steam pipe and then hold it alternatively to my jaw and spleen as there were no aspirins available. Early one morning we reached the Hudson river to land at New York and I left the ship to be admitted to the sick bay in the Armed Guard centre in South Brooklyn. The pain in my jaw was not from the fracture, but a bad wisdom tooth which I had removed. The braces were taken off my left leg as X-rays proved it to be OK. My spleen was another story as it would have to be removed – but I was finally home and glad of it.

From his home in Cumberland, Virginia, Donald recalls:

I had two angels that made my survival possible: the one that was continually with me at sea and the other one waiting for me at home – my wife Betty, who has taken care of me for the last fifty-six years. We have four wonderful children, three daughters, one son, five grandsons and one granddaughter. Every day I think of those 1810 Armed Guard men whose last battle was their final resting place. They should never be forgotten.

Out in the middle of the harbour my four shipmates from HMS *Zetland* and I, stuck in the motor boat, were relieved when at last the propeller was freed. The motor fired, and its weak putt-putting sounded sweet to our ears as we slowly got under way and moved from our vulnerable position near the line of exploding and blazing ships. We searched the surface for any survivors still in the water and though we could not see any we came across a merchant ship with fires along the length of her upper deck. Because of the dense smoke swirling around and the fact that we had been concentrating on the perilous position of the man in dire distress on the outer mole, we had not realised that we were so near to this large ship. Recognising the distinctive lines of an American liberty ship, we decided to assist the crew in fighting the fires and to see what other assistance we could give. She was anchored not much more than a ship's length away from the line of burning ships moored to the outer mole. As she was anchored with her bows facing the harbour entrance we manoeuvred the boat round her stern to board her on her port side, which gave us a measure of protection from the explosions taking place among the line of shipping.

We eventually came alongside, secured the small boat and scrambled up a rope ladder to reach the deck. It was greasy and littered from bow to stern with burning debris which had been blasted aboard from one or more of the explosions, but the most amazing thing was that there was nobody on board to greet us: the vessel had been completely abandoned. Nevertheless our small group dashed for fire extinguishers, buckets of sand and water and attacked the flames. After some time I decided to make a search to see if anybody was still aboard, trapped or injured. Starting at the bridge, I searched cabins, saloons, companionways and everywhere on the upper deck. The ship had evidently been abandoned in a hurry, for lights were still on in the cabins which were in apple-pie order with bunks neatly made up. It was obviously an American ship, as the accommodation was positively opulent. After living on top of one another without any privacy whatsoever in *Zetland*'s cramped quarters, this was every sailor's dream of luxury. It certainly seemed like that to me. I went below decks, shouting and calling, and as no answers were forthcoming I satisfied myself that there was nobody alive on board. I did not see any serious damage, so I returned to my shipmates fighting the fires, using a bed-cover I had come across to beat out the flames.

Some time later, when we at last had the flames under control, we became aware of a boat which drew alongside on the port side. In it were a group of Royal Navy personnel who climbed aboard. It appeared that they were from the shore base. The senior officer, a complete stranger to us, congratulated us on our fire-fighting efforts and then made an astonishing statement, one which over half a century later is still as vivid and remarkable as ever. His words were, 'I have been speaking to the master of the ship.' He said the name which I did not catch but which I knew was Scandinavian. 'He informed me that if I can guarantee that his ship is safe, he will return on board with his crew.' For a split second there was silence, then the air went blue with honest old-fashioned naval language as the full implication of his remarks sank in. There we stood on the slimy, debris-covered deck of the liberty ship, filthy, tired, soaked to the skin, eyes, faces and hands scorched and blistered. We had spent hours exposed to great danger, being battered by explosions aboard *Zetland*, then sailing in a small boat to within a few yards of blazing ammunition ships and tankers we had without any thought to our own safety attempted to rescue a doomed man. We could have called it a day and returned to the *Zetland*, satisfied that we had done our best. But our better instincts told us there was a ship in need of assistance and I am sure I speak for my shipmates when I say we responded without giving it a second thought. And the master graciously agreed to return if it was safe!

Fifty years later to the day on 2 December 1993, at a Coastal Forces reunion at the Imperial War Museum in London, I read a now declassified official naval document which concerned this very ship. It was a US report entitled 'Damage by Air Attack'. In the space for 'Full Christian Name, Surname and Nationality of Master', was the answer: 'Norwegian, name not known'. I also discovered the ship was the US *Lyman Abbott*, named after the editor of *The Outlook*, an influential American political magazine at the turn of the century. She was a liberty ship of 7,176 gross tonnage, registered at Charleston, South Carolina. She sailed from the port of Baltimore in the latter part of 1943 bound for Bari. Her cargo was ammunition, and from another document I have seen, corroborated by members of *Lyman Abbott*'s crew, also mustard gas bombs. For fifty years I had not known the name of the ship, which I had presumed had sunk later in the night. My only clue was that the master of the vessel had a Scandinavian name. As I have said, *Lyman Abbott* was seaworthy enough to sail on 3 December 1943 in convoy to the Sicilian port of Augusta, and was still in service three months after the war ended.

In the copy I have of the Official British Account, Captain Campbell, Naval Officer in Charge, Bari, stated that when he boarded *Lyman Abbott* he found her deserted. Of course this was not so. Our group had boarded the ship at least two hours before he and his party joined us and by that time we had extinguished the fires – the only reason we had boarded the ship in the first place. The reason for this departure from the truth in the official account, written within days of the event, is a mystery to me. I can only think it was a huge lapse of memory on the writer's part, but it was a gross injustice to the five ratings of HMS *Zetland* who risked their lives boarding an abandoned ammunition ship that was on fire and that their efforts could be dismissed in such a cavalier fashion. As a result, our actions were never recognised by the British or US governments. The fact that the document was censored for thirty years allowed no form of protest.

One of the group of men who boarded the ship was an officer who came over to me and 'invited' me to accompany him on a mission he had in mind. I did not know his name and rank (and still do not know them) – it was not an appropriate time for introductions and his clothes were as filthy as mine, making it impossible to recognise any insignia, if he was wearing any. Without a word to the others we immediately made for a rope ladder hanging over the side near the stern. We scrambled down to the bottom, where I was surprised to see a very small motor boat secured. I realised that he had come on his own and not with the base party. We eased ourselves into the confined space of the tiny boat, my new comrade started the motor and off we sailed into the holocaust, my second journey into the smoke and flames. My shipmates were left behind on *Lyman Abbott*.

Arriving at Navy House, Lt Cdr Morgan Giles was informed that the most important objective was to get as many merchant ships as possible out of the harbour because they were carrying mixed cargoes of munitions and high-octane petrol – highly combustible. He had been in his quarters when he heard the spasmodic grunt of Bofors guns. He had wondered if it could be the start of some exercise about which he had not been informed. The intensity of the firing and the crash of bombs, however, made it apparent that it was for real. Quickly making his way out of the hotel, he had hopped on his motor-bike (he found this mode of transport most useful and convenient when making his rounds of the harbour) and set off along the main road leading to the harbour. He made slow progress as he came up against the tide of fleeing survivors and vehicles but eventually came to berth 26, where the battered HMS *Zetland* lay alongside. He wanted to be taken out to a liberty ship anchored in the middle of the harbour, but *Zetland*'s cutter was already away on rescue and fire-fighting operations. As he stood waiting, he felt the most tremendous explosion, followed by a massive blast of hot air which knocked him off his feet and landed him on the deck several yards away. On regaining his feet he realised he was fine, but his cap had disappeared.

Some time later *Zetland*'s boat appeared through the dense smoke, loaded with survivors. After putting the survivors ashore the boat now with Lt Cdr Giles on board, set off towards the liberty ship (which as it happened was *Lyman Abbott*). In order to have the liberty ship towed out of harbour and away from danger, the anchor cable needed to be released. As there was no steam to weigh anchor the only recourse was to blow the cable apart. At the torpedo school at Portsmouth, he had undergone training in the use of explosives and seeing an MTB passing by, he hailed it and asked for one of the scuttling charges that he knew all boats carried in their bilges. The charge, about the size of a large coffee-pot, was delivered to him on a heaving line. The explosive charge was tamped close to the cable with sandbags and after setting the fuse, Giles ran aft to a safer position. The charge fired and cut the cable cleanly in two. The ship was still at anchor, as the cable had been cut near the naval pipe. When the tug arrived it would only be necessary to knock off the slip and let the cable run out. He remembers Captain Guinness being aboard while all this was taking place. Later in the night, he returned to the outer mole to find *Zetland* was no longer there. He never found his cap and was saddened to find his motor-bike in ruins having been the target of a large chunk of flying metal. He now had time to notice that his uniform was scorched and in tatters, hanging from him like a filthy rag. As he stood on the devasted mole, it occurred to him that Captain Guinness must have had the warmest welcome any commanding officer had ever had – unfortunately from the wrong side!

Some time later, he learned that USS *John Harvey* carried amongst its cargo white phosphorus bombs and, even worse, mustard gas bombs which were not fused. The mustard gas bomb casings were very thin and the explosion threw some thirty broken casings onto the mole, where a large patch of mustard gas was found. Many more mustard gas bombs were smashed and their contents thrown into the air and scattered on the water and neighbouring ships in the form of partly mixed mustard gas liquid, oil and water. He recalls:

> Some of the mustard gas sank to the bottom of the harbour, but a lot floated on the oil. Many of the survivors – as well as rescuers, some of whom dived into the water to rescue others – were covered in mustard gas. The gas, oil and phosphorus caused frightful burns. Also when the men reached the hospital in Bari, the heat in the operating theatres evaporated the mustard gas, allowing it to get into the surgeons' eyes, creating dreadful results.

For his part in the night's events Lt Cdr Morgan Giles was decorated, earning the Distinguished Service Order. Shortly afterwards he became Senior Officer, Vis and Liaison Officer with Marshal Tito's partisan forces In 1952 he took command of the cruiser HMS *Belfast*, now a permanent museum moored in the Thames, and was her last sea-going commanding officer. In 1955 he was Chief Naval Intelligence Officer, Far East. He served as a Conservative Member of Parliament for Winchester from 1965 to 1976, and during his parliamentary career he served as Vice-chairman of the Defence Committee. Rear Admiral Morgan Giles was knighted in 1985 and today lives in Hampshire.

In the British Military Hospital in Taranto, Tony Thacker, the Royal Engineer survivor from USS *Samuel J. Tilden*, spent the first three weeks totally blind and then slowly began to regain his sight. Until that time he was unable to do anything for himself and he remembers with gratitude:

> Apart from the first-class medical care and attention I received during the period I was blind, I was cared for by a Canadian soldier, Jerry Radcliffe. It was my misfortune that he was discharged from hospital early on 22 December 1943, before my visit to the operating theatre on that very day to have my bandages removed. So now I am eternally grateful to a man I have never seen.

The survivor from the Danish ship SS *Lars Kruse*, Leonard Walker, after leaving the queue waiting alongside *Zetland*, was picked up by soldiers in a jeep and taken to the 98th General where 'I was carried on a stretcher and placed on the floor in a passageway. I asked for a bucket or basin as I was retching and coughing, bringing up oil and greasy stuff which I had swallowed when blown into the harbour.' He then fell unconscious and when he came round, 'I was in severe pain and bandaged so tightly and extensively, I must have looked like a mummy.' He does not know how long he was in hospital, but several weeks later he was taken on board the hospital ship *St Andrew* which sailed for Bone in Algeria; he was transferred from there to the UK. He had been unable to see for some time but to his relief his sight began to return when he was admitted to the Royal Naval Hospital in Devonport. He told the medical staff his story but, he says, 'They just did not believe me.' He was posted to Poole and when that base closed down he was drafted to HMS *Drake* prior to demobilisation. There he attended an interview where his previous statements were checked.

His eyes were examined daily for weeks by the surgeon and afterwards he was granted six weeks' leave and issued with a 'Hurts Certificate' which said he had sustained mustard gas burns to face, hands and body. He was entitled to a 100 per cent war pension which was reduced in stages to 60 per cent then went back up to 70 per cent. Since then Leonard has undergone several operations, including skin grafts at East Grinstead. He has been registered blind for some years and says of St Dunstan's, the blind institution and hospital, where he still attends, 'They look after us very well and I could not wish for more from them.'

Gunner Tom Yeldman, serving aboard HMS *Zetland*, was detailed off to assist in transporting casualties from the harbour area to the 98th General. A number of Army lorries were being used as emergency ambulances and Tom recalls helping to lift onto the vehicles men pulled from the water who were covered in black oil, fighting for breath, their lungs full of the obnoxious filth. When he and his detail arrived at the hospital with the wounded survivors, 'The scene was no better. There were oil-caked seamen lying on a tiled floor, in exactly the same state as the ones we were bringing in, struggling to get air into their lungs, coughing and retching, attempting to bring up the vile mixture they had swallowed.' Looking back to that time, Tom says, 'There appeared to be no help for them.'

It seemed to be dental technician Bob Wills' lot to be down in the cellars of the 98th General on a permanent basis, laying out the dead head to toe. There were about sixty corpses to start with and a local Italian carpenter was engaged in making rough wooden boxes. For the next few weeks Bob and his small group placed the dead into the makeshift coffins ready for burial at a cemetery south of Bari. Many of the names of the unfortunate men were imprinted in Bob's mind as he recalls collating their effects and identity discs. During this period two Soviet Air Force officers, who were based at the local Bari airfield, arrived to oversee the burial of two of their comrades. On viewing them, the officers were horrified to see the bodies lying naked in the coffins. They returned some hours later with two full-dress uniforms and insisted that their dead comrades be dressed in them. They even placed hats on their heads.

To the surprise of the unit, among the corpses they discovered the body of a young woman. One of the group went upstairs to the main hospital, and helped himself to a white sheet with which they draped the dead woman's body before placing it in the wooden box. Bob recalls, 'Though the soldiers could be as rough and as coarse as any group of men, they treated all the dead with great respect and reverence, handling them all with a gentleness that was touching to behold.'

Working late into the night as the number of victims increased, the cellar took on an eerie and chilly atmosphere. There was very little light; the only illumination was from Tilly oil lamps, the guttering flame throwing shadows over the stone floor of the cellar-cum-morgue as the soldiers carried out their soul-destroying yet necessary task. The cellar was cut off from the rest of the building, which left the men feeling as if they too had been left to their fate. One evening the regimental sergeant major (RSM) appeared, accompanied by two cooks carrying a bucket of tea and a tray of sandwiches. This was the first time the senior NCO had visited the cellar and the three of them looked as if they wished they were anywhere else as they watched Bob and his comrades in the dim half light, lifting the corpses from the cold stone floor to place them in the rough wooden boxes.

As the men halted from their grisly task to eat their supper they were amazed to hear the RSM say, 'Thank you gentlemen', three words they had never heard him say before. He was visibly moved by the sad and depressing scene before him and at that moment he and his men saw one another in a completely different light.

Two days after the raid all the windows in the hospital were ordered to be kept open in case there were more explosions from the still blazing ships in the harbour. During the morning an Army truck drove into the hospital compound with about thirty bodies retrieved from the harbour. Because the corpses were in such a bad shape there was no way they could be taken to the morgue without one man having to climb over them to disentangle arms and legs. Curious heads began to appear at the windows overlooking the gruesome sight, but the RSM bellowed at them with such force that they instantly disappeared. Most of the bodies had no clothes and were covered in the usual black oil. Bob and his comrades wore gloves, though they had no idea that the bodies were highly contaminated by liquid mustard gas.

Bob recalls, 'There were groups of survivors who had been blinded, walking in a line with a hand on the shoulder of the man in front, which took me back to my boyhood when I had witnessed scenes exactly the same in the years following the Great War of 1914–18.' The hospital staff were warned not to mention anything about the raid or the subsequent events afterwards when writing home. They were sworn to secrecy – and what secrecy. Even now, over half a century later, none of the doctors has said or written a word about any incident during that period – a time when they faced a horrific situation such as they had never before encountered. In my opinion it surpasses the secrecy of the Mafia.

During the following weeks the work in the morgue began to take its toll on Bob's state of mind and health. Any sudden noise sent him into fits of uncontrollable shivers, something which he tried to hide from his fellow medics. He was recommended to return to the UK for treatment but before that, the front line moved north and the 98th General became the base hospital. Five years after the war ended, Bob was walking to work in Marshfield, Wiltshire, where he still lives, when alongside him in the road a car back-fired, once again triggering uncontrollable spasms. He

Lieutenant Douglas Barnard on the bridge of LCI *318* (Landing Craft Infantry). Barnard was awaiting orders to sail with 240 fully kitted soldiers on board when the air raid began. He immediately put to sea and disembarked the soldiers on the coast of Yugoslavia some hours later. *(D. Barnard)*

shivered and trembled like a jelly for some time and it left him feeling foolish afterwards.

Immediately after the raid had ended, John Roberts of the Chaplain's Department took leave of the Italian friends with whom he had sheltered underneath the staircase in the shattered church and made his way back to his office, where he lived and slept. The table stood between the door and the window and doubled as a bed at night. He had slept in this fashion every night since the unit arrived, but on this occasion he decided to put his bed in the corner of the room and on the floor. The events of the last hour or two had made such an impression that he was taking no chances, though he had no idea of the carnage taking place in the harbour.

Feeling extremely tired he turned in and the next thing he knew it was hours later and he was absolutely amazed to see that the door was hanging off its hinges and the window frames had been blasted in and flung across the room. Slivers of glass lay everywhere and the table on which he always slept was deeply scored with gashes where pieces of glass and metal had struck it. He realised how lucky he had been in following his intuition the night before. In moving his bed he probably saved himself from serious injury. John believes he must have been suffering from delayed shock or

116

The captain, Lieutenant Douglas Barnard's view from the bridge of LCI *318*, of Bari harbour, showing clouds of smoke from blazing ships at 8 o'clock 3 December. He was ordered not to enter harbour but to turn and make for the port of Barletta.
(D. Barnard)

concussion for he was completely oblivious of the wrecking of the office and the din that must have accompanied it. This state of mind was described time and time again by men who received the force of the blasts after explosions. They remembered some events with amazing clarity and yet were unable to recall what to others were devastating and outstanding moments.

Approaching Bari on the morning of 3 December, Lieutenant Douglas Barnard, aboard LCI *318* saw the huge palls of smoke rising above the harbour. After leaving Bari at the start of the raid, he had safely landed the 240 troops on one of the islands off the coast of Yugoslavia and made his way back in the early hours of the morning to the small port of Barletta. From there he had sailed to Bari, some 25 miles (40 km) to the south. As the landing craft made to enter port, Douglas received a signal forbidding him to enter harbour and telling him instead to return to Barletta. As he turned the landing craft round, he took a photograph of Bari from the bridge. He never returned, and Barletta became his base. In 1944 he moved to the Ionian Sea area, taking part in the liberation of Greece. When the war ended he returned to the Merchant Navy, where he remained until his retirement some years ago.

Driver James Seal of the RASC, after giving a cigarette to the man he found seriously injured and dying on the quayside, discovered that besides his broken thumb, he had many cuts and bruises. He was admitted to hospital suffering from severe shock and contracted double pneumonia. One of the attending doctors told him he would probably lose all his teeth and hair. He kept his hair but some years later, 'I lost several teeth when they just fell out, so at least the doctor's predictions were half right.' Unknown to James, when he was blown in and out of the water, he had been struck by shrapnel. Several pieces were removed while he was in hospital. Other bits of metal painfully worked their way out of his body over the next few years, mostly out of his legs. He died aged 73 in 1976, of acute and chronic leukaemia in St Thomas's Hospital, London. The doctors who treated him were extremely interested in his military record and the horrendous experience he had undergone during that night in Bari.

One of the five Royal Engineers who had been strolling towards the harbour and were sent reeling by the explosion, Bert Staniforth, realised that he had suffered damage to his eyes. He was also badly bruised but when he reported these facts to the local army medical officer, 'I got short shrift.' He was granted two days' rest, sleeping on a tiled floor. When he questioned anyone about the explosion he was brushed aside and after a few days the group were ordered to return to their unit in the Sangro River area, where nothing was known about the raid on Bari and its consequences. Bert later took part in the fighting before Cassino and the advance towards Rome and it was then he was struck down by the first of a series of attacks of dizziness and sickness. He was taken by truck to a field medical unit where the doctor diagnosed food poisoning and blamed 'bully beef' Bert had eaten the previous day. He was then returned to his unit.

The attacks continued during his service and afterwards for many years and in 1975 he was diagnosed as suffering from damaged eardrums. This was followed by tinnitus and Ménière's disease, for which he takes medication every day. He has 60 per cent hearing loss and will, according to his doctors, lose all hearing eventually. He is also disabled by arthritis in all joints, hips, spine, knees, head and shoulders, and walks with the aid of walking sticks. The hospital he attends attributes his condition to the events in Bari.

Once again in a small boat in the middle of the battered harbour, this time with my new comrade, I viewed at close quarters the mass of ships still wreathed in fire and smoke. As the boat was too small to pick up survivors it was obvious we were on some different mission and this was borne out when we headed towards one of the several drifting vessels, which were outlined in the fiery curtain of flame. Drawing alongside the freighter, a smaller ship than the liberty ship we had just left, we tied the boat to a convenient dangling length of rope and scrambled aboard.

Scrambling was the operative word, as most of the usual means of boarding were non-existent during that night, blasted away during the explosions. We made use of scrambling nets, broken mooring lines and single lengths of rope that looked secure enough to hold our weight. Everything we touched was covered in oil and grease, making hand-holds extremely difficult when climbing up and down the steep ship's sides. Once aboard we encountered the same oil- and grease-covered decks, with the ship listing and sloping alarmingly underfoot. The scum had rained down in a torrent after the explosions, leaving the decks of the ships in a dangerous state. Apart from the danger of a spark or falling ember igniting the petrol and oil mixture which could have set the whole upper deck alight, keeping our balance became a problem. I did not know what my comrade was wearing, but I still had on what I had gone ashore in during the afternoon – light naval shoes – and at times found myself almost skating along the greasy surfaces. We had to be careful of jagged edges on superstructures left ripped and torn in the aftermath of explosions and also ugly pieces of metal and shrapnel lying on the upper decks as we staggered and stumbled around. In addition we had to duck for whatever shelter there was when the showers of shrapnel clattered down on us.

The ship was completely deserted (as was every other vessel we boarded during the course of the night), and my companion and I climbed the metal ladder to the bridge and then went down below to the engine room to ascertain that there was nobody left on board and also to assess what state the ship was in and its position in relation to the danger it presented to other shipping.

My comrade must have had orders to try his utmost to make sure that the fairway was kept clear of wrecks and drifting ships; a tall order in that holocaust of fire and flame. The search proved that the ship had not been holed underneath the waterline so, going forward, we managed to let go the anchor. The cable ran out, the ship was secured and stabilised and we scrambled back over the side down into our boat. We set off once more to continue the routine as we approached another drifting vessel, though this one was different: the anchor was missing. In her drifting state she presented a dangerous 'loose cannon' in a crowded harbour of tankers and ammunition ships. My mate dashed back down to the boat and returned with an explosive charge. Without saying a word he disappeared down below and after a short time reappeared as I heard and felt a muffled explosion underneath my feet. The ship was away from the main fairway, so he had placed the charge under the waterline to allow if to settle on the bottom, out of harm's way. Never in my wildest dreams could I have ever imagined that in a space of an hour or two, I would help to keep one ship afloat and sink another.

Once again we went over the side to our small boat. The noise was just as deafening as ever; explosions large and small were erupting, scattering fragments far and wide and rocking our cockleshell boat alarmingly. As more fires took hold, huge clouds of smoke, thicker than ever, billowed out of the blazing ships and was caught by the breeze. It rolled over the harbour and smothered everything, and for us sitting in the boat, it became dangerous to move until it cleared somewhat. The hot, acrid, foul-stinking smog filled our eyes, throats and lungs, but there was no refuge or rest for us; we still carried on and by that time, the early hours of the morning, we saw or passed no other boat on our journeys from ship to ship. We saw no survivors in the water at that late hour as the gallant rescue operations by the small craft appeared to have ended. It was an eerie experience, being seemingly alone and out of contact with anyone as we slowly made our way from one abandoned vessel to another. Twice more we carried out the same searching and assessing routine, and extinguished small fires on the upper deck of one ship, where luckily fire extinguishers were still in place and the blaze was soon under control.

One vessel, though anchored safely, was on fire midships and blazing fiercely. When we searched we could not find any extinguishers, buckets of sand, water or anything else with which to tackle the fire, which was now almost out of control (and certainly out of *our* control). My comrade once again appeared with a charge which he lit and tossed into the middle of the blaze. Both of us dashed for cover as it exploded in a mass of sparks and flame. It was successful; the blaze was put out. I had heard of the operation of blasting out a fire by detonating a charge in the middle of it, but had never expected to see such a successful one first hand.

The next mission, which was to be our last, was to two ships linked together in the middle of the harbour but nearer the dockyard area. As we approached them we saw that during the course of the last few hours the anchor on one, or possibly both, had dragged, and the vessels had circled one another and now appeared to be securely fastened together. We boarded one of them to assess the problem and it was obvious that both ships had received heavy damage from explosions and both looked in a sad condition. All the paintwork on the upper deck of the ship we had boarded had been burnt away and the surrounding ports and windows lay broken and shattered on the deck, which was covered in litter and debris. From what we could see of the other ship, it appeared to be in the same condition.

The ship we were standing on was already well down by the bow, slowly being pulled lower by the weight of the other vessel as she filled with water. It was obvious that, with the anchor cables fastened together, the sinking ship would eventually drag the other down with it. It was impossible to do anything to release either of the taut anchor cables, which were tightening under the terrific weight and stress as more and more water flooded into the vessel. It would have been foolhardy to try. As we both agreed we could not release the cable manually, the only alternative was once again to use an explosive charge. With my comrade clutching the charge in his hand we clambered over the tangled cables to decide where to place it in order to leave the vessel we were aboard still anchored after the parting of the cable and allow the other ship to sink. We packed the charge into position with sandbags and attached the fuse, very much like the touch-paper on a firework. He brought out matches, struck one, lit the fuse (and as in all good firework instructions) we retired to a safer position – in our case behind the shattered bridgeworks.

The previous fuse had been a nine-second one; this time it was only seven seconds. As we dashed for shelter, I started counting, one . . . two . . . three . . . until I reached seven; nothing happened. My companion must also have been counting, because he said to me, 'The bloody thing has gone out.' How ironic that with fire and flame on every side, our tiny ember of a fuse had expired. As he spoke, he took a step forward to the corner of the bridge superstructure behind which we were sheltering. I reacted immediately by throwing myself forward, grabbing his waist in rugby-tackle fashion and dragging him back behind the shattered steel shelter. At that very moment the charge exploded, battering the shelter and sending a barrage of debris bowling and clattering along the deck. Had I not obeyed an instinct and dragged my impulsive comrade back, he could at best have been badly maimed, at worst have lost his life; but luck was still with us and we both survived. We staggered against one another as the bow of the ship, released from the restraint of the cables, shot upwards like a spring to settle on an even keel. We went forward to view the result and we were relieved to see that the explosion had parted the anchor cables exactly as we had anticipated, allowing the ship we were aboard to remain anchored and the other, rapidly filling up with water, eventually to settle on the bottom.

Dawn was almost upon us as at long last and we decided that our work was finally at an end. For the last time we climbed down the side of the battered ship to board the little boat that had served us so well, and turned its bow towards the south end of the outer mole. We reached the mole and climbed wearily up onto the concrete where we stood for a few moments viewing the harbour scene, still a mass of fire and smoke. Ships ahead of us on the outer mole were blazing furiously (and were to do so for several days) and at intervals long tongues of flame shot upwards through the dense black smoke enveloping the harbour. After a short time we wished one another good luck, shook hands and parted, he to his billet or bunk and me to I knew not where. In the smoky half light I could see that the two destroyers were no longer at their berths and hoped with all my heart that they had not sunk after I had left *Zetland*. Walking along the now almost deserted mole, my thoughts went back to the events of the last few hours: hectic, horrendous and awe-inspiring. The mighty destructive power which had been unleashed, overwhelming and frightening though it was, had at the same time been in a curious and perverse fashion thrilling and exciting as the senses reacted with heightened awareness to the danger. Fifty years later I obtained a copy of the berthing plan of the harbour on the night of the raid. I was able to ascertain from the positions of the ships that the last two vessels we had boarded were most likely two of the following: SS *Lars Kruse*, SS *Lom*, SS *Bolsta* and the burnt out *Devon Coast*.

Alongside the mole, near the dockyard, I came across a ship. I boarded, found a corner out of the way, sank onto the deck and succumbed to overpowering weariness. After about three hours I awoke, feeling ghastly. My eyes were painful and almost closed, I croaked when I tried to speak, my tongue felt twice its normal size and blisters had formed on my hands and face. My eyebrows and lashes had disappeared and the hair on my head was singed and covered in grease and sweat, as were my clothes. All the hours I had been exposed to the intense heat, and sweating profusely, not a drop of liquid had passed my lips and, without realising it, I must have been very badly dehydrated.

I explained my position and how I came to be aboard to one of the crew members and he provided me with a breakfast of jam and bread and – best of all – a drink of tea. Soon afterwards I made my way back to the outer mole to see in daylight the scene of our endeavours. As I did so, my thoughts strayed back to the curious meeting with my comrade of the night before. We had been thrown together in a most bizzare fashion, aboard an abandoned American liberty ship in the middle of an Italian harbour. We never knew each other's names, yet had quickly knitted into a team, carried out the many difficult and dangerous tasks, looking out for each other's safety as we clambered aboard the drifting vessels, some of them sinking, others on fire, tinder boxes waiting to explode. Every one of them had been totally abandoned by their crews, as they considered them to be in too dangerous a state to stay aboard. Any of them could have exploded and blown us up at any moment.

During the hours since leaving *Lyman Abbott* we had not come across a living soul, although we had seen several dead on the vessels. After working non-stop for many hours, our rescue and salvage efforts at last at an end, we had said goodbye and gone our separate ways. Was ever the saying, 'Ships that pass in the night' more apt? I never knew who he was – and still do not, over half a century later.

I was surprised and sad to see that neither of the last two ships we had boarded appeared to be above water. I had expected one of them to have been saved and still afloat. In my shocked and emotional state I felt for the first time since I was a small boy, tears prickling my sore and swollen eyes as I imagined that our effort had been for nothing. But it was only passing thought for I now had to make my way back to *Zetland*, news of which lifted my spirits when I learned that she had sailed for the naval base of Taranto. Later in the day I came across a Royal Navy truck whose driver gave me a lift to Taranto.

Late that night I rejoined *Zetland*, berthed in dock. She presented a sad picture. The funnel was twisted out of shape, masts and aerials were missing, large chunks of riven metal still lay on board and most of the composition deck covering had lifted, leaving the steel deck plates exposed. The gun turret shelters and coverings were blasted out of shape and the bridge was a shambles. Her surgeon had been left behind ashore in Bari and I was attended to by the sick-berth attendant, who treated my burns and blisters.

She lay in dry dock in the hands of the ship repairers for some weeks and one sad consequence was the loss to all of us of the captain, Lt Cdr Wilkinson, who entered hospital suffering from facial and body injuries and after discharge left for the UK to take up another appointment. He was later awarded the George Medal for his actions during the night in Bari.

After repairs and refit, *Zetland* sailed from Taranto to resume convoy escort duties, this time escorting ships from Augusta to Naples, where preparations were taking place for the imminent landings at Anzio (in which the repaired *Bicester* took part). In the latter half of February I began to feel discomfort in my right hand and in a very short time it became extremely swollen. The ship's surgeon, now back on board, treated it for two days, but as the hand began to resemble a bunch of green bananas, he decided to send me to hospital. I left *Zetland* at anchor in Augusta harbour and was admitted to a military field hospital on the outskirts of the ancient city of Syracuse. It consisted of several large marquees with rows of beds down each side, and most of the patients were soldiers from the Anzio and Monte Cassino areas, many of them very severely wounded. I felt I was there under false pretences; little did I realise my poisoned hand was serious too. I was immediately taken into the operating theatre, anaesthetised, had my hand drained and came to some time later in a partitioned part of the marquee, unable to understand where I was and what I was doing there.

On 2 December Dennis Brookes of the Pioneer Corps had spent an hour or two with an old school pal serving aboard a merchant ship in the harbour. He had invited Dennis aboard for a meal, which he had enjoyed as a complete change from Army fare. After the meal the two friends stood casually on deck watching the unloading from the ship, ammunition and other supplies which were being stacked in piles on the quayside. At that moment the raid started and the bombs began to find targets on the outer mole and the smoke defences churned out smoke. Dennis dashed off the vessel and as he could not see a thing in front of him, he dived underneath 'something large' on the dockside.

When the smoke cleared a little, he saw he was under a railway truck full of ammunition. Some time later when making his way out of the dock-yard to return to his barracks, he was stopped by an Army captain. He asked Dennis if he was unhurt and together with several more men he accompanied the officer to a store where they were issued with gumboots and waterproof trousers and gloves. They were then taken to one of the jetties where, Dennis recalls, 'there were many bodies floating in the black water – a horrible sight. We had the task of collecting the mutilated and burnt bodies for some hours until I was recalled to my company, not for rest, but to assist in looking for survivors in bombed out houses in the city.' During that time, he remembers hearing the cries of a young girl whose arm was trapped by a large block of masonry. The doctor on hand had to amputate the arm to free her. Both the poor girl's parents were found dead alongside. As dawn broke, Dennis finally left the harbour to return to his barracks.

At an anti-aircraft gun site near the seafront, gunner Robert Ede recalls seeing hundreds of envelopes and scores of parcels and mail bags floating on the rocky shore below the gun position: parcels and letters that would never reach the loved ones for which they were intended. Hundreds more were lying on the harbour bottom. Robert did not know, but the mail had been on board *Fort Athabaska*, one of the ships that exploded.

The gun crews had kept on firing throughout the duration of the air raid and, Robert says, 'we were firing blind, though I believe there was a plan to be followed to create a barrage. With more guns we could have given a better account of ourselves.' From the gun sight he saw men trapped on blazing ships. 'The only escape possible for them was to jump overboard. The flames highlighted the whole scene vividly. It was a terrible sight watching these poor souls leaping into the blazing inferno.' According to Robert, several gun batteries situated on the moles in elevated positions were blasted away during the explosions. 'The morning after brought a most sad and depressing sight – ships still on fire and disaster all around.'

The next day, 'incredibly, in the dark, the still blazing ships were glowing red and hot and the water all around, giving off clouds of steam. In the following days bodies were continually washed up on to the rocks below us and we volunteered to retrieve the corpses. In most cases identification was impossible as the bodies were too mutilated.' The gunners took the remains to the city cemetery where at one end a huge communal grave had been excavated by American Army engineers. When the lorries arrived with the bodies for burial they were placed together in the mass grave, side by side, head to toe. Robert says, 'I know it may sound callous, but what else could be done? They all died together and now they all lie together. I hope that they have erected a suitable memorial there.' He has never been back to Bari. He also recalls, 'During the raid, our gun sustained a direct hit; a burnt out flare floated gently down on its parachute and in a final act of defiance, wrapped itself round the hot gun barrel.'

In the port of Barletta, the British merchant ship SS *Lightfoot* should have sailed to Bari on the morning of 3 December. She had just discharged thousands of jerry cans of petrol and was now due to join a convoy of empty ships leaving Bari later that day. Because of the great damage to the harbour at Bari, she was ordered to remain in Barletta for five more days. When she eventually entered Bari harbour, the upper works of sunken ships were showing, some still smouldering and Robert Foreman, a Royal Navy gunner, remembers with great sadness 'bodies rising to the surface as *Lightfoot*'s screws churned up the harbour water as she moved to her berth.'

One vessel that left the harbour immediately the raid was over was MV *Coxwold*. She was anchored in the outer harbour, near to Molo San Cataldo, and during the raid was subjected to several near misses which caused upper-deck damage. She weighed anchor and sailed to the port of Barletta to discharge her cargo of high-octane fuel and ammunition. Reg Stock recalls, 'Two weeks before, some of my shipmates and myself, looking forward to Christmas festivities, had bought a chicken in Bari, with the intention of fattening it up for Christmas. For that purpose we had made a small wooden hen-coop which was sited on the upper deck. Unfortunately during the raid, this most important part of the Christmas dinner died of a heart attack.'

On the day following the raid, Lieutenant Edwin Farnell of the Pioneers commenced unloading ships again and at this time he heard a rumour which he says was not very convincing, about the presence of mustard gas during the raid. He also heard a rumour that Churchill had made a visit. This last one was not true, though *a* Churchill did visit Bari – the Prime Minister's son Randolph, who at the time was engaged in under-cover operations in Yugoslavia and occasionally stayed in the city. The Pioneers were then given the sad but necessary task, over a period of two weeks, of collecting and burying the corpses, parts of bodies and limbs which came floating to the surface of the harbour. Many of the corpses had the upper part of the head eaten away. This, Edwin was told later, was the work of crabs. He says, 'I am afraid it is impossible to convey the feelings of that night to anyone who did not experience it.'

Later, during his service in Italy, Edwin, an accomplished pianist, gave piano recitals in Assisi and Loreto. After the war he returned to Leeds, qualified as a teacher of music, became head of English and Religious Instruction and taught Italian to adults. He also continued in his role of organist and choirmaster at Salem church, he and his father between them filling the position continuously for over eighty years.

Walter Woodford, an RASC driver, found himself on the ground, face down covering his head with his hands. He then heard, 'the most horri-fying screeching sound coming towards me and then the ground seemed to go away from me. That's funny, I thought, and then the ground came back towards me as I landed flat on my face. I was badly shaken and felt like a rag doll.' He realised he had been lifted into the air by the force of a bomb blast and dumped back again. When he looked round he could see no sign of Major Lumpton and the two junior officers who had been approaching the staff car, but in a short time men began to appear. Several were staggering about in a state of shock and did not appear to realise that they were dangerously near to the water's edge. As he was gazing at the outer mole, where he could see ships on fire, there was a terrific explo-sion which lifted him off his feet again. He was covered in a torrent of water which fell like a cloud-burst around him. He says, 'Because of the smoke I could not see more than a yard in front of me, it was like being enclosed in a black velvet pad.' He heard voices which came from a group of soldiers, one of whom led him to a first-aid post where he had cuts and bruises attended to.

*　　*　　*

In the café/bar near the harbour, Frank Saggers and Andy Carson, the two RAF men, the only customers in the bar at that time, heard the drone of aircraft, left their drinks on the table and with Marcus, the proprietor, went outside to see two white flares hanging over the harbour. They did not attach much importance to them as they knew that the identification colour of the day was white and naturally presumed that the flares had been dropped by friendly aircraft. They soon realised how wrong they were when bombs began to fall. All three men dashed inside and dived under the billiard table. They stayed there until the raid was over, listening and feeling the floor shake as bombs dropped nearby. Frank recalls, 'After the end of the bombing there occurred a tremendous explosion. The doors of the café crashed inwards and the balcony that ran round three sides of the inside of the building crashed to the ground, falling on top of the billiard table and the bar, causing a great deal of damage.' When the three men crawled out from beneath the billiard table they discovered that besides the damage, the whole area was covered with broken glass.

The two airmen decided that they should return to the airfield as quickly as possible. The streets were packed with fleeing people, running in a panic to and from shelters, and when they tried to hitch a lift, none of the vehicles would stop. It was some time before an Army lorry did and gave them a lift to near the airfield. To their surprise and great relief they discovered that it had sustained no damage whatsoever. Frank Saggers, who by an amazing coincidence now lives next door to me, says, 'Today, whenever I see a billiard table, it brings back memories of that day when I am certain one saved my life.'

At 2 a.m. on 3 December, Ian Peyman, the survivor from SS *Norlom*, recovered consciousness in the 98th General in Bari. He found himself staring at a clock on the wall facing his bed, and looking round he saw he was in a corridor surrounded by other patients. His first sensation was an irritation on his right elbow; when he tried to shake it off he realised it was a blood/plasma transfusion drip. It began to dawn on him that he could not move his right leg, which he discovered was encased in plaster, as was his left wrist. He recalls, 'It was quite some time before I found out that my head had something round it, and it wasn't a hat.'

When he became more in touch with the world at large he asked what had become of his uniform and wallet and the answer was that they had been destroyed because of contamination. This statement made Ian wonder. 'Although I knew that bombs had been dropped, normally the results would not require decontamination. Many of the patients around me had been covered in bandages but I was not aware whether these were from ordinary burns or something worse.' After nine days in hospital, during which time he learned that the body of his comrade, the Norwegian Radio Officer Halvor Stensrud, had not been found, he was transferred to Catania in Sicily by plane. Afterwards he remained a further six weeks in hospital in Algiers, where he discovered he had a broken right femur and left wrist, which was also badly burned. He returned to Britain in time to celebrate his twenty-first birthday. Several months later, *Norlom*'s administration company Nortraship, based at that time in London, informed Halvor's mother in Norway that her son was never seen again and that it was believed he did not get off the ship. Ian was able to put them right about that, but he could not tell them what had happened to his young comrade after they were thrown into the water together.

Realising that he was not going to be able to pick up his hand pumps, Bill Moran of No. 544 Bulk Petrol Company made his way back to his lorry. Although the bodywork had been damaged, the motor started and he was able to begin his journey back to his billets in the town of Trani. He arrived in the early hours of the morning, tired and dazed and with his eyes beginning to feel sore, something which he attributed to the smoke in the harbour. Once in his billet, which at one time had been a winery, he had a shower, tea and sandwiches and went to bed. He woke up feeling very stiff and bruised. His blistered eyes felt worse and his throat was also raspingly sore. As he was shivering with a high temperature, he was placed in the care of a medical orderly. On Sunday, 5 December, after a visit from the unit's medical officer, he was informed that if there was no improvement in his condition the following morning, he would be transferred to hospital. Next morning, he felt worse and was transferred to the 83rd General. On 12 December he was discharged from hospital and posted to the 2nd Independent Parachute Brigade attached to the New Zealand Division who were at that time stationed at the approaches to Monte Cassino.

In later years he applied for a War Pension, claiming that he had been contaminated with mustard gas at Bari. The War Pensions Board refused his application, so he took his case to the High Court, who decided in his favour and he was consequently awarded a pension.

6

THE AFTERMATH

A n extract from the official British account written some days after the raid gave the following:

Outline

The AA Defences of Bari as at 2nd December consisted of:

British: 32 H. AA guns (5.7")
          36 L. AA guns (40mm)
          18 20mm guns
          12 Searchlights

Italian: 20 H. AA Guns (76/40s) and 75/27s.
          8 L. AA Guns (57/54s.)
          16 L. AA Guns (20mm).
          20 Searchlights

Shipping: Arrangements in force at the time for the control of heavy AA fire from HM ships and merchant ships and of Light AA guns of HM ships and merchant ships are as set out in Appendix VI.

These defences were controlled by a British GOR [Gunnery Operations Room]working to the Italian part of the defences through an Italian Gun Operation Room.

Smoke barrage was established round the port and was directly under the control of GOR. Smoke was in short supply and was sufficient to maintain the barrage for 2 hours only and there were gaps in it for which no satisfactory remedy had been evolved.

Balloon barrage was up at 2,000 feet.

Fight Patrol was provided at dawn and dusk.

GOR received raid information from SOR from SOR Grottaglie and passed the information on to the Navy and other essential services by direct line telephone.

Initiation of Red Warnings to the port was a Naval responsibility but it had been agreed by all services that those for the port and therefore incidentally, for the town (inasmuch as the means of giving the Warning to the Operation Room), should be given by both day and night for not less than 3+ hostile or unidentified within 40 miles of Bari. Captain Campbell had repeatedly represented to both to the Flag Officer, Taranto, and to the Brigadier, 62 AA Brigade, that this scale of defence was not commensurate with the importance of the Port to the Army's effort and also that for the enemy its congested state made it the most attractive target in the Heel.

In Action – 2nd December

Barrage The ammunition expended represented a high rate of fire per gun. GL sit were unaffected by 'window' and two aircraft were claimed as destroyed.

Searchlights SLCs were badly cluttered by 'window' and as a result few, if, any targets were illuminated.

Smoke Conditions were very favourable for smoke and cover good when once it had time to spread. Unfortunately it was by then too late. In short, lack of any early warning completely negatived this invaluable means of defence.

Fighter Patrol The patrol aircraft had just landed from their dusk patrol when the raid commenced. Three aircraft went up when the raid was known to be hostile but did not reach the scene until the raid was over.

Another extract gives the following information:

Generally speaking the number of Merchant ships in the port had averaged 35/40 for some time and the peak of 40 on 2nd Dec is accounted for by the fact that 3 ships were being held for *Ortona* and *Puck* had arrived to replace *Brittany Coast*. It was the practice to hold ships for Barletta and on 2nd December 2 full and 2 empty ships were so held.

The only means, other than double banking, of fitting in so many ships, a substantial portion of which were deep draughted Libertys, was to berth the latter on the Outer Mole 'stern to'. Captain Campbell had from the start repeatedly represented the risk which this almost solid line of ships entailed. On this particular occasion no less than 14 ships had to be berthed in this way between 25 and 31 berths inclusive, of which 25 had never before been used in order to avoid obstructing the entrance to the Eastern basin. On this occasion *Devon Coast* was used because her small size reduced the extent of the obstruction caused to a minimum.

It was of course known that *Devon Coast* was carrying 100 octane in bulk as she was a Naval Auxiliary, but the actual amount remaining on the 2nd December was only 45 tons. On the other hand it was known to the Port Manager that *Lom* also carried a dangerous cargo, and the same applied in the case of *Lars Kruse* (100 octane in drums). The fact of the matter was that the general practice in case of forward ports, Bari included, being to load mixed cargoes, it was seldom possible to practise any sort of segregation that, except in the case of bulk tankers, no attempt was made to do so or even to ensure that advice of the nature of the cargo of a store ship was received before allocating a berth to her. As regards the tankers, the San Cataldo Mole was reserved for bulk oil traffic of all kinds. It can accommodate one large (29 ft) tanker and one small (20 ft) tanker, and up to three more small tankers can be conveniently anchored in the vicinity. So long as only one large tanker is in port at a time 100% segregation is possible and has always been practised. It is when more than one large tanker has to be accommodated in winter that difficulties arise. In summer a second tanker can be accommodated at the western end of the Outer Mole, but in winter this berth is untenable and the nearest approach to segregation is possible that can be achieved is 11b berth, 'stern to' on west side of Molo Ridosso. The strong North-Westerly winds experienced for long periods in winter would inevitably drive burning oil from this berth through the entrance to the eastern basin, and in the case of a black oil tanker, this berth is unsuitable for fuelling destroyers. In practice one of the alongside berths has to be used, preferably No. 11 which though deep is too short (375 ft) for a Liberty ship and therefore less in demand for discharge of stores than any other deep berth.

Maybe one reason for taking the risk of having extra ships in harbour was intelligence information giving details of recent German Air Force operations in the area. The report indicated that the *Luftwaffe* in Italy had virtually ceased to operate after the stabilization of the Allied front line north of Naples at the beginning of October. The Sicilian campaign and the Allies' occupation of southern Italy, in which the *Luftwaffe* suffered heavy losses in pilots and aircraft, had taken a heavy toll of its resources. The record of the *Luftwaffe* in the autumn of 1943, however, was less than encouraging; between 15 October and 2 December, long-range German bomber groups based in Italy had operated on seven occasions, six on Naples and one on La Maddelena (northern Sardinia), a total of 300 sorties. During one of the raids on Naples, only twenty aircraft out of ninety airborne were reported to have reached the target. Of the 105 that were engaged in the attack on Bari on 2 December, approximately thirty-five bombed the target. The Allied Command obviously did not realise that the depleted enemy force could plan and deliver such a devastating precision attack which culminated in one of the most successful *Luftwaffe* raids of the war, and one for which the Allies were totally unprepared.

The report stated:

(a) *Reconnaissance*
The enemy had carried out two recce's at 1915 and 1050 on 2nd December, the second by two Me 109s in company. Although a single recce was a by no means unusual or infrequent occurrence, the fact that two were carried out at such a close interval was at least a straw in the wind to show which way the wind might blow. I am not aware, however, that any special precautions were taken.

No warning from intelligence or Y sources was received.

Radar sets had been set up for the defence of the port at an RAF post a few miles up the coast from Bari. There was an RAF set at Molo di Bari that had only been set up for a few days and was sited primarily for surface warning, to which more importance was attached at that time. On the San Cataldo Point another surface set had been sited but with only a limit of 12 miles (19.3 km) which detected low-flying aircraft, but was out of action waiting spare parts.

The Official Account continues:

Section 11. Early Warning
In action – 2nd December

About 1923 Light AA opened up on a sound plot followed immediately by heavies firing barrage.

Although as a result of the breakdown of communications no one was aware of the fact at the time, sector gave a 'doubtful' plot reading at 1917 as no hostile reading until 1925, by which time BARI defences were already in action.

(a) *As Available*

Early warning sets in the vicinity of Bari were:
1. RAF GCI a few miles up the coast from Bari. This kept constant watch and toe-in to Sector Filter Room, Grottaglie (situated midway between Brindisi and Taranto). GOR Bari had a tee-in to this line and kept constant watch on this toe-in.
2. RAF 277 set at Molo di Bari. This had been set up a few days previ-

ously and was sited primarily for surface warning to which more importance was attached at the time (because of German 'E' boats and submarines sowing mines on the vicinity of the harbour entrance). It was in contact on two separate direct lines to Navy Operations Room, Bari and Sector Filter Room, Grottaglie.

3. 271 surface RD/F set at San Cataldo Point, Bari. Sited primarily as a surface warning set for Naval use and having a range limit of 12–15 miles. It could detect low-flying aircraft within that range. It was in contact on two separate direct lines to Navy Operations Room, Bari and GOR (Gunnery Operations Room), Bari. This set was out of action awaiting essential spare parts.

4. Plots from RAF sets at Foggia and Vieste were filtered by No. 1 Moru and sent on by W/T broadcast, to which SOR Grottaglie listened in.

5. Each Heavy AA Battery had its GL and there were two GLs permanently on the air by night. These, of course, tell-only to GOR.

6. Failures on the direct line GOR/SOR were frequent, communications common-user line was uncertain and subject to serious delays, whilst the W/T link was completely unreliable. This weakness was apparent from the outset and with a view to its elimination, the Navy and Army had repeatedly pressed the RAF to establish an SOR at Bari itself. The RAF had, however, stated that this was impossible owing to the general shortage of communications.

(c) *In Action – 2nd December*

The direct line S/OR Grottaglie/GOR Bari, was inoperative on the 2nd December and had been faulty for 24 hours. The line between SOR Grottaglie/GOR Taranto, the first of the alternative links on the common-user connection and the W/T link, were also 'out', as a result communication was not established until the raid was in progress. The weather and atmospheric conditions were such that 'mush' similar to 'window' effect had been experienced earlier in the day. A force of Halifaxes was expected back from a bombing mission on or about the time of the raid.

No positive plots were received until the enemy was only 25 miles away. At 1918 hrs, GCI reported to SOR three separate plots 25 miles North of the harbour, followed immediately by indications of 'window'. These reports were heard by GOR on their 'tee' to the GCI/SOR line and passed onto Navy Operations room as 'A lot of responses which could not be identified as aircraft'.

At 1920 hrs, GOR went 'Red' on this information and because one of the duty GL sets picked up a single target at 40,000 yards at this time, Navy did not go 'Red' due to lack of information and of definite plots and there being no question at this time of 3+ [3 or more aircraft] within 40 miles.

About 1923 hrs Light AA opened up on a sound plot followed immediately by Heavy AA, firing a barrage. Although as a breakdown of communications no one was aware of the fact at the time, sector gave a 'doubtful' plot reading at 1917 hrs and no hostile reading until 1925 hrs, by which time the Bari defences were already in action. The 277 set on the mole at Bari picked up nothing prior to the raid.

It was fortunate that GOR possessed the tee-in on the GCI/SOR as thanks to the unfiltered information which it gave them, they were able to have the guns ready for what proved to be a surprise attack. 'Window' had not been used by the enemy on the East coast. Not enough publicity had been given to window or its uses. Many officers and men in responsible positions on 2nd December in the defence organisation of Bari had never even heard the word, much less any idea of its significance. Had the word been widely understood, the significance of all the clutter on the GCI's screen would not have been the mystery that it was.

In actual fact, on this occasion, no early warning was received at the scale and range at which Early Warning is intended to be provided. First warning or plots were at 25 miles from GCI Bari, whereas, a satisfactory W/T link early warning should be 100 miles or more.

On 28 or 29 November a representative of the US Port Officer went on board *John Harvey* and was told she carried a cargo of mustard gas. There was some evidence that the presence of mustard gas was discussed between the Docks Superintendent, the acting Port Commandant and the Sea Transport Officer, and it was considered, in view of her low priority and the berthing space available, that she was in as safe a place as could be found.

It was obvious that not just one or two people had prior knowledge of the mustard gas aboard *John Harvey* but a number of service personnel, probably as many as ten, were fully aware of its existence. One person who was not aware and certainly should have been was, NOIC Bari, Captain Campbell, RN. Even as late as the morning of 3 December when the 98th General Hospital made enquiries of Navy House as to the possibility of gas in the harbour, it was denied. Had Captain Campbell been aware that mustard gas was in the harbour its information could have been authoritatively confirmed during the admission of the casualties to hospital on the night of 2 December and possibly many lives that were lost, could have been saved. Even the Base Medical Officer, RN, stated that the first definite knowledge he had about the mustard gas was on 3 December at about 1030 hrs. It would appear that not one of the several people who knew of the mustard gas were capable of releasing the true facts to the hospital. On the other hand they probably did not want to take the responsibility for being the person who revealed the secret.

The official report:

> At 2200 hrs it was impossible to get beyond 24 Berth and burning oil and petrol on the surface of the water prevented approach by water, while smoke and flame made identification of the remaining ships still afloat inside the inferno uncertain. On the assumption that *Puck* had been destroyed by the first explosion, the second still left two Liberty ships, one of which might be *John Harvey* with more than 5,000 tons of bombs, including a quantity of them believed to be 500 tons of Mustard Bombs.
>
> Under the circumstances Captain Campbell came to the conclusion that 'disaster on a major scale was extremely possible' and advised the Area Commander to evacuate the town. After some discussion it was decided to evacuate the Docks area only, leaving a small Operational Staff and representatives of No. 6 Base Sub Area and Port Commandant at Navy House. In conformity with the above all RN personnel, except for an operational nucleus, were evacuated to country, together with all CBs and Signal Logs.

(d) *From midnight till dawn*

Explosions of varying severity continued intermittently throughout the night. By midnight all that could be had been done or was in hand. Appeals for help had been sent to Taranto and Naples, survivors were being brought ashore by all possible means and conveyed to hospital, or to the Fleet Club, which had been converted into a survivors' shelter and resting place. Measures to clear ships in danger had been taken or were in hand. Everything outside the actual conflagration was under control unless either another major explosion occurred or the wind shifted. It became a question of waiting for the conflagration on the Outer Mole to expend itself.

John Harvey

It was not known until shortly after the first major explosion, viz; at about 2015 (NB Captain Campbell states 2100 but various reports show it to be have been earlier than this) that the *John Harvey*, confirmed later by the Port Commandant and the Docks Superintendent, cargo of 5051 tons of USAAF Ammunition included some Mustard Gas bombs. This information was brought by two American Officers and confirmed shortly afterwards by the Port Commandant and the Docks Superintendent. The quantity mentioned was 500 tons, although I understand that in actual fact it was only 100 tons.

Nothing was known of *John Harvey*'s condition except that the whole area in which she was berthed appeared to be a mass of flames. A message addressed to her Master was, however, sent by four different means – two by land and two by water – ordering him to scuttle his ship if there was any danger of her catching fire. At least one of these is known to have been delivered. After the first major explosion, Lieutenant Bateman proceeded by motor-cycle to a point on the mole within shouting distance and passed the message verbally to an officer who was on the poop, after confirming the ship was in fact *John Harvey*.

Lieutenant Bateman states that she was not then on fire. A ship in the next berth East (*Testbank*) was, however on fire as were also another two berths West (presumably *John Bascom*), with the berth between, where *John Motley* should have been, empty.

On this evidence it was believed she was a potential source of danger, although it is of interest to note that it was in the form of vapour that it was assumed it would manifest itself. The possibility of the black oil, which by then had covered the harbour, contaminating survivors by contact was not realised, even when daylight revealed that *John Harvey* had sunk. Indeed the first reaction was that the disappearance had at any rate disposed of this particular menace.

From the preceeding paragraph it would appear that Lieutenant Bateman and presumably the person who gave him the information and orders to contact *John Harvey*'s master, were fully aware of the mustard gas bombs aboard the American ship. If these officers knew about the existence of mustard gas, it was quite evident that they withheld the information from the hospital staff. Many lives could have been saved if the truth had been relayed to the medical teams as soon as possible. Instead fudged rumours and counter-rumours clouded the issue and valuable time was wasted when men's lives were in peril and in many cases – lost. It was not until the next day that the hospital authorities became aware that they were dealing with mustard gas-contaminated patients.

From the Official Account:

The Effect Of The Gas

Most of the contamination arose through contact with the oily clothing of survivors who had been in the water, and ships who took survivors on board suffered worst, notably *Vienna, Bicester, Zetland, Vulcan* and *MBT*'s. A number of cases which could have only have arisen through direct contact did, however, occur in these ships and in *La Drome*.

The death rate amongst those contaminated was relatively severe and the tendency has been to attribute this to the fact the hospitals were not officially aware of the gas risk, or at any rate the particular form of that risk, until about 1000 hrs on 3rd December – the time when the symptoms themselves were beginning to appear.

It is, however, a matter of speculation whether even an official warning of the existence of mustard gas would have made a great deal of difference in the actual event, in view of the fact that fuel oil was the medium of contamination and under the circumstances the only practical method of decontamination was removal of the oil. In the absence of red oil this had to be done with soap and water, a process laborious and lengthy in the extreme.

A higher death rate than the normal would appear to be the logical consequence of the large area and long duration of the contact with mustard oil to which the casualties were subject – unavoidably under the circumstances.

In actual fact two warnings of a general nature from Naval sources were given to the 98th General Hospital. At about 2200/2nd December Surgeon Lieutenant Gray of 30 Commando took three casualties up to this hospital and warned the Medical Officer to whom he delivered them that he had heard a rumour that one of the ships in the harbour had gas bombs on board and that there was therefore a gas risk. Surgeon Lieutenant Gray left for UK shortly after the raid and his own evidence on this point has not therefore been available.

However, Surgeon Lieutenant Cosh my Base Medical Officer, who discussed this matter with him the following day, has the impression that the warning he gave was a general one, and he did not suspect the casualties delivered by him to be [contaminated], nor did he at that time realise the possibility of contamination through the medium of oil fuel.

On his return to Navy House about midnight Surgeon Lieutenant Gray went to Operations Room to get information on the gas situation and when he discovered that the rumour he had heard was well founded he asked Lieutenant Shearer, the Duty Operations Officer, to telephone the hospital to that effect.

This Lieutenant Shearer did, with Captain Campbell's approval. He asked specifically to speak to a Medical Officer and informed him that there was a gas risk and asked for and received his assurance that this was passed on to all hospitals concerned. Unfortunately the fate of this message is obscure.

It certainly was unfortunate, especially for the pour souls admitted to hospital, for the men who were left in contaminated clothing and for those who were wrapped up in blankets which facilitated the absorption of mustard through the skin. It was also unfortunate that the doctors were unaware of the contamination. Had they known of the existence of mustard gas they could have done much more for the men who suffered needlessly and indeed the many that died.

According to Surgeon Lieutenant Cosh, the first definite knowledge he had about the existence of mustard gas was at 1030 hrs 3 December. He went round with the Port Defence Officer to sites suspected of contamination. He boarded HMS *Vienna* where he found that sick-bay personnel had their eyes affected and the doctor a blister on one foot. He also inspected the French tanker, *La Drome*, which he thought might have been affected, but found no signs of contamination. The quay was closed and sentries posted to forbid anyone going there for unessential purposes. The initial treatment given in the hospitals, first aid posts and ships was for shock, burns, exposure etc. and survivors were wrapped in blankets, which aggravated the danger from the mustard gas on the skin and clothes. The hospitals were puzzled by the nature of some of the casualties they were receiving and their subsequent development. Such warnings as they may have received (if any) about the possible presence of gas certainly did not reach the appropriate quarters, and there is some evidence that, on a telephone enquiry being made by the 98th General Hospital (where the majority of the casualties were) to Navy House on the morning of 3 November no confirmation of the presence of mustard gas could be obtained. Whether the alleged informant was ignorant of the facts or was impressed with a supposed desirability of secrecy is not clear.

According to the evidence of the Medical Specialist, 98th General Hospital, Surgeon Lieutenant Gray's warning reached him, together with the former's caveat that it was entirely unofficial and only based on rumour. Shortly afterwards he was informed that 'someone': it was not known who, and enquiries failed to discover whether from the Army or Navy, had telephoned to state specifically and authoritatively that there was no foundation for the rumours which were current as to a possible gas risk. No further information on the subject was received at the hospital until the following morning.

It was fortunate for many people that Surgeon Lieutenant Gray left for the UK shortly afterwards. Some important questions needed answering and had he stayed he might have cleared up the matter and pinpointed who was to blame for the abysmal lack of communication between the port authorities and the hospital.

The Official Account continues:

Fire-fighting

(a) The extent and weight of fire quickly assumed the proportions of a major conflagration which swamped the limited equipment available. In fact after the second explosion, it was clear that the situation was completely out of control.

Fire-fighting efforts during the night were accordingly confined to attempting to prevent the spread of fire eastwards along the outer mole from the most easterly ship involved in the conflagration. These efforts were successful to a point, but not enough to prevent the fires on *Lom* and *Devon Coast* from getting out of control. This was chiefly due to the fact that they were lying too far off the Mole for fire-fighting from the Mole itself to be effective. Two fire-floats, Italian manned, were given a roving commission in the harbour.

By dawn considerable reinforcements had arrived from all over the Heel and at 0600 hrs 3rd December a battery of fire pumps had been embarked in each of two 'Z' lighters and an attempt under Cpt. Duffet RN (NLO 15th Army Group) made to tackle the fires on the Outer Mole. Unfortunately intense heat and recurrent minor explosions, including fusillades of small arms ammunition, forced the 'Z' lighters to withdraw, and it was not until the afternoon that they were able to get close enough to have any effect.

Remarks

As a precautionary measure the whole of the Outer Mole from Berth No. 19 westwards and the whole of Molo Ridosso (Berths 11 and 12) were put out of bounds from the time the ships that had been using them had sailed until they had been freed from contamination by Colonel Shadle, Chief Chemical Officer, AFHQ who reached Bari on 5th December.

No evidence of contamination could be found on Molo Ridosso, which was re-opened at once, but a number of mustard bombs, 40 of which were damaged and leaking or empty, were found on the Outer Mole in the vicinity of 29 berth and 200 yards of the Mole; [ships] centred on this berth were cleared, decontaminated and re-opened on 9th December.

Tugs

Lack of tugs from the very outset was undoubtedly the reason why several ships which could have been towed clear in the early stages were ultimately lost. The Italian crews of all tugs took shelter during the raid and could not be found for long afterwards. 'PORTO PISANO' the duty tug was sunk in berth 9, the salvage ship 'INSTANCABILE' did not have any steam up and even when this had been raised [the crew] had to be driven to get under way.

'CAPODISTRIA' was manned by an RN crew, who failed, however, to master her machinery. She was eventually got under way about midnight

139

when the Skipper and Chief Engineer had been located, and thenceforth gave valuable service.

The crew of the fourth tug, 'RESISTANTE', did not appear until the following morning.

This failure of the tug crews was one of the most trenchant lessons of the raid.

Rescue Work

Rescue of survivors continued until well after midnight and was carried out by all conceivable types of craft including MTB s and HSL [High SpeedLaunches] who all performed invaluable service with courage and skill.

At various times during the night parties of men seen to be trapped, both on the Outer Mole and on wrecks themselves, were rescued. A small boat manned by two American seamen under command of a British Coast Defence Officer was responsible for bringing in a large number of men, including wounded, cut off on the end of the Outer Mole.

HSL 2581 went alongside the Outer Mole outside the harbour to rescue another party of trapped men who were not located until nearly midnight.

Many MTBs went alongside ships or wrecks to take men off – often under extremely hazardous conditions, and several wounded or unconscious men were rescued from between decks of burning ships.

During the evening a lookout serving in an AA battery on Molo San Cataldo picked up signals of distress from a number of men cut off on the end of the outer mole. The flickering signal was SOS in Morse code. The operator was Signalman Bob Kelly of USS *John Bascom* who had found shelter with the rest of his shipmates in the concrete shelter on the end of the mole. When abandoning ship, Bob had had the presence of mind to take with him the signal lamp. The information was reported to a Royal Engineer officer, Captain Williams who, finding a 20-foot American steel motor boat in the charge of two men belonging to one of the vessels in the harbour, took the boat across to rescue the men. Because of the burning petrol and oil on the surface and flames which were lapping the mole to within a few feet of the trapped men, which made rescuing them from inside the harbour impossible, Captain Williams took the boat outside the harbour and rescued the men over the sea wall.

The crew of the abandoned *John Bascom*, including the master, Otto Heitmann, were rescued and landed safely. Welshman Captain Williams eventually received the MBE for this very resourceful and courageous operation.

HSL *2582* went alongside ships or wrecks to take men off, often under hazardous conditions, and several wounded were rescued from between decks of burning ships. HMS *Vienna* and HMS *Bicester* each turned themselves into reception and clearing stations. Unknown to any of them, the water was soon to be contaminated when *John Harvey* blew up. The surface of the water was coated with fuel oil and petrol and masses of dunnage, wreckage and debris was also floating on top. It is difficult to imagine the foul state of the water, but a harrowing film, taken some days later in which British soldiers are clearly seen retrieving bodies and parts of bodies from the glutinous swamp-like water, shows it admirably. What the film does not show, was the nightmare that was created when the surface of the water ignited. The survivors, attempting to swim to safety had then to contend not only with the foul water conditions, but fire as well. It must be said that the vast majority of the rescue operations during the night were carried out by Royal Navy personnel.

It might be worth commentating that the headquarters staff residing in the glorious splendour of Caserta Palace, Naples and in Algiers would have had no comprehension of the conditions created in the harbour during the raid and for several hours afterwards. It was certainly a disaster nobody could have envisaged; there was no time lag between the end of the raid and the holocaust that followed. If there had been time for a thoughtful evaluation of the situation followed by a practical plan of action, perhaps many lives would have been saved. As it was, the magnitude of the task presented to the port authorities was awesome.

The loss and damage of so many ships was in itself a major setback. The continuous explosions of ammunition and petrol provided a constant deadly deluge of shrapnel and flying chunks of metal. It was a hazard everyone carrying out rescue work had to contend with, indeed to everyone who was out in the open. In addition, the two huge explosions and the resultant tidal wave created a situation where central control had ceased to exist. The dense thick black smoke of the burning ships together with the port smoke defences, made visual communication impossible. Radio contact was lost as aerial masts on ships and shore were put out of action, and at that time it was obvious that ships commanders, Army company commanders, units of men and single individuals had no recourse but to fend for themselves.

After Jack Manning had left the toiling soldiers desperately trying to move the ammunition from the dockside he rejoined his ship, SS *Fort Assiniboine*. Steam had been raised when orders had arrived for the ship to clear harbour if at all possible. The risk of staying alongside with a volatile cargo which included blockbuster bombs was too great. The order to chop away mooring lines was given and with great skill on thepart of the deck officers, the vessel made a tortuous passage through the harbour on her way out to sea. Once clear, she made for the port of Augusta, where she awaited orders to return with her now ever more precious cargo of munitions; they would be needed to replace the thousands of tons lost: for the northward push of the 8th Army and Allied forces.

Some days later the order to sail for Bari finally came through and the ship arrived back there on 9 December. She made her way through and round the wrecks to tie up at the same No. 6 berth in order to discharge her cargo, but this time she had great difficulty in going alongside. As the vessels churned up the water near the berth, mutilated bodies were revealed. As the corpses rose to the surface they had to be retrieved before the ship could go alongside. It was a sight and experience Jack has never forgotten.

In daylight he was able to see the enormous damage the port had suffered, upper deck works sticking up out of the water at grotesque angles, some vessels lying on the bottom, their backs broken and split into two halves, funnels marking the graveyards of the once proud ships, all blackened by the fires that had raged aboard them. Jack recalls, 'One hulk was lying on its side and I was able to see down the three funnels as *Fort Assiniboine* passed it on our way to the berth.'

A distasteful incident occurred when one of the ship's crew stole a coat from one of the corpses lying on the quayside, much to the disgust and consternation of the rest of the company. The thief was punished in a manner he could never have imagined. After wearing the coat for a day or two, he discovered to his horror rashes and ugly blisters on all parts of his body, face and hands. He was rushed to the New Zealand General Hospital and diagnosed as suffering from exposure to mustard gas, treated with ointment and a certain amount of disgust and kept in for several days. This incident was to prove to Jack and the rest of the crew, in later years that although the Ministry of Defence denied the existence of mustard gas at Bari, they knew the truth.

Fort Assiniboine sailed from Bari after discharging and safely crossed the Atlantic to the exotic port of Rio de Janeiro where Jack going ashore for the first time, bought a newspaper which carried a front page report of the raid on Bari and its aftermath. Some thirty years elapsed before any inkling of the news of the catastrophe appeared in Britain and the United States.

Lieutenant Graham Scott had helped with the rescue and transport of survivors to the hospital, and remembers that by daybreak the hospital

142

resembled a refugee camp. The survivors were given the usual treatment for shock, warm, sweet tea, a shot of morphine and rest.

On receipt of secret intelligence, the doctors ordered all men to be woken up, stripped of all clothing and rushed through the hurriedly constructed decontamination units. For many of the patients it was too late. Owing to a decision of the War Cabinet in London, their fate had been sealed hours before.

Graham Scott reported to the shattered Navy House later the following day. When he entered the dockyard he had to pick his way carefully through the piles of debris and wreckage. He viewed a scene of, 'Utter desolation, such fantastic, twisted, chaotic black and grey destruction that it seemed impossible that any one of us who spent the night in that other-world shambles could have survived.'

As the exploded upper deck of the ship fell back to the ground, wireless operators John Adams and his sergeant comrade Mac dived for what little cover there was, knowing full well that there would be a huge blast: and there was. They had dug themselves into the sand and most of the upheaval passed over them. They staggered to their feet to discover that the pink planks which had formed the bed and which were only 3 feet (1 metre) above their heads, had vanished. John found them two days later, ¾ miles (400 metres) away, embedded a foot into the ground. The blast damaged property 7 miles (11 km) away John recalls:

> Sailors were trying to abandon blazing ships, but many had no choice, jump onto a burning ship near to the mole or jump into the water, which by that time was on fire. I saw only one ship escape to sea during that period. Explosions were taking place, the acrid smoke was overpowering. Burning oil, burning ships, burning debris and above all a sickly smell which we likened at first to onions, but later garlic. In the chaos and confusion the significance of this escaped me. Mustard gas never occurred to me.

About 0200 hrs John and Mac had brewed up using their famous brew-can, flavoured with wood-smoke of many open fires in North Africa. The gunners in the near-by gun-pit had grown accustomed to its unique taste. John took three mugs of tea across to the gun-pit but found all the gunners had been taken to hospital, blinded. Their blindness was attributed to oil-laden spray entering their eyes. John says:

> The lesson of the raid was quickly learned; during the next morning civil-ians streamed past us on the way out of Bari. In the reverse direction AA regiments and searchlight batteries poured into the area. The searchlights

were warmed up in readiness and the guns aimed to form a box barrage. We noticed that the line of barrage started just over our truck and then in a straight line over the north side of the harbour. We thought that the planes on the previous day must have come in from the sea or slightly south. The barrage seemed concentrated on planes coming directly from the north.

John and Mac were still at their posts in the wireless truck nicknamed 'Gin Palace' as dusk approached on the next evening.

We heard on our W/T – 'Five doubtful, map square Manfredonia' immediately followed by 'Five hostile': Tin hats on again. At that moment an Italian man who was leaving Bari stopped beside us. I pointed to my steel helmet and explained to him in my best Italian that in a few minutes it would be *molto pericoloso* (very dangerous). He decided to stay with us. The next moment the searchlights were switched on. Having been warmed up they came on immediately to maximum intensity. In their light, though it was not completely dark, I saw a flight of five bombers, not very big ones. All the guns opened up and I could see the leading pilot screaming into his microphone. The planes were only just above ground level. My immediate impression was how white the pilot's teeth were. The planes were in a very tight formation and they banked fiercely but were too close to the barrage. The leading plane's wings crumpled and the same happened to the following planes. None got through the wall of steel. A terrible waste for the Germans as there were no vulnerable ships left in the harbour but slight compensation for all the men and material we had lost; but not much.

I looked round to check on the Italian as shrapnel was pattering down on our steel helmets. I was just in time to see a large piece of shrapnel hit the unfortunate man in his neck as he looked up. He died within seconds: one more casualty.

Some time after the war had ended, John was admitted to his local hospital where an X-ray showed a lesion at the top of his right lung which in the absence of any knowledge of the existence of mustard gas was attributed to tuberculosis. At the time he was in the middle of a law degree, which he was advised to give up. He had an artificial pneumothorax to protect the lesion and spent more than seven months in hospital, all the while being treated with streptomycin. The wonder drug did not remove the lesion, much to the surprise of the medical staff.

In the 1970s, the British official accounts were released and for the first time John learned about the existence of mustard gas at Bari. His doctor, an ex-RAF surgeon who had studied the effects of mustard gas, was extremely interested and when he and John discussed the subject, he looked up his records and remarked that he was 99 per cent certain that the lesion was the result of exposure to mustard gas. By that time John had qualified as a solicitor and was senior partner in a local law practice in Leicester. He says, 'Bearing in mind what happened to so many in Bari, I was content to be in one piece.'

The morning after the raid, the minesweeper HMS *Hazard* entered the harbour and moved cautiously among the many obstructions to tie up at her berth. The night before she had sailed out to sea and cruised up and down the coast until daylight. As the minesweeper moved to her berth, Robert Forrest recalls many bodies floating in the water. When the captain saw them, he ordered duty watch to retrieve the corpses. 'There were sailors, soldiers and Italian civilians all covered in a black mess. We pulled them from the dirty, yellow water, placed them on stretchers covered with a union flag and took them ashore to be transported to a communal grave.'

He says of the burials, 'The road along which the tragic procession wound its way was flanked by hundreds of Italians, mostly women, sobbing and praying at the sight they were witnessing.' *Hazard* carried on with minesweeping duties for several months before being recalled to the UK.

After abandoning the Norwegian ship SS *Vest* when it suffered a direct hit in the hold full of coal, Radio Officer Bob Anderson and his shipmates spent the next few days attending several funerals of unknown sailors. Later they were allowed back on board the stricken vessel, but nothing of a personal nature remained. All their clothing and belongings had been burnt and destroyed, leaving nothing that could be salvaged. Most of the crew were repatriated to the UK. Bob Anderson's most vivid memory is 'How such a pleasant evening could change without warning, into the holocaust that it became.' As Bari was the first port of call on his maiden voyage as a sailor, he endured a baptism of fire of the first order.

A man not concerned in the raid on Bari but much involved in the consequences was Patrick McKenna, a native of Glasgow. Patrick had joined up in 1939 and served three years in the infantry before transferring to the Pioneer Corps in July 1942. At the end of that year he was posted overseas to North Africa and after the Allied landings in Sicily, he worked with the Pioneers in southern Italy. In May 1944, Patrick and three companions were ordered to report to the company commander. He explained to them that a war cemetery was to be opened up and he was giving the task of constructing it to the four men.

Lines of immaculately kept graves in the British War Cemetery sited near the village of Triggiano some 5 miles from Bari. This is the cemetery that Patrick McKenna of the Pioneer Corps helped to build in 1944. *(R. Bennett)*

Gravestone of R.F. Baldwin of the SS *Fort Athabaska*, which blew up with the loss of all forty-three men on board. She was empty and had on board 238 bags of mail and two captured German rockets which were to be examined by technical staff in Algiers. *(R. Bennett)*

The gravestone of H.A. Jones, master of the British coastal tanker SS *Testbank* berthed on the outer mole during the raid. It blew up and disintegrated. Only the master and one other body were recovered from the crew of seventy on board. *(R. Bennett)*

The gravestones of Olav Jacobsen a Norwegian merchant seaman and an unknown soldier, both killed in Bari. *(R. Bennett)*

147

The plan was to build the new cemetery a few miles from Bari and to transfer to it all the bodies that were already buried in the municipal cemetery in Bari. The graves followed the normal fashion of a military cemetery and Patrick recalls, 'I think my comrades and I made a good job of them and during that time we interred 375 Allied servicemen's bodies.' He remembers that when the re-interment was completed a church service was held after which, Patrick, his task finished, was posted to his unit, north of Naples. Shortly afterwards he fell ill and after X-rays were taken it was discovered he had contracted tuberculosis. In January 1945 he was shipped back to the UK where he spent several months in hospital. After a number of operations, he had his right lung removed. He later received a 100 per cent War Pension. Of his experiences, Patrick, who still lives in Glasgow, says, 'I underwent two serious operations and had a lung removed but I have something to be thankful for, because all this happened well over fifty years ago and I still survived.'

Ted Fry – he was overseeing the unloading of Royal Engineers stores from the merchant ship SS *Empire Meteor* at berth No. 11 in the dockyard when the raid began. *(Ted Fry)*

A scattered pile of bombs dislodged during the raid when a bomb landed not far from the stack. The vibration from the explosion caused the stack to collapse, but luckily without causing any damage. *(J. Risbridger)*

British soldiers standing over a dead man. There is wreckage in the background. *(Ray Bennett)*

Ships on the outer mole burning fiercely several days after the raid. *(A. Peterson)*

The traffic jam in the road leading to the harbour. Smoke can be seen rising from the harbour in the middle distance. *(A. Peterson)*

On Vecchio Molo were three identical buildings used as dockyard offices in peacetime. On 2 December, 131 Battery 7th Regiment, Light AA were manning Bofors gun emplacements on the roof of each building. The buildings had doors on each side, giving access to two oblong rooms connected by several steps to a central platform from where a further flight of steps led to the roof, which was some 20 feet (6 metres) high. The gunners' billets were on the ground floor. Richard Gamble was one of the gunners manning the middle gun of the three. After landing in Sicily, his unit had moved up to the Italian mainland to set up the gun position in Bari in October, on the promenade overlooking the harbour. Three weeks later they were moved into the harbour to the battery on the mole. Each gun team consisted of ten men, including sergeant, bombardier, two drivers and six gunners, though all were capable of manning the guns.

Richard's gun crew continued firing throughout the raid until the planes had departed. Afterwards, a massive explosion shook the building. The gunners were hurled off their feet and drenched with oil. The sergeant was dashed against a concrete wall, his face taking the full force. All his front teeth were smashed, severely cutting his lips and cheeks and rendering him voiceless for several weeks. The bombardier dived down the staircase to his billet, and as he drew level with the outside doors he caught the full blast of the eruption. It catapulted him against the inner wall, killing him instantly. Richard almost had the same experience, as he dashed down the steps for his steel helmet. He picked up the helmet and just as he reached the top of the staircase to step out onto the roof, the blast hit him, hurling him down to bottom of the steps. He received a massive blow on his thigh which he believed was from an ammunition box which crashed down on him as he lay on the floor. For many months afterwards, he could not sleep on that side.

Richard remembers pulling an American seaman from the water after the raid was over. He never saw what happened to him and he was the only swimmer that he saw that night, though he noticed many bodies floating in the harbour in the following days. He says, 'We usually received the Red Alert when the raiding party was about 40 miles (64 km) away; something went wrong this time, as they were over the top of us by the time we had dashed upstairs to man the guns.'

Cyril Simpson, signalman aboard *Empire Meteor*, was standing on the bridge with other members of the crew. At 0800 hrs Friday 3 December:

> We witnessed another outstanding happening. The Italian armed merchant cruiser *Barletta* was moored on the central quay of the harbour [Vecchio Molo]. We observed men leaving the ship, some moving to

mooring ropes with no degree of urgency in what they were doing. They cast off the lines fore and aft, there was a pause for a few seconds and as we watched in amazement the ship started to list to port and within half a minute she completely capsized and disappeared.

The whole of the harbour wall was breached at the point where the main explosions had taken place and Cyril remembers that on 5 December, a small ship was towed out of the harbour and scuttled in the gap to stop the winter seas washing into the anchorage. *Empire Meteor* sailed to Augusta where Cyril 'Wangled a posting on a ship returning to Bari. The fires had burned out by the time I returned to the stricken harbour and bodies were beginning to surface from the sunken ships and were floating mangled and bloated in the water. A sad sight and sad reminder that there but for the grace of God, go I.'

The USS *John Bascom*, built in Panama City, Florida, did not have a long life. She entered service in January 1943 and sailed after loading a cargo of ammunition at Baltimore, Maryland to arrive in Bari on 1 December. She was able to lower a lifeboat which with some survivors clinging to the sides, was able to reach the outer mole, from which they were rescued later. Out of the ship's personnel of seventy two, fourteen were missing.

The USS *John Motley* was hit by a bomb which caused tremendous damage as deck and hold cargo immediately burst into flame. She was one of the first ships to explode. Her life was even shorter than that of *John Bascom*. She was built in May 1943 at Baltimore and had loaded in Philadelphia, Pennsylvania, and departed Lynnhavan Roads, Virginia, on 25 October to arrive in Bari on 28 November. From her complement of seventy-three, there were only ten survivors (all ashore at the time). Constantin Tsimenis, the master, was one of the men who did not survive.

The USS *Joseph Wheeler* caught fire and blew up at almost the same time as her sister ships. She was built in Mobile, Alabama, in November 1942. She had sailed from New York on 11 November, arriving in the same convoy as *John Bascom*. Most of her personnel, including the master, Patrick Morrissey, were lost. Out of the complement of sixty-nine there were eighteen survivors (all ashore at the time). All that was visible the next morning was a burned out blackened hulk.

No one knows exactly when USS *John Harvey* exploded. Like *Joseph Wheeler*, she was showered with burning debris and probably blew up together with another vessel. She was built in Wilmington, North Carolina, in January 1943, and had sailed from Baltimore to Bari with mustard gas bombs among her cargo of ammunition. Her master, Elwin Foster Knowles, perished with seventy-seven of the crew, which included ten chemical warfare personnel. There were two survivors, a cadet and an able seaman who were ashore at the time.

The two British ships, SS *Fort Athabaska* and the tanker *Testbank*, which were berthed adjacent to the American liberty ships, were also destroyed about the same time. All of the crew of seventy-one on board *Testbank* at the time, perished. All of the forty-three crew on board the *Fort Athabaska*, at the same time, perished. From the combined ships' crews of 114, only four bodies were recovered.

At 0800 hrs 3 December, Ted Fry was on duty in the dockyard, just as his sergeant had forecast the night before. 'A coal ship moored off berth 12 was a mass of fire and it was still burning a week afterwards.' Ted discovered what the loud rumbling that he heard on the previous night was. The same bomb that had rocked *John Schofield* and *Louis Henepin* had also shaken a huge stack of bombs on the dockside which had collapsed. The large 100 lb (45 kg) bombs rolled all over the quayside in a great untidy mess.

Apart from these two incidents, Ted was not aware of any bomb damage in his vicinity and his section carried on working as usual for the rest of the morning. Though he did not know why at the time, he noticed that from berth 19 to the end of the mole was cordoned off and sentries were posted to stop anyone going further along. In the next berth to the *Louis Henepin* was the small refrigator ship *Spero*, which carried on discharging her cargo of frozen beef.

7

THE COVER-UP

THE strict censorship, the dearth of information from government sources and the lack of follow-up of hundreds of survivors and patients who were contaminated by mustard gas, leaves us with unanswered questions about the long- and short-term effects on men who were contaminated. Therefore, the story of Bert Stevens is worth recounting.

When Bert arrived home after his spell in hospital in Brindisi, it was the end of January 1944. He reported to the Royal Naval Barracks at Portsmouth, was not examined, stayed overnight and the following day was sent on four weeks' leave. He decided to give his family a surprise by arriving unannounced. He knocked on the door, which was opened by his younger sister, who had been eight years old when Bert had last seen her. Now eleven, when she got over her shock, she did not know whether to laugh or cry. The sailor followed her indoors to be reunited with his mother and three other sisters.

After the tears of joy, the first words his mother said were, 'My God, what have they done to you?' He explained that nothing out of the ordinary had happened to him except that he had been involved in an air raid. After requesting aspirins for a headache, which he had seemed to have developed since the bombing, he decided to clean himself up and have a bath. The events that followed 'lived with me for the rest of my life'.

He had just lowered himself into the bath when there was a tremendous crack. He went rigid with shock, then began to shake like a leaf. He got out of the bath and dashed downstairs, shouting, 'What the hell was that?' His mother replied, 'It was nothing, son, only the gun battery practising, as they do every day.' It transpired the gun battery was at the end of the road. The shock of the last few weeks had caught up with Bert. He says he must have looked a sight, with a towel round his waist, his eyes streaming and deep brown patches showing on his skin. The woman broke out in a flood of tears and his mother asked him once again what had happened to cause the state of nerves he was in. He eventually calmed down, dressed himself and went to see his future in-laws.

When he explained what had happened to his future father-in-law, an ex-soldier and holder of the Military Medal, he took him to one side. Bert said he showed a lot of understanding and said, 'Try and ignore it, it will pass in time.' Bert says:

> I then made the most disastrous mistake of my life when I asked him if I could marry his daughter Betty, who is now my wife. If we could have known at the time what Betty and I would go through, I am sure my father-in-law would have explained the position and refused permission. I would have taken his advice gratefully and would never have put this wonderful lass of mine into this life of hell we now live.

Completely unaware of what the future had in store for them both, the wedding went off without a hitch and nobody took any notice of Bert's regular 'shakes'. At that time Betty was serving in the ATS in an anti-aircraft regiment. On returning to Portsmouth after leave, Bert says, 'I took no further part in the war and was moved from one camp to another during the remainder of my service.' As for the events in Bari, not a mention. He did not have a medical examination or X-rays during this period. When the war ended he served eighteen months aboard the Officer Cadet Training Ship HMS *Frobisher* before the ship was taken out of service. Bert, though, was still suffering from recurring headaches and running eyes, which were put down to tension.

His service expired on 8 January 1948, at the finish of leave due to him. He never met any of his old shipmates, although *Vulcan* was Portsmouth-based. The only medical he had was 'a short arm one, arms above head, bend over, touch toes, then cough'. The Royal Navy said they were discharging him as A1 but he would not have to serve the five years in reserve. Bert and Betty talked the situation over and decided not to protest, as Betty did not want him to stay in the Navy.

He came home to his young wife and son, Michael, to commence a civilian career. He was bewildered when, as early as 1952, in deteriorating health, he discovered he had become impotent. He was also suffering from bouts of gastric trouble, bronchitis and conjunctivitis. He agreed with his doctor's diagnosis at that time, though neither Bert nor his doctor were aware of the reason for his condition. He found his eyes were so painful that he had to wear glasses continually because they watered uncontrollably. He found walking difficult as large blisters had formed on the soles of his feet and his breathing became laboured. From 1968, he was so often ill that he never managed a full year's employment.

His state of health steadily worsened, and on 18 November 1982, suffering from extremely painful earaches, he suddenly felt a crack in one ear from which a discharge appeared. He was also suffering from sores on the back of his neck and one appeared on his bottom lip. He made an appointment with his doctor when he realised that the sores were not healing, and after undergoing a series of tests at Whitechapel Hospital, London, cancer was diagnosed. One of the two doctors attending him, asked Bert why he always wore dark glasses and why his eyes watered so much. He informed him that his eyes had been in that condition since 1943, when he had been involved in an accident in which several ships had blown up.

After consulting his colleague, the doctor asked Bert if he could have a chat with him when next he visited the hospital for treatment, in two weeks' time. Bert agreed and two weeks later, following his admission, nurses took his blood pressure and temperature every hour until the following Tuesday. At 7 p.m. the same day, the doctor turned up to have his chat, during which he explained the details of the operation and post operative treatment. He then said, 'What do you remember of the night of 2 December 1943 at Bari?' Bert had never given much thought to the events in Bari all those years previously; his constant ill-health and its effect on himself and his family over many years had concerned him far more. It took some time to gather all his thoughts together but at last he began to recount some of the events of that fateful night. The doctor listened intently, breaking in to ask him, 'Did you notice anything unusual such as a garlic smell during that night?'

Bert replied, 'There was a smell of garlic, but that smell was prevalent in Italy at any time. What I do remember was a smell that reminded me of old English pear drops.'

The doctor said, 'Well done, can you remember anything else?' By this time Bert was recalling more of the events and recounted his experience of the raid, the ships exploding, his drenching and his memories of the passage to Brindisi. The doctor said that was enough for that night, saying 'I have to go home to enter into my report, what you have told me. In the meantime have a good think of what else you can remember and we will have another talk tomorrow and then I will tell you what I know.'

The following morning the doctor arrived but this time with a group of other young doctors, about ten in number. He pointed at Bert sitting up in the hospital bed and said, 'Take a good look, for in front of you is something you will never see again. The things Mr Stevens could tell you would make your hair stand on end. Gentlemen, he is a relic from Bari harbour during the last war.' He turned to Bert. 'I will see you this evening, Mr Stevens.' They trooped out leaving Bert to mull over what the doctor had said, especially about him being a relic, and it worried him so much he began to feel apprehensive. The doctor came back later in the evening and asked Bert to carry on from where he had left off. He recounted how *Vulcan* had been smashed against the quayside and set adrift, how survivors had been pulled aboard, his shipmates taken to hospital, and the symptoms that appeared. Bert finished by recalling being admitted to the tented field hospital in Brindisi. The doctor asked 'Did at any time anyone tell you the cause of your irritations?' Bert replied, 'No.'

The doctor explained his interest in the case, but because of medical security he could not reveal all he knew. He said that about six years after the war had ended, a group of medical personnel, himself included, were sent to Bari to investigate why some citizens of Bari were dying suddenly. On arrival they were told about the night of the bombings and explosions and the aftermath.

That year, 1982, marked the end of Bert's narrative, as he became too ill to make further notes. Nowhere in his story is mustard gas mentioned, which confirmed that even at that late date, he and Betty were totally ignorant of his exposure to mustard gas almost forty years previously.

Bert had encountered the British establishment's obsession with secrecy. The doctor wanted to know all about what had happened to Bert and had promised to tell him what he knew about the affair. But although he listened and made notes, he told Bert absolutely nothing about what he knew or even his thoughts regarding Bert's condition. He had visited Bari, evidently as part of a fact-finding and evaluation team and for many years must have known full well of the mustard gas contamination. Yet he never volunteered one word about mustard gas. Such secrecy is almost paranoid.

Bert's case highlights the injustice in the way the survivors were treated. It was not until the 1980s that the Government finally admitted that there had been mustard gas at Bari and that men had suffered from the effects. Bert's devoted wife, Betty, had witnessed the change in the young man she married in 1944 and had endured with Bert his long-drawn-out years of illness and distress. In 1983, Bert was diagnosed as having cancer of the throat and after discussions it was decided to operate. Betty recalls, 'He died on the operating table, but was revived.' She also says, 'I found out what had been the cause of all Bert's illnesses when quite by chance I overheard two doctors discussing his condition. This was at the first cancer diagnosis, when I heard the words "mustard gas" mentioned.' From then on, Betty never gave up the fight for justice. She contacted members of Parliament, appeared on television and wrote to the then Prime Minister, Mrs Thatcher, from whom she received a negative response.

After forty years Betty realised what had been the cause of her husband's debilitating illness. Had she not overheard those two fateful words, perhaps neither Bert nor anyone else would have been granted war pensions or compensation. On 24 February 1995, Bert Stevens gave up the struggle. He died on the date of his fifty-first wedding anniversary. He was the first survivor to be officially recognised as having been contaminated by mustard gas at Bari, and the first to be awarded a pension; it was grudgingly awarded in 1985, and was not back-dated. Betty again dug her heels in and after more months of protesting and lobbying, perseverance and determination, the pension was finally back-dated to the time Bert's illness was first recognised.

In a letter dated 5 March 1986, the Department of Health and Social Security stated that they were taking steps to investigate the other 600 or so casualties. Presumably that figure was the number that was hospitalised in the 98th General Hospital in Bari. Where the Department got that figure from is a puzzle, particularly as according to the RAMC, they have no record of the incident at all. Up until 1993, ten years after admitting that there had been contamination by mustard gas, the Department had granted thirty-five war pensions and disbursements. Hundreds more affected survivors were never admitted to hospital, but were treated by ship's surgeons, sick-berth attendants and first-aid personnel, and some received no treatment at all.

From the medical point of view the secrecy about mustard gas has been total. All medical personnel had been told not to mention anything concerning mustard gas when writing home and had then been sworn to secrecy – as it has turned out, a life-time's secrecy. Medical records are not due to be released until 2018, by which time no one who was in Bari in 1943 will be around to refute it. To the best of my knowledge there has never been a comment or letter published concerning mustard gas by any doctor who was serving in Bari at the time. Even when the news media gave a great deal of coverage and detail of the use of chemical weapons during the Iran–Iraq war, it elicited no comments whatsoever. In my appeals throughout the country, not one doctor has replied. It is of course possible that none are alive. How many more people suffered like Bert Stevens and his family, totally unaware of the real reason, we shall never know.

On 22 April 1915, at Ypres, Belgium, mustard gas was used for the first time when the German forces deployed 150 tons of chlorine against unprotected French troops. It was used again on 24 April, against the 1st Battalion Canadian Brigade, on 1 May against the 1st Battalion Dorset Regiment and on 5 May against the 2nd Battalion The Duke of Wellington Regiment. When the clouds of poison gas rolled over the pock-marked battlefields of Flanders, up to and over the Allied lines, causing hundreds of casualties among unsuspecting soldiers, there was no censorship of the information. As the enemy was the first to use chemical weapons it was roundly condemned. There was no need for secrecy and the general public were kept fully informed of this new weapon. It was good propaganda.

In the years following the armistice in 1918, many ex-soldiers who had been exposed to mustard gas suffered illness and sickness. Most families knew about or had family members who had been afflicted. In some cases the onset of illness occurred many years later. These ex-servicemen had one advantage that the survivors of Bari were denied. A great number of general practitioners had returned from war service and had experienced life in the trenches of Flanders and the effects of mustard gas. They had an affinity with their patients which was apparent in the way they helped them and procured war pensions for many of them.

There was no such help for the contaminated at Bari, though that was not the fault of general practioners. There were no medical records showing exposure to mustard gas, which could have assisted in diagnosing various ailments brought on in later years. Any enquiry to the RAMC would elicit the same reply as I received to my request for information.

A significant point in my research has been the fact that I have not had one reply to the many appeals I made through newspapers and magazines from any man pulled from the water after the main explosions which was the time when the mustard gas was released. Considering the vast number who were rescued by boats and taken to HMS *Vienna* and other ships, plus the line of men I saw waiting to be sluiced down aboard the *Zetland* and the many survivors treated aboard *Bicester*, it seems very strange that no one has contacted me. This runs counter to the law of averages, for every hundred men, most of them in their early twenties at that time, at a conservative estimate I would expect at least fifteen to be alive today. It raises the question, has every one of them died since? Another surprising fact is that though the rescuers were overwhelmingly outnumbered by the rescued, I was contacted by at least five men who had assisted in manning the Royal Navy's small craft which carried out most of the rescue operations.

A derestricted document from Allied HQ Algiers, Office of the Surgeon, dated 27 December 1943, gives the following information:

> It seems remarkable that no general alarm of gas was released that evening, but very few survivors identified any characteristic odour. In the fire and excitement any specific odour either was not detected or escaped recognition. On direct questioning, some of the survivors spoke of commenting

earlier on a 'garlicky odour', some even joked about it during the evening, attributing it to the quantities of garlic consumed by the Italians . . .

It probably seemed remarkable to the HQ Staff in Algiers that no gas warning was given, but there was not the slightest reason for the hundreds of sailors, soldiers and Italian workers in the harbour (apart from the personnel who did have the knowledge and for whatever reason remained silent throughout the night) to assume the existence of mustard gas. If it had been general knowledge, the hospitals would have been alerted instantly, thereby saving many lives which were lost during the hours of ignorance. Speaking as a participant, if I had heard a gas warning, I would have interpreted it as meaning that the German planes had deployed it, not a spillage from our own ships.

On the other hand, there were individuals in Bari who knew that mustard gas was aboard one or more ships in the harbour, yet deliberately withheld the information from the hospitals, and the blame must rest with them. To receive the consignments of mustard gas bombs and shells, there must have been a chemical warfare unit in the vicinity of Bari. Someone in charge of unloading the bombs and shells from the ships and despatching them to the dumps, and of course the captains of the ships which carried the cargo, must have known. In addition there were the recipients of the ten copies of *John Harvey*'s manifests, forwarded from Algiers HQ.

Because of the great secrecy surrounding the movement and stockpiling of mustard gas weapons, it would appear that co-operation between those responsible for their delivery and reception was almost non-existent. Perhaps it was a case of 'head in the sand' or the fact that the words 'mustard gas' were too controversial to be mentioned, so compounding the secrecy. The Official Account admits that many men died because of the lack of information, or more to the point, bungling secrecy.

> At some time in the evening, somebody aboard the USS *Lyman Abbott* called 'Gas'. The *Lyman Abbott* was lying in the harbour, later to be destroyed. Many of the crew put on gas masks for about an hour. None had recognised gas themselves. Masks were remove of their own volition. The *Lyman Abbott* suffered considerable damage which necessitated the Master to order the abandonment . . .

In my opinion, little credence can be placed on these remarks, which were hopelessly inaccurate. *Lyman Abbott* was the American liberty ship that a small party of ratings from HMS *Zetland* (myself included), boarded during the early part of the night and found deserted and probably given up for lost. Fires were blazing along the length of the upper deck, probably caused by burning debris landing in the wake of the many explosions. But though she had fires on deck, which after some time we managed to control, she appeared to be in no danger of sinking, and in my search of the vessel, I came across no damage below decks. On the other hand she was anchored, nakedly exposed only a short distance from the line of fiercely blazing ships, had already received and survived one tremendous explosion and could have possibly been involved in others at any time. Contrary to the report of her sinking, she was seaworthy enough to sail the very next day in convoy to Augusta. She was still afloat and carrying cargo on November 1945, three months after the end of the war.

One reason for the call of 'gas' and the use of gas masks when there was no reasonable assumption of the existence of mustard gas, could have been the knowledge that some of *Lyman Abbott*'s crew may have had. According to one US document from naval sources, *Lyman Abbott* was the only ship carrying mustard gas. When she left the United States she loaded her cargo in Baltimore, the same port that *John Harvey* sailed from, and the place to which the mustard gas was dispatched from the chemical warfare plant in Edgewood, Maryland.

There is not one report, other than this one, of anyone during the night using a gas mask, and of the survivors from the ship who forwarded their accounts to me, not one of them mentions anything about the shout of 'gas' or the donning of gas masks. And when *Lyman Abbott*'s Damage Report was made out only a short time later by the senior officer on board, how could he have not known the name of the master? Under Master of the ship was written 'Norwegian, name not known'. If the report was written by the master, he must surely have known his own name; he was not injured during the night and was capable of speaking to Captain Campbell about returning to his ship, if it could be guaranteed safe. And if the report was made out by a junior officer, he would surely know the name of his captain. It was evident that when the report was submitted to a higher authority, they were quite content to allow 'Norwegian, name not known' to suffice. However, from an American source I obtained the name; it was Carl P.R. Dahlstrom.

Lt Cdr Morgan Giles parted the anchor cables aboard *Lyman Abbott* to free her from the Italian ship *Barletta* which had drifted alongside after I had left with my unknown companion. This allowed the American ship to be turned over by the senior British naval officer to her master and three of the ship's engineers. The rest of the crew boarded her the following morning.

161

Censorship allows certain individuals, particularly those in positions of responsibility, the opportunity to rewrite history and, if need be, to display themselves in a favourable light. After all, who is in a position to oppose any of the statements if they are secret for many years? If the thirty years' censorship was a grave injustice to the survivors, it may have been very providential for several personnel of all three services based in Bari. Had it not been in force there would most likely have been a full inquiry and the person or persons responsible for withholding the vital information from the hospital authorities might have been brought to book. As it was, they were probably commended.

The Official Account says:

> **First Aid Treatment**. It must be repeated that rescue squads at the port and hospital personnel at the hospital had no idea or information that the casualties were, or had been, exposed to mustard. The casualties were covered in crude oil and, under the supposition that they were suffering from immersion and exposure, the casualties were wrapped in blankets and given warm tea. Surgical cases were given priority care and those just covered with oil were left wrapped in blankets for as long as 12 hours or even 24 hours. No attempt was made to decontaminate this mustard-in-oil solution from the men. Oil-contaminated clothing was not removed. A few individuals, on their own initiative, cleaned all the oil from themselves promptly that night. These individuals sustained only minor burns. No anti-gas treatment was employed . . .

Why should anti-gas treatment be employed when the hospital authorities had no knowledge of the existence of mustard gas?

> Many of the cases, after several hours, appeared to be in good condition and were permitted to be sent to an Auxiliary Seaman's Home (still clothed in their oil-contaminated clothing). All cases showing shock or other injuries were given concentrated care and resuscitation. In the hustle and rush of work no odours were detected, and in many cases [survivors] covered in oil remained wrapped in their wool blankets for many hours awaiting their turn for special care. Very few of the medical attendants sustained burns, although several had irritation of the eyes, which would tend to indicate that, for the most part, the solution of mustard-in-oil was quite dilute. Cases were hospitalised in the 98th British General Hospital, 14th Combined General Hospital (Indian), 3rd New Zealand Hospital, 70th British General Hospital and the 84th British General Hospital . . .

When one considers that the 98th General Hospital in Bari dealt with over 650 gas-contaminated casualties alone in addition to other wounded and injured, it gives some indication of the scale of casualties overall.

162

The main explosion in the harbour that evening was of tremendous violence. Window glass seven miles [11 km] away was shattered, and considerable other damage done in Bari. With this in mind, it was expected by the hospitals that many blast injuries would be admitted, and cases initially were considered either as such or as immersion and exposure. The first indication of unusual proceedings that evening was noted in the resuscitation wards. Men were brought in supposedly suffering from shock, immersion and exposure. Pulse rate would be imperceptible or just barely palpable, blood pressure would be down in the realms of 40–60 mm hg, and yet the cases did not appear to be in clinical shock. There was no worried or anxious expression or restlessness, no shallow rapid respirations, and the heart action was only moderately rapid, 110–120, considering the condition of the pulse and blood pressure. These cases did not complain of chest pain, have altered respiration, injured ear-drums, or blood-tinged sputum as in typical blast injuries.

They were rather apathetic. Upon being spoken to they would sit up in bed and would state that they felt rather well at a time when their pulse was barely perceptible and their systolic blood pressure perhaps 50. A striking feature was the lack of response of the hypertension to the usual resuscitation measures. Plasma infusions, at best, gave only a small and transient rise of blood pressure, and in most cases showed no response to plasma, warmth, stimulants, and morphia. Adrenaline gave no rise in tension, even when given as intravenous infusion. Coramine gave a transient, but not significant, effect.

About six hours after the disaster, cases began to have eye symptoms. Patients in the hospital and cases yet not admitted noted burning of the eyes and lachrymation (an outflow of tears) became very marked and was associated with severe blepharospasm (spasm of the eyelid) and photophobia (extreme sensitivity to strong light). Within 24 hours, the eyes were swollen and the individuals complained they were blind. There was no actual loss of vision but the blepharospasm was so severe that they would not open their eyes. Erythema (inflammatory redness) of the skin was noticed early the next morning as it became light. Blisters were noted also about this time some 12–24 hours after initial exposure. It was at this time that the hospitals first were notified of the possibility of 'blister gas' exposure among their casualties.

Nausea and vomiting were present in nearly all cases upon admission. Little information was gathered as to the character of the vomitus. The first death occurred 18 hours after exposure. Several other deaths occurred at 24 hours. There were 14 deaths within the first 48 hours. The type of early death within the first 48 hours deserves special attention as it was as dramatic as it was unpredictable. Individuals that appeared in rather good condition, save for hypotonia, conjunctivitis, and skin erythema, within a

163

matter of minutes became moribund and died. There was no respiratory distress, marked cyanosis (body acquires bluish tinge), or restlessness associated with their deaths. Cases that were able to talk and say they felt well, would be dead within a few minutes after speaking, and there were no prognostic signs of this possibility noted.

Some cases just went downhill, as for example: one case was pulseless but warm, and able to talk, though still with a clear sensorium (his wits about him) – he next was pulseless but cold, and soon his heart stopped beating. Their hearts, lungs, abdomens and CNS showed no or only very minimal findings at these times. They did not complain of chest pain or have any blood-tinged sputum. The general apathy of the patients was quite consistent and impressive. They could be roused, but when the external stimulus was removed, they returned to their apathetic state. Thecasualties included men of at least twelve nationalities or races and the apathy was as striking in one as in the other.

Secondary infections were not as severe and did not play a large part in the acute picture. In the small, somewhat more severe group, infection was not a tremendous problem, though it must be remembered that the eye lesions, on the whole, could not be classed as severe, or comparable to liquid mustard splash lesions, or saturated vapour lesions. On the other hand, the significance cannot be over-emphasised. For example: the destroyer *Bistera* [HMS *Bicester*] was in the harbour that night, and after picking up about thirty casualties from the water, put to sea for Taranto. Six hours out of port, eye symptoms appeared in the ship's officers and most of the crew. This became so severe that it was only with great difficulty that the ship was brought into Taranto harbour eighteen hours later, as the staff was practically blinded by their eye lesions . . .

If this gives the impression that the crew of *Bicester* were contaminated by the survivors they picked up, this was not so. *Bicester* and *Zetland* were alongside at berths 24–26 on the mole when the explosions took place. Both ships received a torrent of harbour water which was mixed with oil, petrol and liquid mustard gas, and all men on the upper decks were drenched in the foul mixture. The survivors *Bicester* picked up were in the water outside the harbour, most of them from *Samuel J. Tilden*, which of course never entered harbour, and therefore the men were not contaminated. It would be more likely that the reverse was the case – survivors that *Bicester* picked up could have been contaminated by their rescuers. The Official Account admits that both destroyers were heavily contaminated during the evening and night.

Burns were found where mustard-in-oil had been in contact with the skin. Some that were immersed were burned in all areas. Those individuals that had only their feet or arms in the water (and oil) were burned in those areas. Individuals in PT boats (motor torpedo boats and motor launches) that were showered with oil and water from the harbour were burned where the mustard-in-oil landed. Vapour burns were more marked on the exposed areas. Several who had sat in the mixture had burns only of the buttocks. The soles of the feet and the palms of the hands were remarkably free from burns.

The subcutaneous oedema was most severe and distressing in the genital region. The penis in some cases was swollen to three times or four times its normal size and the scrotum was greatly enlarged. The skin here, and in the fold of the groin, sloughed and local sepsis rapidly began in the region, as well as within the prepuce of the penis. Paraphimosis (a painful condition in which the prepuce [foreskin of the penis] has been retracted behind the glans penis and cannot be replaced) was common. These local lesions were quite painful and, in addition, caused mental anguish.

As there was no thought of toxic agent in the oil, no attempt was made to wash or decontaminate the men. Many men in wet, oil-contaminated clothes were wrapped in blankets, given tea and allowed to lie with the oil on their skin all night. The opportunity for burn and absorption must have been tremendous. A few cases were cleaned with liquid paraffin and then with warm water and soap. They showed only a diffuse and mild erythema and no toxic effects, and it is certain that early cleaning saved many lives. Only a few of the doctors, nurses and attendants sustained injuries to their hands, and/or mild eye lesions. All of these did well. This also points to the solution of mustard-in-oil being rather dilute. A longer period of exposure would have been necessary to sustain significant lesion.

Respiratory tract. There were no respiratory complaints in the first 36 hours. After that, the hoarseness began to develop, accompanied by roughness and soreness of throat. This was followed by a cough. By the fifth and sixth day, these had progressed to severe degrees. There was voluntary aphonia [loss of speech through paralysis of the vocal cords] in several cases and marked pain in swallowing. At this time, they started raising sputum, progressively purulent. There was some blood showing at this period, but none before, but respiratory distress and cyanosis were not features of most of the early deaths.

Warning must be given that it is still too early to evaluate properly all the factors in this group of cases, and that study of the collected data and pathological material will permit a more nearly complete and factual presentation. This preliminary report is believed warranted in the effort to have such information as is now available dispatched to the centres in Porton (HQ Chemical Warfare UK) and Edgewood (HQ Chemical Warfare USA) for early consideration. Pathological specimens of forty representative cases, dying within the first twelve days, also will be despatched to these centres for microscopic examination and study . . .

As I have said, medical records are not due to be released until 2018 and it could be that one reason for the secrecy is that the release of the information could cause distress. I am sure that is not the case today, however. Public awareness has undergone enormous change since the war. The advent of television and the use of satellites bring to every family scenes of tragedies, wars, shipwrecks, erupting volcanoes, trapped people, earthquakes, road, rail and plane crashes and the violence of terrorism around the world. More personal to us in Britain were the scenes from the Falklands when ships were set on fire after being hit by missiles, and the pictures shown on television from Valley Parade, Bradford's football stadium, when we witnessed spectators on fire as they tried to escape from the stand which was blazing furiously.

In Bari that night, and since, no records were kept of patients discharged from hospital or survivors and participants who could have been contaminated. There were no checks and follow-up examinations – on the contrary it appeared that survivors were widely dispersed, making any sort of check almost impossible, as most of the men were not aware of their own exposure to mustard gas. A copy of a telegram from the War Office to the South African High Command reveals that secrecy was urged in the way casualties were described. It says all mustard gas symptoms should be described as 'dermatitis'. The same telegram admits that the mustard gas element was widely known in Italy. If it was widely known in Italy, it would certainly have been known in Germany.

One must conclude that the secrecy surrounding the affair was an attempt to keep the British public in the dark. That the censorship was successful there can be no doubt. Even today, well over half a century later, people in Britain, including most ex-servicemen, know nothing about the unique disaster that befell the Allied servicemen. The event is unique in that a chemical weapon was 'deployed' by accident, by a tragic quirk of fate; the designers of the weapon never intended mustard gas to be deployed in water.

Though the existence of mustard gas was successfully concealed from most of the servicemen concerned for over forty years, others not involved in the raid knew almost immediately. Second Engineer Roy Nichols, who was serving aboard SS *Nyanza*, kept a diary in which he made entries late at night when his watches were completed. *Nyanza* had sailed from Cardiff on 3 November 1943, calling at Gibraltar and Syracuse before arriving at Brindisi where she hove to, entered harbour and moored alongside the jetty. Roy's entries from 2 to 15 December are:

> Thursday 2nd Dec . . . Busy. Quite cold today. Played cards. Air raid at 9 p.m. No damage.

Friday 3rd Dec . . . Went in motor boat again. Quite cold. Wish I was home. Air raid on Bari last night. Played cards and draughts and cards.

Saturday 4th Dec . . . Busy. Believe heavy damage on Bari. Mustard gas trouble. Played draughts and cards.

Sunday 5th Dec . . . Small ship came alongside. Was submerged in Bari by explosion of munition ship and refloated. Was in bad mess, no water on board. All men dirty and suffering from mustard gas. Got Italian bullet from her deck. Moored alongside at 4 p.m. Played cards again.

Monday 6th Dec . . . Cold. Busy. Played cards. Ship alongside with smallpox.

Saturday 11th Dec . . . Arrived Bari at 8 p.m. 17 ships sunk in harbour. About 600 lives lost. Still smell of petrol and burning. Coal, petrol and ammo ships lost. Started work at once, short notice. 5 p.m. curfew. Watched them fishing bodies out of dock all day. Air raid at about 11 p.m. Terrific barrage, heard no bombs drop. Soldiers and Italians working ships.

Tuesday 14th Dec . . . Lot more bodies in dock this morning, about 16. Believe 500 men killed altogether from 17 ships. Just lucky we had our destination changed at last minute. Moved from quay to anchor, saw all sunken ships. Unfortunately moved into wreckage by quay wall and some more bodies were in it. Felt a bit sick. We did not stop too long.

Wednesday 15th Dec . . . Took Captain ashore again in afternoon. Part of another body was on quayside. Soldiers took it away, just too late, we landed there.

Nyanza left Bari at the end of December bound for Augusta. Both the Axis and Allied forces held stocks of mustard gas for retaliatory purposes; neither side ever intended to use it as a strike weapon, and indeed never did. That reassurance meant nothing to hundreds of victims that night and afterwards when choking and fighting for breath.

Unlike the British and American authorities, the Italian Military Hospital in Bari gave full details of injured and wounded men admitted. Giuseppe Agneli, born on 4 May 1923, enlisted in the Italian Navy at the naval base of Taranto on 4 May 1943 and was serving aboard the motor vessel MV *Barletta* as a mechanic. She was anchored in Bari harbour close to the line of shipping and to *Lyman Abbott*. Giuseppe was admitted to hospital on 5 December 1943 suffering from extensive second- and third-degree burns to his body. He died at 4.10 p.m. on 8 December. He was unmarried. There are eleven sheets of information including death certificate, hospital charts, operating theatre cards, hospital reports, diet sheets and authorisation to take the body from the mortuary. This contrasts with the complete lack of information from the Allied authorities and the denial that the event ever took place.

Throughout the Second World War, the USA and Britain feared that Germany or Japan would use poison gas against them, and they wanted to develop better protective clothing and gun masks. Because tests using animals did not go well, the researchers decided in 1942 to use human beings. These experiments, the worst of which were at the Naval Research Laboratory in Anacostia in Washington and the Edgewood arsenal in Maryland, got out of control. The US Army, with strong memories of the effects of mustard gas in the First World War, refused to let its men be used as human guinea pigs. The US Navy, on the other hand, not only volunteered its own men, but for decades after the war also refused to compensate them for crippling injuries caused during the tests.

In 1942 the US Navy locked 17-year-old Glenn Jenkins into a gas chamber within sight of the dome of the Capitol in Washington. It then poisoned him with mustard gas and lewisite (arsenic) gas. He never recovered his health. Norman Schnurman, another 17-year-old, was asked to test summer uniforms for the Navy. 'I thought it meant a trip to Florida,' he says. Instead the Virginian was taken to the small Army encampment at Edgewood in Maryland, where he was issued with a gas mask and told the experiment was really about how well Navy equipment resisted poison gas. He was locked in a small hut heated by a furnace and with a door that could only be opened from the outside. 'I looked up at the ceiling and saw the dark yellow oily mist rolling in.' When something went wrong with his mask he asked over the intercom to be let out, but was refused. He vomited into the mask, passed out and had a heart attack, coming to later to discover that somebody had dragged him into the fresh air.

All the survivors (now in their seventies) tell the same stories. Russell O'Berry, then also seventeen years of age, says, 'After eight weeks at boot camp, an officer came to us and said by taking part in secret experiments we could shorten the war. At seventeen or eighteen, everybody is gung-ho, so we said yes.' Russell had a physical examination which he passed – the last time he was able to do so. Only when he got to the Naval Research Laboratory in Anacostia did the officer tell him the experiment involved mustard gas. He says, 'Some of the men refused to go into the gas chamber and were given a direct order. We were told that if we did not go through with it we would get forty years in Fort Leavensworth in Kansas [the Army prison].' With nine others he was locked in a small, dark room with a thick door, like a bank safe, that could only be opened from the outside. He did not see the gas being pumped into the room through a hole in the ceiling, but he felt it beginning to burn 'around my right eye, my buttocks and genitals'. As the experiments continued, 'I developed blisters as big as hen eggs on my buttocks'. As the gas ate into his lungs, he developed a hacking cough.

The gas was of the type first used by the Germans against the British at Ypres during the First World War, when it caused 400,000 casualties. The short-term disabling effects were severe skin blistering and damage to the eyes and respiratory tract. Victims died if the gas was heavily concentrated. What the US Navy ignored in its experiments in the 1940s was a series of studies of First World War gas casualties showing that they also suffered serious long-term health damage. Lewisite, of later invention, also had catastrophic long-term effects.

The bitterness of the veterans who were used as guinea pigs at Anacostia and Edgewood stems from the refusal of the armed forces to acknowledge what had happened to them. Until 1991, they had to prove that their ailments were the result of poison gas, an almost impossible task. Many, who had been told that the Espionage Act would be used against them, did not even tell their doctors what had happened to them. Doctors at Saipan in the Pacific diagnosed Glenn Jenkins as having tuberculosis until a doctor with experience of the First World War realised that his lungs were showing signs of mustard gas damage. Russell O'Berry returned to Richmond, Virginia, went blind in one eye and, unable to get a better job, ran a sandwich bar.

The plight of these and 2,500 other sailors who were used in what the US Navy called 'man break' experiments with poison gas has remained a secret for five decades. Only very recently, under pressure from the victims, did the Pentagon agree to let them tell their stories. The US Navy's own reports entitled 'Chamber Tests with Human Subjects', dated 1943 and now declassified, are extraordinarily blasé about the results of the experiments. They say, 'Occasionally there have been individuals or groups who did not co-operate fully. A short explanatory talk and if necessary a slight "verbal dressing down" have always proved successful.' Surviving sailors say the 'dressing down' consisted of a threat of immediate court martial and forty years in prison.

In Britain in 1960, after completing a course which gave him a trade qualification, James C. Dornan returned to RAF Stafford where, after leave, he waited for his anticipated promotion from corporal to flight

169

sergeant. Some months later he saw a notice in the station routine orders inviting personnel from all three services to volunteer for tests at Porton Down for which extra money would be paid. There would be no tests involving any danger to health.

As a young man saving up for marriage, he volunteered and at the end of June he was transferred to Porton Down, where he joined a group of about twelve servicemen from the Navy, Army and Air Force. Over the next ten days, under medical supervision they were tested wearing protective clothing against mustard gas. They were also given some injections, and to this day, James still does not know what they were. 'We were then exposed without any means of protection to Adamsite, which I discovered is an organo-arsenic substance in the form of droplets.'

At the end of July, back at RAF Stafford, he was taken seriously ill and was admitted to the base sick quarters where, during the next ten days, 'my temperature reached 103 at one point and I had severe breathing problems and was unable to swallow anything. I was given large doses of a drug called Christopen which I gather saved me. Later I was released from sick quarters to return to normal duties.'

During the next few years, he served in the RAF Police and in August 1970, after discharge, he became a police constable in Woolwich, London. After a probationary period and several moves, he was eventually stationed at Corsham, Wiltshire. 'In 1992 I had two minor heart attacks within 24 hours and was admitted to Bristol Infirmary where after all the usual tests they discovered a problem with my left lung.' He was later retired on medical grounds.

He applied for a war pension, but the War Pensions Agency turned him down. He appealed against the decision and at the hearing in Cardiff in August 2000 which lasted fifteen minutes, the case was suspended to a later date because certain pages of his service medical documents were missing. At the next hearing, the War Pensions Agency will be required to give an explanation for the missing pages. They have admitted that he was exposed to Adamsite, a highly toxic chemical/nerve gas which affects the lungs and respiratory systems, but in their opinion this is not the cause of his present illness.

At the present time, James says, 'I am suffering from pleural thickening of the left lung, angina, diabetes, hypertension, arthritis of the left arm and Dupetrens contracture of the right hand and although this is an operable condition, because of my lung and heart condition, the surgeons will not take the risk of operating.'

Though all medical personnel in Bari were sworn to secrecy and ordered not to refer to mustard gas in any way, one doctor did get round the order.

I have in my possession a copy of a 'Hurts certificate' issued some months after the raid. Its full title is 'Report of Wounded or Hurt' dated 16 June 1944, and it is signed by a medical officer. It gives the name, rank and number of a Royal Navy seaman who was serving aboard HMS *Vulcan* at the time of the raid. In the space provided for the description and nature of the injury sustained, is the following: 'Conjunctivitis and MG burns of skin and legs and abdomen.' The space provided for particular marks or scars was left blank. So although the censorship did not allow the use of the words mustard gas, the doctor still made his point by using the initials MG instead.

On 5 December 1943, the Chief Chemical Officer Allied Forces Headquarters (AFHQ), the Technical Officer (CW) AFHQ and the Technical Officer (CW) 8th Army visited the docks. The latter gave this report.

> Samples were taken on the 5th December of the oil still remaining on the surface of the water and no trace of mustard gas was found. The fact that samples, tested nearly three days after the raid, contained no mustard gas does not in any way discredit the conclusion that mustard had been dissolved in the oil, as most of the mustard was doubtless destroyed by the fire which burned on the surface of parts of the harbour for some 36 hours. Any remaining trace would have been dissolved from the oil into the water by that time and would have sunk to the bottom.
>
> On the 6th December an area of about 200 by 10 square yards on the mole beside Berth 29 was decontaminated under the supervision of the Technical Officer (CW) AFHQ. This area contained numerous heavy patches of mustard and one ton of dry bleach powder was scattered (this is the standard laid down in the text books, viz 1 lb per square yard). The treatment was completely effective, and the next day the mole was hosed down in order to wash the paste into the sea . . .

The captain of HMS *Vienna* gave this report on 10 December.

> From the time of the raid, and throughout most of the night, dozens of survivors from ships in the harbour were being taken from the water by various boats and HMS *Vienna* was used as a clearing station; the men being given any emergency treatment, placed on stretchers and then loaded on to trucks and sent to hospital. It was quite impossible to take details of those men owing to pressure of work and lack of space. This would be done at the hospital. The injured men were brought over the gangway and carried down to the sick bay just below the quarter deck. After the sick bay and the flat were filled, the Petty Officer's recreation

space was also filled. A large number of men had been in the water and were soaked and also covered with thick oil. In some cases, part of the men's clothing was removed and thrown aside.

Towards early morning, it was noticed that many of the crew's eyes were becoming inflamed. This could not be attributed to the smoke from burning ships as the wind was from the South, and no smoke came in the direction of the ship. Still later, five or six men were vomiting, and eye cases becoming more severe and more frequent. The ship's Medical Officer could not account for this . . .

On 3 December 1943 at 2.15 p.m., a day after the raid, a meeting was convened at HQ No. 2 District. Attending were: Lt Col Sismey, General Staff Officer No. 2 District; Major Fabor, 12th United States Air Force (Chemical Warfare); Colonel Hradel, 15th USAAF (Chemical Warfare); Lieutenant Steiner; US Adriatic Base Command (Chemical Warfare); Major Bolland, Supply Officer No. 6 Sub Base Area; and Captain Cannaway HQ No. 2 District (Chemical Warfare).

Lt Col Sismey informed the meeting that *John Harvey* in berth 29 had carried 540 tons of American mustard gas bombs and white phosphorus. As a result of the raid on the night of 2 December this ship was reported to be on fire forward and sunk aft. Colonel Hradel stated that the bombs were not fused and that the only danger would occur if the bombs were split and the fumes dissipated by heat. The men were unanimous in their opinion that the concentration was unlikely to be dangerous outside the dock area and that precautions were only necessary within the dock area.

The following immediate action was to be taken. A reconnaissance was to be made at once. Senior Officer No. 6 Base Sub Area, working in conjunction with Major Fabor, was to post two sentries (one American, one British) at HQ 58th First Class Fire Brigade in the dock area to watch the direction of the wind and test for gas and give warning to Navy House and No. 6 Base Area of any sign of it. In the event of the wind changing and blowing gas towards the shore, a danger area was to be picketed off by the above sentries working in conjunction with dock military police. Notices saying 'Danger', 'Fumes' and '*Pericolo*' would be displayed.

Gas masks and anti-gas clothing were released for the use of naval decontamination squads. This equipment was held at HQ 58th First Class Fire Brigade inside the docks and the Naval Officer in Charge had been informed.

8

CONCLUSION

O NE of the most urgent problems to be solved was the decontamination of ships and boats in order to bring them back into service
as quickly as possible and this was addressed by the following
message:

6th December 1943, Staff Officer Operations to the Captain Coastal Forces
Mediterranean

Subject: Mustard gas contamination of HMS *Vienna*, MTBs *287, 289, 290,
296, 81, 86, 242, 243*, and ML *361*.
Copies to: NOIC, Brindisi, Commanding Officer HMS *Vienna*, Passive
Defence Officer Malta, Senior Officer 20th MTB *Flotilla*.

(1) On the night of 2–3 December 1943, enemy aircraft raided Bari and a
number of ships were lost either by receiving direct hits or being set on fire
from the hit ships. The MTBs and two of *Vienna*'s boats were employed in
picking up survivors from the water and rendering sundry assistance whilst
Vienna was used as a Casualty Clearance Station, all boats disembarking
survivors to her. Early in the morning it was decided to evacuate the
harbour of most shipping and the MTBs and ML sailed shortly before noon
for Brindisi, the *Vienna* followed two hours later.

I think the staff officer could have chosen his words more carefully;
'rendering sundry assistance' sounds akin to helping out in a grocer's
shop on a busy afternoon, instead of men risking their lives in extremely
dangerous rescue operations.

(2) Unfortunately one of the stricken ships contained mustard gas and the
water of the harbour became contaminated with liquid mustard, a fact that
was not known until some twelve hours later. On arrival at Brindisi all casualties were sent to hospital whilst the remainder of MTBs' officers and
ratings, and most of the *Vienna*'s complement, were decontaminated
ashore and sent to the Transit Camp.
(3) The decontamination of the *Vienna*, MTBs and the ML presented a
peculiar problem in that this was the first case to be tackled in this war [and

any war] and it was not known what part of the ship and Coastal Force craft were contaminated either by liquid or vapour. Survivors had been placed on the upper decks and mess decks of the MTBs and men could thus contaminate all parts of the craft by having previously walked or sat where the survivors had been. Similarly the *Vienna* could have been completely contaminated.

(4) However it was imperative to get the Coastal Forces craft either operational or fit for repair work as soon as possible whilst the *Vienna* was required for repairs, no mean number, to the craft. Therefore, it was decided to assume that certain parts were contaminated and others not.

The assumption arrived at was as follows: MTBs (a) Contaminated. All upper decks, bridges, guns, torpedo tubes, depth charges, and all other gear on the upper deck such as fenders, ropes, wires, canvas covers, rafts etc. Mess decks, wardrooms, wheelhouses, heads, galleys and bilges. (b) Very slightly, if at all contaminated. Engine rooms, tanks spaces, W/T offices. ML *361*, only 2 slight casualties occurred in her, one who had been in the *Vienna*, with sore eyes and the other with a small blister on his arm. The boat was not used for rescue work, etc. and lay alongside a quay further away from the burning ships than the *Vienna*. (c) Slightly contaminated. The upper deck, bridge, funnel, guns, depth charges and all other gear on the upper deck. (d) Very slightly if at all contaminated. Mess decks. HMS *Vienna*. (e) Contaminated. Sick bay, sick bay flat, Chiefs and PO's recreation space and certain officers' cabins, the former where survivors, mustard and casualties lay, the latter belonging to officers who had been tending the casualties or who had been in the water carrying out rescue work. Motor boat, whaler, skimmer, and copper punt which had been in the water. (f) Lightly contaminated. Fo'xle. All other gangways, passages, mess decks, messes, heads and bathrooms, decks and mess tables, stools and chairs.

Decontamination of MTBs. It is obvious that a systematic method must be evolved to carry out this work quickly, as approximately only 20 'labourers' at one shift are available for the boats. This is due to lack of men, suits, boots, and bleach, coupled with the problem of fitting in of transport (road and sea), meal hours, and the fact that the dressing and undressing stations have perforce to be at Navy House. That means that the 'working hours' on the boats must be about 0830–1200 and 1230–1630hrs.

It appears best to tackle three boats at a time, secured alongside each other at a quay. It is reckoned that, when the organisation gets going, the group of three boats can be decontaminated in two days as follows: (a) First half-day. Remove all ropes, canvas covers, etc. from upper deck to quay. Wash down upper decks, bridges, torpedo tubes, depth charges, then scrub them with mixture of bleach, sand and water.

The scale of the disaster caused AFHQ to make the following conclusions and recommendations.

Notification of despatch . . . So far as we are able to ascertain, the present procedure does not require any special notification of the despatch of toxic ammunition. In the particular case under consideration, 12 AFSC did in fact notify the addressees referred to previously, but the message was not received until the 28th November, the day on which the convoy arrived. The ship's manifest arrived in good time but does not appear to have been circulated. It does not always happen that the manifest arrives before the ship and in any event it does not give any prominence to the fact that a toxic cargo is carried.

We consider that toxic ammunition is of such a nature that it calls for special notification, and that a cable should be sent from the port of dispatch as soon as the ship sails, to the Area HQ and the appropriate Port and Ordnance Authorities at the port of discharge, setting out the name of the ship, details of the toxic cargo carried, and expected date of arrival. Ports of call should also be notified.

Stowage . . . We recommend that storage of toxic ammunition and explosives on the same ship should, wherever possible, be avoided. It was the explosion aboard the *John Harvey* of the ammunition she was carrying which was the principal cause of mustard being scattered over the harbour which such unfortunate results. The explosion of such a mixed cargo in port is bound to have the most serious and somewhat incalculable consequences.

Ports to which despatched . . . It is tempting to recommend that toxic ammunition be not sent to large, busy ports in forward areas. Many factors however outside the scope of the inquiry, affect the question. Operational and shipping requirements must come first; the number of ports likely to be available in any theatre of war in the early stages of operations is limited, and we do not consider that the danger from toxic ammunition, provided appropriate precautions are taken, justifies a recommendation which might dislocate normal shipping arrangements.

We should point out, however, that if toxic ammunition were loaded and discharged only at certain ports, the necessary anti-gas stores and equipment and the personnel required to use it could be much more easily prepared. Moreover, adequate equipment and training, at least in personal decontamination, might be given to the civil population. It follows that small ports with a small civil population are the most suitable.

Dispersion and quick unloading . . . It is not the practice in an operational port like Bari to treat a ship carrying toxic ammunition as an abnormal risk. In view of the particular danger which this raid has illustrated, however, we consider that such a cargo should be given a high priority of discharge and that while the ship is waiting in port she should be isolated from other ships, particularly ammunition ships, as far as circumstances permit.

Similar considerations apply at a port of loading, if the area is subject to air raids.

Warning . . . The outstanding fact which emerges from our inquiry is that a number of persons suffered from mustard poisoning which might have been allayed and possibly prevented if the true nature of the injuries had been appreciated from the beginning. The risk present in the minds of the persons who considered the matter after the raid was that there might be splashes of mustard on the moles and on other ships with possible strong concentrations of vapour. It was not to be expected that the particular, insidious danger which in fact caused so many casualties would occur to them. So far as we are aware this phenomenon of mustard dissolved in oil has never occurred before in anything approaching similar circumstances or on a similar scale.

It is probable that had the appropriate medical authorities received information that a ship carrying mustard had exploded in the harbour they would have been able to make a true diagnosis a good deal earlier. As it was they were confronted with patients exhibiting the ordinary symptoms of shock, exposure, burns etc., who therefore received initial treatment actually favourable to the spread of the poison. The particular form which the poisoning took was unusual; the burns were not typical of mustard because they had been brought on by long exposure to a solution of mustard in oil, aggravated by resuscitation treatment involving in some cases a long period in blankets.

We recommend that, following the signal notifying the shipment of toxic ammunition, the Port Authorities should notify the Area (Garrison etc.) HQ when and at what berth the ship will discharge. If there is a reason to believe that the gas has escaped from the ship, through an air raid or otherwise, the Port Authorities should immediately warn the Area HQ and the COs and Masters of ships, giving the fullest information available. Area HQ must be prepared to pass on the warning for the information of hospitals, first aid posts etc. and definite arrangements for the speedy dissemination of this information should be made beforehand . . .

On discharge from the military field hospital on the outskirts of the Sicilian city of Syracuse, I returned to the Royal Navy base at Augusta, anticipating rejoining my shipmates aboard HMS *Zetland* on her next visit. Sadly it was not to be, for I had only been there for two days when

I received orders to join the draft pool in Malta, where I spent seven aimless days scanning the draft lists which were pinned on the notice board every day. Eventually my name appeared on the list; I had obtained a draft to the Royal Navy base in Naples. On arrival in Naples I was billeted with dozens of other sailors in barracks situated in a four-storey building near the seafront and overlooking a football pitch which was bare of grass.

The boring life in barracks was not to my liking and when one morning there appeared a notice that volunteers were required to train as stores assistants, I put my name forward. Some days later I was lucky enough to receive my draft – as in all service procedure, not to naval stores but to the military police! The group I joined consisted mainly of soldiers, though there were one or two Royal Marines and sailors. We were based in a large elegant house off Via Roma, the main street of Naples. Its previous occupants, before the Allies requisitioned it, had been the Gestapo. For my first patrol I was paired with a soldier from Oldham and we strolled along the roads and the seedy back streets adjacent to Via Roma. We heard gunshots which we thought had been aimed at us. We dashed to cover by the side of the building, only to discover that fireworks had been thrown down at us from a window in the tall tenements.

Another of my regular duties was on the dock gate with American soldiers, mainly stopping sailors taking bottles of wine and spirits aboard their ships. When we confiscated the bottles we immediately threw them into a concrete pound where they smashed up against the wall – it stopped all arguments.

One morning we all looked in surprise when one of the American soldiers said, 'Get this!' and we spied an American merchant seaman approaching the dock gate to have a run ashore. He was wearing an unusually loud and long jacket that came down past his knees. It was the first time any of us had seen a 'zoot suit'.

Very soon my original request was granted and I became a supply assistant based in the ancient Castel de Nuovo right on the seafront overlooking the Bay of Naples. There I became friendly with a man who came from the Lancashire fishing town of Fleetwood. He surprised me one day when out of the blue he said, 'George, how long have you had that cough?'

I said, 'What cough, I didn't know I had a cough?' He went on to say that I was constantly clearing my throat. This surprised me greatly because I certainly had not had a cough previously; it would have been noticed and remarked on in no uncertain manner aboard *Zetland*, living as we did in close proximity to each other. I still have that cough today, and it has been a source of embarrassment to me for more than half a century.

In the dock area of Naples, the Royal Navy had a small single-storey room in a warehouse where goods were stored awaiting transport either to or from ships arriving or leaving the port. Quite a number of the items stored there were personal ones such as kit-bags, hammocks and suit-cases, some belonging to sailors who had been killed or had died. I was in charge of the warehouse and had a working party of about ten Italian civilians. Though I was based and slept in Castel de Nuovo, I sometimes had to work the night shift and had a camp bed at the warehouse.

It was at the Castel de Nuovo that I first saw Italian-style graft in action. On pay day, when the men left the Navy pay office after collecting their weekly wage packet, a very large and menacing individual would be standing outside the doorway. As the workers filed past they would meekly hand over a percentage of their wages. It was all carried out quite openly and without any word spoken. If anyone refused to pay, he would not stay on the payroll afterwards. It appeared that the Royal Navy left the hiring and firing to the Italians themselves.

One of my duties was to collect stores from ships which arrived at the port and to carry out this task I received a daily list of all arrivals and departures. At our disposal was an Italian keel-boat (built in Goole), in the charge of an English-speaking Italian, one of hundreds who came back from America just before the war, and most of whom had been living illegally in New York without passports or papers. One day I had to collect naval stores from HMS *Zetland*, which was anchored in the bay, and I spent an enjoyable hour or two with my ex-shipmates whilst collecting them. While I was on board I was informed by Lieutenant John Benstead that for my actions in Bari, I had been awarded the British Empire Medal (Military). I received the medal some two years later, nine months after the war had ended. It arrived in a small red cardboard box about 3 inches (7.5 cm) square, delivered by the postman as a registered packet.

In June 1944, King George made a visit to Naples and I was due to go on parade but was laid low by a throat infection and could not attend. In August the Navy in its wisdom sent me aboard an armed trawler to the island of La Maddalena where they had had a small base. I arrived there and nobody seemed to know why, so I spent a very pleasant two weeks on my own, roaming the island and enjoying its marvellous views over-looking the Straits of Bonifacio and the island of Corsica beyond. Two weeks later I arrived back in Naples, landing at the small quay of Santa Lucia in the late evening, and spending the night sleeping on the cobbles of that romantic location. Again the Navy did not know what to do with me so in order to give them time to make their minds up, they sent me with John Ogden, an 18-year-old supply assistant from Manchester, to a small family hotel on the north-east coast of the island of Ischia.

We spent another pleasant week there before the powers that be decided to return us to the drafting pool in Malta. In Naples we embarked on an Italian cruiser as passengers and the next day we were once more scanning the draft lists in Malta. In a day or two both John and I had received drafts to HMS *Hamilcar*, which turned out to be the Royal Navy base in the Sicilian port of Messina. Named after Hamilcar Barca, the father of Hannibal, it was situated at the end of a long breakwater and consisted of several modern buildings and a large berthing area for small craft. The base's main purpose at that time was to pay off landing craft, of which there were dozens stripped of all gear, awaiting passage back to America or Britain.

When we arrived there the gates were closed after us and the base put out of bounds because of an outbreak of poliomyelitis. A short time before, a supply assistant had arrived from Britain to join the base staff after completing his initial training. Soon afterwards he was discovered to be suffering from polio and within a day or two he died. He was eighteen years of age and though of course I never knew him, his name has remained in my memory. His name was Becket and he was buried at sea in the Straits of Messina on the day we arrived. I was his replacement. Of the twelve months I spent in Messina I spent three weeks in the municipal hospital, suffering from tonsilitis and jaundice.

On my return to Portsmouth I was granted four weeks' leave and on 17 December 1945 I arrived home. My wife Kay was waiting at Leeds station when I got off the train. Her description of my appearance is worth including. It predates by some thirty years our knowledge of the mustard gas element in Bari and I had just spent two and a half years in the Mediterranean with three summer months in Britain in between. 'George stood on the platform and I hardly recognised him. He was clad in an ill-fitting suit and had a green face.' Today I realise that the description 'greeny-brown' had also been applied to most of the victims of mustard gas poisoning during and after the First World War. With hindsight I ask myself why I should have had that pallor after all that time in the warm climate of Italy and a good deal of the time spent outdoors. In my service record on entry I was described as 'fresh complexioned'. On demobilisation I suffered a series of boils culminating in an extremely painful carbuncle on my nose.

Kay and I moved to Scarborough in 1948 to run a restaurant business near the seafront for twenty-five years. In 1972 I became ill and lost a lot of weight. My doctor asked, 'Have you always had that pallor?' After marrow-bone and blood tests I was diagnosed as suffering from pernicious anaemia.

I was one of the lucky ones that night in Bari. I had been in the middle of the harbour from the time the first bomb was dropped to almost dawn next morning, repeatedly soaked, and I had breathed in the fumes, from which it was impossible to escape, and had scrambled on and off several filthy contaminated ships. It is remarkable that I did not succumb. During research spanning many years I have come to the conclusion that only a small percentage of those servicemen who were in the harbour that night are living today and hardly a single one who was immersed in the harbour water lived a very long time afterwards. Sadly, because no records were kept, we shall never know the true situation.

Captain J.V. Wilkinson, RN, guest of honour, breaking a bottle of champagne during the 'launching' after refurbishment of the Zetland Arms, Bute Street, South Kensington, London, 1976. It was the first reunion of ex-*Zetland* crew members, and when most men learned for the first time about the mustard gas in Bari thirty-three years previously. *(G. Southern)*

Captain Wilkinson being presented by the landlord with a framed photograph of HMS *Zetland* at the reunion at the Zetland Arms. *(G. Southern)*

Peter Bickmore (right) with Bob Davies at the Coastal Forces reunion at the fiftieth anniversary of the Bari episode, at the Imperial War Museum, London, on 2 December 1993. *(G. Southern)*

Rear-Admiral Sir Morgan Giles (left) with the author at the Coastal forces 50th Reunion. *(G. Southern)*

Vic Webster, ex-crew member of the minesweeper HMS *Sharpshooter*, at the Coastal Forces reunion. *(G. Southern)*

Bob Davies having dinner at a naval reunion in Portsmouth in 1999.
(R. Davies)

In July 1976 I organised the first reunion of the *Zetland*'s ship's company. The venue was the Zetland Arms in Bute Street, South Kensington, London. Captain John V. Wilkinson, GM, DSC, was guest of honour. About forty of the ship's complement attended and it was at that time that most of us learned of the existence of mustard gas, and also the number of ships sunk and the scale of casualties. We also learned that the thirty-year rule of censorship had applied to the episode. Sadly, a short time after the second reunion in 1978, Captain Wilkinson took ill and died after a brief illness.

During my research I directed an enquiry to the RAMC in the hope that they would be able to furnish me with details of the sterling work performed by the medical staff of the 98th General Hospital in Bari – probably the most difficult incident dealt with during the whole course of the war. The answer I received was 'Our records show no mention of the incident.'

To similar requests to the RASC and the Royal Corps of Transport, I received the reply, 'I have scoured our archives but regret I have been unable to unearth any detail about the heavy air raid on the port of Bari about which you enquired.'

The British Army Command in 1944 appointed Luigi Fidanza as Director of the Port Authority for Bari. Salvatore Farinato, who was at that time an NCO, remembers that in the summer of that year a gathering took place in great secrecy in the Navy offices in Bari. Officials of the Port Security Section and several high-ranking naval officers attended. It was explained to the assembly that the port of Molfetta, some 50 miles (80 km) north of Bari, had been singled out as a disposal point for a certain quantity of mustard gas still in Bari.

To safeguard fish stocks, it was proposed to dump the chemicals in the Adriatic Deep, at a depth of 1,000 metres (3,300 feet) and at that depth it was envisaged the shells and bombs containing the mustard gas and phosphorus would be buried safely for ever. In due course, military lorries began to arrive at the small port of Molfetta and though the port workers did not know why they were dumping the munitions, Salvatore and his fellow soldiers gathered that there was an air of mystery about it.

The Port Authority had requisitioned barges and motor launches to be used in the transportation of the shells and bombs to the deep-water disposal area. It was agreed between the Port Authority and the Italian firms contracted to carry out the disposal operation, that payment would be based on the quantity transported and dumped. Because of lax supervision by the authorities concerned, the proper procedure was not adhered to and the consequences of this failure is evident today.

In order to save on fuel oil, and not knowing the nature of the materials they were dumping, the barge and boat owners cut corners by jettisoning the highly toxic cargoes in an area of the sea 40 miles (64 km) north-east of Molfetta. This area, though not as far, was of course much shallower than the designated one. When fishing was resumed after 1945, incidents began to occur. Nobody knew what the metal bomb and shell casings dragged up in the fishing nets contained. Some cases split open when landed and others were deliberately opened by crew members in the hope that the contents would be recoverable and saleable materials. But the fishermen soon learned to fear these 'catches'. One of them, Cesare Giacaspo says, 'I was young then, mustard gas covered my hands and arms – they were burning, but above all, my eyes were hurting so much that even today they still go red and burn.' Salvatore Farinato remembers, 'In about 1947 the captain of our motor boat died from breathing in mustard gas.' Another fisherman, Ignazio Salvemini says, 'Five in total died from breathing in mustard gas but even when death was avoided, burns and periods of blindness occurred, which could last up to two months.' He goes on to say, 'My brother, who was on board with another nine fishermen, was contaminated and blinded, but fortunately managed to get back to port relying on instinct and knowledge of the sea. Only the mechanic was partially saved, at least from the burns, thanks to the protection of engine grease which covered his hands.'

From then on, according to Ignazio, 'Grease was used as a defensive barrier in case of contact. My brother remained in hospital for a month before regaining his sight; from that crew of ten fishermen, not one is alive today.' A similar thing happened to another boat in which Salvatore Farinato's nephew was working. Fortunately they returned to port, but they were temporarily blinded. Nobody knew exactly what it was; even the doctors who dealt with the first cases were amazed at the strange symptoms. With experience, the fishermen protected themselves by smearing grease on hands and faces. At times when mustard gas was escaping from the seabed, they put the boat's bow into the wind to avoid breathing in the fumes.

The most sensible precaution was to keep well away from the area, but because it was a traditionally rich fishing area, many of the fishermen took the risk. In some cases when bombs and shells caught in the nets were heaved aboard, the fishermen dumped the containers in other areas, thus possibly spreading the contamination. Many containers were scattered by the currents and other marine causes and cases of contamination have continued up to the present time. Four occurred in 1994, and others have not been reported by fishermen to save their nets and tackle from being impounded. Molfetta fishermen have also come across phosphorus bombs, which burn on contact with the air, probably dumped in the Adriatic at the same time as the mustard gas.

Dr Angelo Neve is the enthusiastic co-ordinator and director of a group studying the long-term effects of the contamination of the seas around Bari. Working with him is Professor Giorgio Assenato, lecturer in legal medicine, Professor Roberto Gagliano Candela, lecturer in toxicology, and Professor Giovanni Marano, Director of the Institute of Marine Biology. Dr Neve sent me a video tape filmed aboard a diving support vessel, where he was being interviewed with another diver as part of a programme for RAI, the Italian state television company. The diver turned round to show viewers his leg, on which ugly red blisters covered a large area from his knee to his thigh. It showed contamination still occurring more than fifty years after the disaster.

The tape contains underwater scenes of several divers from a sub-aqua

Angelo Neve, co-ordinator of a group who monitor, collect and collate artifacts found at sea and washed up on the shoreline adjacent to Bari. He is holding a shell casing and a boot recovered by a member of the local diving club during a dive off the coast near Bari. *(A. Neve)*

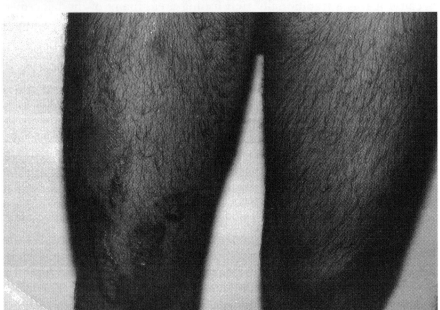

A member of the diving club showing burns and blisters on his thigh, caused by contamination during a dive when inspecting a wreck on the sea bottom off the coast near Bari. *(A. Neve)*

Bari harbour today showing ships berthed on the outer mole, the Nuovo Mole, where the fifteen ships were berthed stern-on on 2 December 1943. *(R. Bennett)*

A scene in Bari harbour today. *(R. Bennett)*

club (of which Angelo Neve is a member) examining a wreck in very clear water. It appears to be lying in one piece on the seabed in an upright position. Angelo asked me if I could identify the vessel, which he believed was a warship. I concluded that it was not a warship, but a merchant vessel. I spent some time comparing photographs of the one remaining wartime American liberty ship still afloat, the USS *Jeremiah O'Brien*, with the video scenes, and though the wreck is covered in barnacles, the shape and positions of the derricks, masts, stays and gun turrets on both sides of the bridge fore and aft are clearly visible and match exactly. In my opinion, the wreck is a liberty ship and as there is no record of any other liberty ship being sunk in that area, it is almost certain to be USS *Samuel J. Tilden*, the ship that was anchored outside the harbour and was eventually sunk by torpedoes fired from MTB *297*. I sent Angelo the copies of the photographs to assist him and the divers in the hope that they can ascertain the name of the wreck. I also suggested that if they were able to get into the holds and make a search and found trailer units there, then it would almost certainly be *Samuel J. Tilden*.

In the apartment block on Corso Trieste at 7 a.m. on 3 December 1943, the Lugli family trooped back upstairs from the basement where they had sheltered throughout the night. When she surveyed the shattered apartment, Alberto's mother realised that it was impossible to stay there and in the afternoon the four of them collected some of their more necessary possessions and reluctantly took leave of their home. Walking out of the stricken city, they headed for the small town of Triggiano, some 8 miles (13 km) from Bari, where they found shelter in a convent. They stayed there for some weeks and each morning the children walked the 8 miles to school and back, though after the first week or so they were given lifts by British servicemen who took pity on them. Some of Alberto's soldier friends, learning about the children's long walk, organised a lorry to pick them up each day.

Seven weeks later the family thankfully returned to their home, which had been cleared and made habitable. Exactly one year later, on 2 December 1944, and at the time the raid had started the year before, Signora Lugli received news that her husband had died. From that moment young Alberto became the bread winner. He lived in Bari until 1966, when his work as a surveyor took him to northern Italy where he worked for the Italian Finance Department until 1976. He then worked in a private capacity until 1993, when he retired. Today he lives in the scenic town of Moreno in the Italian Dolomites and has a summer residence in the resort of Monopoli, some 25 miles (40 km) south of Bari. Alberto recalls, 'The British friends I made were extremely kind and humane to me and my family during that time of peril and stress, and I still remember them with affection.'

In 1946 Nurse Gwladys Rees, now Mrs Gwladys Rees Aikens, travelled aboard the liner SS *Queen Mary* as a war bride and arrived at pier 21, Halifax, Nova Scotia. During her war service in North Africa and Italy she had met a young Canadian Army doctor, Robert Aikens and at the ending of hostilities, they had married. She has lived in Canada ever since. Sadly Robert died in 1972 but Gwladys brought up their four children and still lives in Halifax. Of the events in Bari she says, 'Most of those dear boys probably lie buried somewhere in Bari. Some may not even have names, but they will never be forgotten by the QAs who were with them as they quietly slipped away.'

Bari today is a modern seaport and industrial city with a population of almost half a million. Besides its normal shipping trade, it has thriving car ferry services to Corfu, mainland Greece and Egypt. Unlike many regions of coastal Europe, it is not a centre of mass tourism. The surrounding countryside, once neglected, has over the years become one of the finest agricultural regions in the country. It is now and has been for many years the Adriatic port where NATO ships have been maintained and serviced during the years of unrest and uncertainty in the Balkan region. Unfortunately it has gained a reputation for petty crime such as muggings, bag-snatching and stealing from cars when vehicles come to a stop at traffic lights etc.

Some years ago a friend of mine learned about the events in Bari in 1943 from an article I wrote for my local newspaper. He told the story to his son, a Royal Navy officer, who took a rather sceptical view about the affair. Two years later, his son was serving aboard the aircraft carrier HMS *Illustrious* as an engineering officer. In the course of operations the carrier visited Bari. While the ship was anchored, he mentioned the story of the mustard gas episode which had occurred fifty years previously to some of his fellow officers. Not one of them had heard anything about it, even though the Official Account had been derestricted since 1973.

Royal Navy ships have visited Bari for many years, and the crews have enjoyed all the comforts and relaxations of a safe haven. Few if any of today's mariners realise that in the very same harbour half a century ago, one of the worst disasters of the Second World War occurred. Then, seaman relaxed in what they also thought was a safe haven, but what was shortly to become a hell, a holocaust and to many fellow sailors on that fateful night, their last haven and their last resting place.

*   *   *

John J. White, the son of John White, the Chief Engineer who died with all his shipmates on aboard the USS *John Harvey* when she blew up, remembers living at that time with his mother and family in Lindhurst, New York.

> I knew how and where my father died because of a visit in January 1944 from some of his former shipmates, a month after his death. Our family were also visited by officers of the FBI and the few mementoes we had, an engraved 20 mm shell, a table lamp made from a 5 inch (125 mm) shell and other small items, had to be surrendered because the name *John Harvey* was engraved on them. We were also ordered by the officers not to mention anything about the incident. Now I have nothing left except a copy of a drawing of my father made by an Italian prisoner-of-war.

Four men who lost their lives in Bari were remembered and commemorated by the United States government by naming four liberty ships after them. They were Elwin F. Knowles, master of the USS *John Harvey*, Able Seaman Donald Holland of the USS *John Motley*, Cadet Edwin D. Howard, of the USS *John Motley* and Third Mate Allen G. Collins, of the USS *John Bascom*.

On the peaceful evening of 2 December 1993, a lone tall figure made his way along Bari's outer breakwater, the Nuovo Molo. He was making the same journey he had made exactly fifty years previously, but in very different circumstances. Now deserted, the mole evoked many sad and painful memories: of bodies lying in grotesque positions where the blasts had hurled them like leaves in an autumn wind, of vehicles overturned and blazing, of panic-stricken servicemen and civilians shouting and screaming, of the acrid, foul-smelling smoke, of the rain of shrapnel and, above all else, of the tremendous ear-splitting noise.

His thoughts turned to the grief-stricken moment when he cradled an unknown dying sailor in his arms to give him what brotherly love and comfort he could during the last few moments of life left to him, at the start of his incredible perilous dash along the mole to obtain sailing orders from Navy House.

Robert (Taffy) Davies had made the long overland pilgrimage by train from his home in Anglesey, North Wales. It was not a holy pilgrimage but one to commemorate the fiftieth anniversary of the raid. It was a journey of remembrance he had promised himself for some years. The local council had contacted him on his arrival, with an invitation to be guest of the mayor. Interviews were arranged on local television and radio and he was escorted to the War Cemetery. The poignant visit to the cemetery, a few miles south-west of the city, alongside Highway 100, near the village of Triggiano, had been made on the previous day. There he had paid his respects to the fallen and to those who had no known grave, of which there were many as a consequence of that long, long night. As he had wandered around the immaculately kept gardens of the quiet peaceful resting place he had noticed many headstones bearing the names of fellow-Welshmen.

On the mole he slowed his pace as he looked for his destination: berth 26, where HMS *Zetland* had been moored alongside HMS *Bicester* during those fateful hours. He halted at the very place, to gaze forward further along the curving mole to where the doomed line of ships had been moored.

His emotions ran wild. He could see in his mind's eye the burning ships, the explosions, the hysterical and anguished cries and calls of drowning men beyond the thick black curtain of smoke. He recalled with amazing clarity the utter chaos in the harbour and the never-to-be-forgotten moments he had experienced on *Zetland*, when in one split second of an unstoppable surge of awesome power, all of the bridge staff became a jumble of bodies in the wake of the explosion when the destroyer was lifted out of the water.

Suddenly, without any warning, Bob was roused from his thoughtful, sad reminiscences. A vivid flash of lightning patterned the sky above the harbour, brilliantly illuminating the scene for an instant, to be followed immediately by a heavy rumble of thunder, which reverberated around the harbour. Glancing at his watch, he saw the time: 7.30 p.m. – the time of the raid all those years before. Throughout those years, the heroic and sad events in Bari had been a closed book to the vast majority of Britons, but could it be that at that very moment, as the thunder rolled around the harbour, through the medium of St Nicholas, the patron saint of sailors, whose body lies in Bari's cathedral, Robert Davies was given a sign that some greater being than us poor mortals, has not forgotten?

INDEX

Page numbers in *italics* refer to illustrations.